Praise for *Fisher's Decoding the Ethics Code*

"This indispensable volume stands alone in the range and quality of information it provides and in the insight and guidance it offers about how to integratively conduct psychological research and practice and, as well, serve the interests of and promote human welfare. All psychologists, and all citizens served by their work, may be grateful to Professor Fisher for this extraordinarily significant and uniquely important book."

—Richard M. Lerner,
Bergstrom Chair in Applied Developmental Science, Tufts University

"This book is a must, 'one stop' ethics read as it integrates the old code with the new code and the new code with HIPAA. The icon alerts that direct the reader to relevant sections based on professional work are real time savers."

—Robert J. Resnick, Ph.D., ABPP,
Past-President, American Psychological Association,
Randolph-Macon College

"Decoding the Ethics Code *offers a kind of 'behind the scenes' view of why changes to the code were made that I expect readers will appreciate. People will be encouraged to follow the code if they believe it's sensible, and such discussions help make the case that it is."*

—Deirdre Knapp, Ph.D.
Human Resources Research Organization (HumRRO)

"The primary strengths of this book are the thorough, well organized, clear explanations and examples of the new Ethics Code. Dr. Fisher's passion for ethical awareness, concerns for making compliance an essential and realistic goal, and ability to express the ideas of the code in readily accessible language make the book readable and engaging."

—Tamara Shulman, Ph.D., FAACP,
Board Certified in Clinical Psychology, ABPP

"This book is an excellent guide to interpreting the 2002 APA Ethics Code. It provides useful discussions and helpful examples that psychologists can use in their daily work to alert them to potential ethical conflicts. The ethical decision-making model presented in the final chapter should be used by all psychologists, even those with considerable experience, to avoid ethical breaches and better serve others."

—Georgiana Tryon, Ph.D.
Professor, Educational Psychology, The Graduate Center, CUNY

"An excellent reference book which all present and future psychologists should read. The icons facilitate access to specific standards and the examples are not only easy to understand and apply but are very relevant to many situations which psychologists may be faced with."

—Noreen Vail,
Doctoral Candidate Clinical Psychology, Hofstra University

"In her book, Dr. Fisher not only 'decodes' but demystifies complex ethical issues as well. I love the way the book is organized and the clarity with which the Ethics Code changes are explained. As both a practitioner and an academic, I was delighted to find the ethical issues in education and training easily accessible and new practice questions such as HIPAA and the ethics code clearly explained. This is the ethics book I've always wanted, and I intend to use it as the text for my fall 2003 Ethics class and as a major resource in my practice."

—Patricia M. Bricklin, Ph.D.,
Professor, Institute for Graduate Clinical Psychology, Widener University

DECODING THE ETHICS CODE

To my parents, Helen and Norman Burg,
who taught me by example the importance of moral principles;
my husband Gary, who lovingly supported my ethical quests;
and my children Brian and Erica,
who taught me how to combine responsibility with care

DECODING THE
ETHICS CODE

A Practical Guide for Psychologists

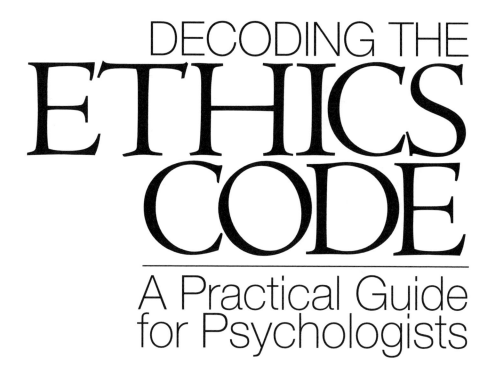

Celia B. Fisher
Center for Ethics Education, Fordham University

SAGE Publications
International Educational and Professional Publisher
Thousand Oaks ■ London ■ New Delhi

For information:

Sage Publications, Inc.
2455 Teller Road
Thousand Oaks, California 91320
E-mail: order@sagepub.com

Sage Publications Ltd.
6 Bonhill Street
London EC2A 4PU
United Kingdom

Sage Publications India Pvt. Ltd.
B-42, Panchsheel Enclave
Post Box 4109
New Delhi 110 017 India

Printed in the United States of America

Library of Congress Cataloging-in-Publication Data

Fisher, Celia B.
Decoding the ethics code : a practical guide for psychologists / by Celia B. Fisher.
    p. cm.
Includes bibliographical references and index.
ISBN 0-7619-2619-4
    1. Psychologists-Professional ethics. 2. Psychology-Moral and ethical aspects. I. Title.
BF76.4.F57 2003
174´.915—dc211

                        2003006141

Printed on acid-free paper

06 07 08 09 10 9 8 7 6 5 4 3 2

Acquiring Editor:	Jim Brace-Thompson
Editorial Assistant:	Karen Ehrmann
Production Editor:	Claudia A. Hoffman
Copy Editor:	Kate Peterson
Typesetter:	C&M Digitals (P) Ltd.
Indexer:	Molly Hall
Cover Designer:	Michelle Lee

Contents

Part I. Introduction and Background / 1

TOPICAL TABLE OF CONTENTS FOR ENFORCEABLE STANDARDS

Selected Work Settings

Psychologists Working in and Consulting to Businesses and Other Organizations

Psychologists Working in or With Health Maintenance Organizations and Other Third-Party Payors

Psychologists Working in or With Health Maintenance Organizations and Other Third-Party Payors, continued

Work Conducted Over the Internet and Other Electronic Media

Psychologists in the Military and Public Service

Psychologists Working in Schools

Psychologists Working in Schools, continued

Standard	Page	Standard	Page	Standard	Page
3.06	71	5.05	111	9.02c	186
3.07	73	6.01	115	9.03a	188
3.08	74	6.05	129	9.05	196
3.10b	77	8.02a	146	9.07	201
3.11a	80	8.04a	155	9.08a	202
4.01	85	8.05	156	9.08b	203
4.02a	90	9.01a	179	9.11	208
4.04b	95	9.01b	180	10.09	229
5.01a	103	9.02a	183		
5.01b	105	9.02b	185		

Ethics and Law

Forensic and Other Court-Related Activities

Standard	Page	Standard	Page	Standard	Page
1.01	33	4.02a	90	9.02a	183
1.02	34	4.02b	92	9.02b	185
1.05	39	4.03	93	9.03a	188
1.07	41	4.04a	94	9.03b	190
2.01a	45	4.05a	96	9.03c	191
2.01f	51	4.05b	98	9.04a	192
3.04	63	5.01a	103	9.04b	195
3.05a	65	5.05	111	9.05	196
3.05c	69	6.01	115	9.07	201
3.06	71	6.02c	121	9.08a	202
3.07	73	6.04a	123	9.08b	203
3.08	74	6.04c	126	9.09c	206
3.10a	76	6.04d	127	9.10	207
3.10b	77	6.04e	128	10.01a	211
3.10c	80	6.06	130	10.02a	219
3.10d	80	9.01a	179	10.02b	221
3.11b	82	9.01b	180	10.03	222
4.01	85	9.01c	182	10.08a	226

Health Insurance Portability and Accountability Act (HIPAA)

Standard	Page	Standard	Page	Standard	Page
1.02	34	3.01	59	3.08	74
1.04	37	3.04	63	3.10b	77
2.05	54	3.07	73	3.11b	82

Ethics and Additional State and Federal Laws

Selected Work Roles

Counseling and Therapy

Research

Teaching

Diverse Populations

Childhood, Adolescence, and Family
see also Psychologists Working in Schools

Individuals With Disabilities

Racial, Ethnic, Cultural, and Linguistic Diversity

Frequently Cited Ethical Practices and Issues

Aspirational Principles

Avoiding Harm

Avoiding Harm, continued

Standard	Page		Standard	Page		Standard	Page
3.10a	76		8.07c	164		10.05	224
4.05b	98		8.08c	166		10.08a	226
4.07	101		8.09b	168		10.08b	228
8.05	156		8.09d	168		10.10a	230
8.07a	163		9.04a	192			
8.07b	163		10.04	223			

Confidentiality

Standard	Page		Standard	Page		Standard	Page
1.04	37		6.01	115		8.15	176
1.05	39		6.02a	119		9.03a	188
1.06	40		6.02b	120		9.03c	191
2.05	54		6.02c	121		9.04a	192
3.07	73		6.04e	128		9.04b	195
3.10b	77		6.06	130		10.01a	211
3.10c	80		8.01	145		10.01b	217
3.10d	80		8.02a	146		10.02a	219
3.11a	80		8.03	154		10.03	222
3.11b	82		8.05	156		10.10b	233
4.01-4.06	85		8.14a	175			

Informed Consent

Standard	Page		Standard	Page		Standard	Page
2.04	54		4.06	100		8.07c	164
3.04	63		4.07	101		9.03a	188
3.10a	76		6.01	115		9.03b	190
3.10b	77		6.04e	128		9.03c	191
3.10c	80		6.07	132		9.10	207
3.10d	80		8.01	145		10.01a	211
3.11a	80		8.02a	146		10.01b	217
3.11b	82		8.02b	151		10.01c	218
4.01	85		8.03	154		10.02a	219
4.02a	90		8.04a	155		10.03	222
4.03	93		8.05	156			
4.04a	94		8.06b	162			

Multiple Relationships and Conflict of Interest

Acknowledgments

In August 2002, the Council of Representatives of the American Psychological Association (APA) voted unanimously to adopt the ninth revision of the APA Ethical Principles of Psychologists and Code of Conduct (APA, 2002). The 2002 APA Ethics Code is the product of an extraordinary 5-year revision process built on APA's 50-year tradition of applying a group dynamics approach to create a living code of conduct with which psychologists can identify and use in their everyday professional and scientific decisions (Hobbs, 1948). I was privileged to chair the APA Ethics Code Task Force (ECTF) responsible for developing, implementing, and completing the 2002 Ethics Code revision. Our mission was to create a process and product that reflected the values of the discipline and that would assist APA members in meeting ethical challenges in the new millennium.

The ECTF was composed of remarkable individuals representing the public and the diverse constituencies within APA. Each member was committed to developing an ethics code that would reflect the ideals and merit the trust of psychologists and consumers. Over its 5-year journey, the ECTF continuously sought member input on the revision process through critical incident surveys, calls for member comments, and open meetings encouraging lively exchange among the ECTF, APA members, and observers from APA constituencies. ECTF members brought to the revision process their professional, ethical, and scientific expertise. But perhaps more important they demonstrated a special ability to listen to member concerns and a unique willingness to challenge their own ethical preconceptions. I greatly benefited from the wisdom and friendship of the ECTF members: Peter Appleby, Bruce Bennett, Laura Brown, Linda F. Campbell, Nabil El-Ghoroury, Dennis J. Grill, Jessica Henderson Daniel, Samuel J. Knapp, Gerald P. Koocher, Marcia Moody, Peter E. Nathan, Thomas D. Oakland, Mary H. Quigley, Julia M. Ramos-Grenier, Abigail Sivan, Steven N. Sparta, Elizabeth Swenson, Melba J. T. Vasquez, and Brian Wilcox.

The ECTF had a dedicated and talented APA staff navigating the revision process through what often felt like a voyage through the Scylla and Charybdis of seven Ethics Code drafts. Stan Jones as Director of the Ethics Office and later ECTF consultant was a treasure trove of knowledge about the history of past APA ethics codes and ethics adjudication. In the middle of the revision process, Steve Behnke dived into the role of Director of the Ethics Office with a perfect combination of scholarly expertise, administrative acumen, and personal warmth. Steve and Stan, with the able assistance of Jonathan Tin, created the innovative interactive Web site that enabled APA members to comment on the revisions over the Internet. Debbie Felder, Revision Coordinator, was the ECTF's gatekeeper, librarian, scribe, grammarian, minutes keeper, and schedule maker and performed many other essential roles with a competence and commitment remarkable to find in a single individual. If there is a perfect attorney, it is Nathalie Gilfoyle, APA General Counsel. Nathalie continuously helped clarify the legal parameters and challenges of the ECTF's work, nurturing the construction of standards sensitive to but not dictated by law. Along with Lindsay Childress Beatty, Deputy General Counsel, Nathalie made sure that the ECTF was up-to-date on continuously evolving federal regulations. Stan, Steve, Debbie, and Nathalie were my personal lifelines during the revision process, and their contribution to the success of the ECTF was equally invaluable.

As chair of the ECTF, I also benefited from the support and guidance of the APA Board of Directors, committee chairs, and division representatives. I am particularly grateful to Pat Bricklin, Charles Brewer, Jean Carter, Stuart Cooper, Pat DeLeon, Mike Honaker, Norine Johnson, Deirdre Knapp, Ron Levant, Katherine Nordal, Russ Newman, Ruth Paige, Stuart Pizer, Norma Simon, and Phil Zimbardo and to the more than 1,300 APA members who shared their kudos and concerns with the task force. This book has benefited from the wisdom and kindness of everyone who participated in the Ethics Code revision process, but I take full responsibility for the interpretations and opinions expressed.

It is also a pleasure to record indebtedness to Deirdre Knapp, Tamara Shulman, Noreen Vail, and Georgiana Tryon for their careful and kind critiques of the first draft of this book and to James MacDonall for his help with animal research cases. I am fortunate to have had the wonderful guidance and support of my editor Jim Brace-Thompson and his assistant Karen Ehrmann, and the assistance of senior production editor Claudia Hoffman and copy editor Kate Peterson at Sage Publications. I owe a great debt to Fordham University for providing me with the faculty fellowship to complete this book, Nancy Busch for her years of administrative support and friendship, Adam Fried for his help in preparing the final manuscript, and the many Fordham University graduate students who provided valuable feedback on the different drafts of the Ethics Code. I am also grateful to colleagues and friends Margaret Farley, Don Green, Robert Levine, and Carol Pollard, who as Executive Committee members of the Yale University Bioethics Project made Yale feel like a second home during my year as bioethicist-in-residence.

My husband, Gary, read each draft of the book, and in addition to providing loving support, continuously urged me to use periods instead of semicolons, dramatically reducing the number of paragraph-length sentences in the final draft. I am also grateful to my daughter Erica for providing the title for this book, and to both my children, Brian and Erica, for their many late-night instant messages.

PREFACE
Navigating This Book

The purpose of this book is to introduce psychologists to the 2002 American Psychological Association's (APA) Ethical Principles of Psychologists and Code of Conduct and to assist psychologists in effectively using the ethical principles and standards to conduct their work activities in ethically responsible ways, avoid ethical violations, and preserve and protect the fundamental rights and welfare of those with whom they work. The book seeks to place into practical perspective the revised format, choice of wording, aspirational principles, and enforceable standards of the code. It provides in-depth discussions of the rationale and application of each ethical standard to the broad spectrum of scientific, teaching, and professional roles and activities of psychologists. It gives clear examples of behaviors that would be in compliance with or in violation of enforceable standards. The goal of the book is to help psychologists apply the Ethics Code to the constantly changing scientific, professional, and legal realities of the discipline.

How to Use This Book

Decoding the Ethics Code: A Practical Guide for Psychologists was written to provide an in-depth yet easily accessible guide to applying the Ethical Principles of Psychologists and Code of Conduct (APA, 2002) to psychologists' everyday ethical decision making. The book has several features designed for easy reference to a wide range of information and practical guidance on each component of the APA Ethics Code.

How the Book Is Organized

The APA Ethics Code consists of the Introduction and Applicability section, the Preamble, five General Principles, and 10 specific sections putting forth enforceable standards for ethical conduct. Although the chapters of this book are organized around the format of the Ethics Code, the book does not have to be read from cover to cover. Each chapter and the discussion of each standard is designed to stand on its own. Cross-references to other parts of the code are provided when they are helpful to ethical decision making. The book is organized around 14 chapters.

Chapter 1. A Code of Ethics for Psychology: How Did We Get Here? Chapter 1 presents an introduction to the history, goals, controversies, major advances, and revision strategies associated with the APA Ethics Code since its inception a half century ago. It contains specific examples of the innovations and controversies associated with the 1992 Ethics Code and how these innovations and challenges were expressed during the process of creating the 2002 Ethics Code. It familiarizes readers with the value of the Ethics Code to the profession and the public. This chapter also explains the history of a revision process that includes broad APA member involvement as a critical element in the construction of an Ethics Code that reflects the values of the discipline.

Chapter 2. The Introduction and Applicability Section, Preamble, and General Principles: What Do They Mean? Chapter 2 provides a guide to the practical meaning of the Ethics Code's Introduction and Applicability section, Preamble, and General Principles. It includes discussion of to whom and what activities the Ethics Code applies; the rationale and meaning of the language used in the Ethics Code; the relationship between the Ethics Code, APA guidelines, and the rules and procedures for enforcement of the code; the relevance of the Ethics Code to sanctions applied by other professional bodies and state licensure boards as well as to litigation; and the meaning and practical significance of the General Principles.

Chapter 3. Changes From the 1992 Ethics Code: What You May Need to Know Right Now. This chapter briefly explains the major changes in ethical requirements from the old to the present Ethics Code that psychologists may need to know immediately to ensure continued ethical compliance. Standards highlighted include those with relevance to informed consent, the release of test data, test security, student disclosures of personal information, student authorship, forensic activities, conflict of interest, use of the Internet, and the implications of the Health Insurance Portability and Accountability Act (HIPAA).

Chapters 4-13: Enforceable Standards. Chapters 4-13 provide in-depth explanations and practical examples of how to apply the 151 enforceable standards. The chapter titles correspond to the titles of the 10 sections on enforceable standards in the Ethics Code: Resolving Ethical Issues, Competence, Human Relations, Privacy and Confidentiality, Advertising and Other Public Statements, Record Keeping and Fees, Education and Training, Research and Publication, Assessment, and Therapy.

Chapter 14. The APA Ethics Code and Ethical Decision Making. Chapter 14 provides a model for ethical decision making and discusses how the Ethics Code can be applied to new and emerging areas of psychology as the discipline continues to evolve.

Alternative Table of Contents

In addition to the traditional table of contents, a topical table of contents is provided to help readers quickly identify discussions of standards relevant to five major areas: work settings (industrial-organizational and consulting activities, health maintenance organizations, hospitals, companies, work conducted over the Internet, the military, and schools), ethics and law (forensic and other court-related activities, HIPAA regulations, and ethics and state and federal laws), work roles (counseling and therapy, prescription privileges, psychological testing, publication, research, and teaching), populations (childhood, adolescence, family; gender and sexual orientation; geriatric populations; individuals with acute or chronic health problems; individuals with disabilities; and racially, ethnically, culturally, and linguistically diverse populations), and frequently cited ethical practices and issues (aspirational principles, avoiding harm, confidentiality, informed consent, and multiple relationships).

Discussion of Ethical Standards

Most of the enforceable standards in the Ethics Code were written broadly so they would apply to psychologists in varied roles and work contexts. As much as possible, this book attempts to explain the overriding purpose of each standard, help readers understand the implications of critical terminology, provide examples of the range of psychological activities to which the standard applies, and offer suggestions for ethical "dos" and "don'ts" quickly identified by these icons ☑ ☒. In the examples of ethical dos and don'ts in this book, the terms "client" and "patient" are used interchangeably.

Comparisons With the 1992 APA Ethics Code

For seasoned psychologists, new Ph.D.s, and graduate students practicing under or trained on the 1992 APA Ethics Code, bracketed notations placed at the end of each standard indicate the extent to which the new version of the standard differs from its corresponding standard in the 1992 Ethics Code. These notations are as follows:

"No Significant Change." This notation alerts readers to instances in which the meaning and overall wording of the 2002 and corresponding 1992 standards remain unchanged.

"Modified for Clarity." This notation indicates instances in which major wording changes clarify the meaning of the 1992 corresponding standard. For example, the 2002 Ethics Code Standard 1.06, Cooperating With Ethics Committees, includes the sentence "However, making a request for deferment of adjudication of an ethics complaint pending the outcome of litigation does not alone constitute noncooperation." Although this sentence did not appear in the corresponding Standard 8.06 in the 1992 Ethics Code, it was always the case that a request to defer APA Ethics Committee adjudication of a complaint was not in and of itself an ethical violation.

"Expanded." This notation draws attention to wording in a 2002 standard that expands the meaning or application of a corresponding 1992 standard. For example, the 1992 Standard 7.02b, Forensic Assessments, required psychologists to provide forensic reports or testimony about the psychological characteristics of an individual

only after they had conducted an adequate examination of the individual. The corresponding 2002 Standard 9.01b, Bases for Assessments, expands the scope of this requirement beyond the forensic context to opinions about psychological character-istics expressed in any recommendation, report, or diagnostic or evaluative statement.

"Significant Change in Meaning." This notation alerts readers that a 2002 standard has been reworded to prohibit or require ethical behaviors in a manner that significantly changes the meaning of a corresponding standard in the 1992 Ethics Code. For example, the 1992 Standard 6.12, Dispensing With Informed Consent, only required that psychologists consider applicable regulations and institutional review board requirements before determining whether their research did not require informed consent. In contrast, the corresponding 2002 Standard 8.05, Dispensing With Informed Consent for Research, lists the specific conditions under which it is ethically permissible under the Ethics Code to dispense with informed consent.

"New." This notation indicates there is no corresponding standard in the 1992 Ethics Code.

Readers interested in a redline/strikeout comparison of the 1992 and 2002 APA Ethics Codes should refer to http://www.apa.org/ethics/codecompare.html.

Psychological Activity and Work Setting Icons

The Ethics Code is divided into six general sections representing ethical standards that apply to a broad spectrum of psychological activities and four more sections putting forth ethical rules explicitly for teaching, research, assessment, and therapy, respectively. Although this format is an improvement over the 1992 Ethics Code, it does not provide a precise way to locate standards directly relevant to other common work roles and settings. To help readers quickly navigate the Ethics Code for direct application to work roles that do not have special sections in the code, icons for the following areas of psychology are strategically placed before the discussion of standards in which such activities are mentioned:

 This icon alerts readers that the standard is particularly relevant to psychologists who apply the science and practice of psychology to enhance human well-being and performance in organizational and work settings, including consulting, personnel screening and promotion, marketing research, employee counseling, executive coaching, and research on job or organization effectiveness. Throughout the Ethics Code, the term "organizational client" refers to organizations to which the psychologist provides the services described above, whereas the term "client/patient" refers to individuals receiving therapy or other health services.

This icon indicates that the standard applies to work involving forensic, court-ordered, or other activities relevant to the legal system, including forensic examinations, expert testimony, testimony as a fact witness, research on a psycholegal issue, trial behavior consultation, or correctional or forensic mental health services.

When readers see this icon, it means that the standard mentions or is directly related to research about the schooling process, consultative services to schools, or delivery of psychological services to children, adolescents, and families to assess, remediate, or otherwise address school performance and related psychological skills or vulnerabilities.

This icon indicates that a standard is particularly relevant to psychological practice, research, training, or policy formation in military, criminal justice, police, or other public service settings.

The science and practice of psychology are continually responding to societal changes in health care management, federal oversight of health care practices, and the use of the Internet and other electronic media for research, psychological services, record keeping, and the transmission of information.

This icon highlights standards for which examples are provided for psychologists working within organized systems of care or who otherwise have professional associations with health maintenance organizations (HMOs).

This icon draws readers' attention to discussion of standards that include the implications of the federal Health Insurance Portability and Accountability Act (HIPAA) to ethical practice. (See "A Word About HIPAA," below.)

Although to date only a small subset of psychologists has obtained prescription privileges, the number of psychologists obtaining training and competence in this area is anticipated to increase over the next 10 years with changing state law. This icon alerts readers to standards that are particularly relevant to psychological services that include prescribing psychopharmacological medications.

This icon draws readers' attention to standards that explicitly mention or for which examples are given for research or services using the Internet, telephone, fax machines, video-conferencing, or other forms of electronic transmission.

The special areas for which icons were selected are not exhaustive but represent areas outside of teaching, research, assessment, and therapy that are repeatedly referred to in the standards or in the explanation and illustrations provided in this book

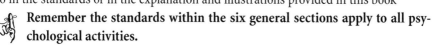
Remember the standards within the six general sections apply to all psychological activities.

A Word About HIPAA

In 1996, Congress enacted HIPAA in response to the increasing costs associated with transmitting health records lacking standardized formatting across providers, institutions, localities, and states. Recognizing that uniform standards for creating, transmitting, and storing of health care records would require additional patient protections, Congress included in HIPAA regulations standards giving patients greater access to and control of their records. The Ethics Code Task Force (ECTF) responsible for the 2002 Ethics Code revision was aware that the scope and detail of HIPAA regulations would change the nature of health care practice and research in the United States. The ECTF sought to ensure that ethical standards would reflect sensitivity to and avoid inconsistency with the new HIPAA regulatory landscape.

Throughout this book, the relationship between HIPAA and relevant Ethics Code standards is identified and explained. A brief overview of the new regulations and relevant terminology is provided below. Additional information regarding HIPAA appears throughout this book under discussion of individual standards. Readers can also obtain more detailed information about HIPAA from the U.S. Department of Health and Human Services (http://www.hhs.gov/ocr/hipaa/finalreg.html and http://aspe.hhs.gov/admnsimp/, http://www.cms.hhs.gov/hipaa/hipaa2/), the American Psychological Association Insurance Trust (www.apait.org/hipaa), or the American Psychological Association Practice Directorate (www.apa.org/practice).

HIPAA standards. HIPAA has three components: (1) *privacy standards* for the use and disclosure of individually identifiable private health information (Privacy Rule, effective April 14, 2003), (2) *transaction standards* for the electronic exchange of health information (Transaction Rule, effective October 16, 2003), and (3) *security standards* to protect the creation and maintenance of private health information (Security Standards, effective April 21, 2003; compliance date April 21, 2005). These rules seek to protect individually identifiable health information through regulations that

- standardize the format of electronically transmitted records related to individually identifiable health information,

- secure the electronic transaction and storage of individually identifiable health information,

- limit the use and release of individually identifiable health information,

- increase patient control of use and disclosure of private health information,

- increase patients' access to their health records,

- establish legal accountability and penalties for unauthorized use and disclosure and violation of transaction and security standards, and

- identify public health and welfare needs that permit use and disclosure of individually identifiable health information without patient authorization.

To what does HIPAA apply? HIPAA regulations apply to *protected health information* (PHI), defined as oral, written, typed, or electronic individually identifiable information related to (1) a person's past, present, or future physical or mental health; (2) provision of health care to the person; or (3) past, present, or future payment for health care. For health information to come under the definition of PHI, it must be created by an employer or by the following *covered entities:* a health plan, a health care clearinghouse, or a health care provider who transmits any health information in electronic form in connection with financial or administrative activities related to health care. Educational records covered by the Family Educational Rights and Privacy Act (FERPA), employment records held by a covered entity in its role as employer, and de-identified records (in which all individually identifiable information has been removed) are *not* considered PHI.

What do covered entities need to do to comply with HIPAA? Under HIPAA, covered entities must (1) provide information to patients about their privacy rights and the covered entity's privacy practices, called a *notice of privacy practices;* (2) permit patient access to records and upon patient request provide an *accounting of disclosures* of PHI made to others over the past 6 years; (3) obtain patient *authorization* for use and disclosures to others in a manner and for purposes specified in the regulations; (4) implement clear privacy procedures for electronic transmission and storage of PHI; (5) designate a *privacy officer;* (6) implement security procedures that prevent unauthorized access to health records; (7) train and ensure that employees comply with privacy, transaction, and security procedures; (8) reasonably ensure that business associates, individual contractors, consultants, collection agencies, third-party payors, and researchers with whom PHI is shared comply with privacy and transaction rules; and (9) attempt to correct violations by these other entities if they occur or cease the relationship.

Are researchers, industrial-organizational, or consulting psychologists affected by HIPAA? Most researchers or members of their team who create, use, or disclose PHI as part of a randomized clinical trial or other forms of health-relevant intervention research will be considered covered entities. Researchers who are not involved in intervention research but who plan to use in their research or consulting services PHI created by a covered entity must provide to the covered entity written assurance that they will comply with HIPAA standards.

PART I

Introduction and Background

CHAPTER 1

A Code of Ethics for Psychology
How Did We Get Here?

> In a field so complex, where individual and social values are yet but ill defined, the desire to play fairly must be given direction and consistency by some rules of the game. These rules should do much more than help the unethical psychologist keep out of trouble; they should be of palpable aid to the ethical psychologist in making daily decisions.
>
> —Hobbs (1948, p. 81)

Beginnings

The American Psychological Association (APA) has had five decades of experience constructing and revising an ethics code that strives to reflect both the aspirations and practical aspects of ethical decisions made by members of the profession. The creation and each subsequent revision of the APA Ethics Code has been driven by the desire for standards that would encourage the highest endeavor of psychologists, ensure public welfare, promote sound relationships with allied professions, and promote the professional standing of the discipline (Hobbs, 1948).

Discussions within APA regarding the need for an ethics code in psychology arose in response to an increase in professional activity and public visibility of its members before and after World War II. During this period, the societal value of the still young discipline of psychology was evidenced as psychologists developed group tests to help the armed services quickly determine the draft eligibility of young men in wartime and provided mental health services to hospitalized soldiers when they returned home. In 1947, the first APA Committee on Ethical Standards for Psychologists was appointed. The committee, chaired by Edward Tolman, wanted to create a code of ethics for psychologists that would be more than a document with an imposing title (Hobbs, 1948). The members were committed to producing professional standards that would provide members of the profession with a set of values and practical techniques for identifying and resolving moral problems.

To achieve these goals, the committee decided to draw on the knowledge of the field to create a process of developing a code that would "be effective in modifying human behavior" (Hobbs, 1948, p. 82). According to Hobbs, "This is an old and familiar task to psychologists, their very stock in trade, in fact. The only difference here is that human behavior means specifically the behavior of psychologists" (p. 82). Drawing on the knowledge of group processes during that period, the committee conceived the task of developing ethical standards as one of group dynamics (Hobbs, 1948). The process chosen was the critical incident method (Flanagan, 1954), a technique that involved asking the members of the APA to describe a situation they knew of firsthand, in which a psychologist made a decision having ethical implications, and to indicate the ethical issues involved.

A second committee, chaired by Nicholas Hobbs, reviewed more than 1,000 such incidents submitted by APA members. The committee identified major ethical themes emerging from the incidents that focused on psychologists' relationships with and responsibilities to others, including patients, students, research participants, and other professionals. Many of the incidents reflected the political climate of the postwar period, including confrontations between academic freedom and McCarthyism and dilemmas faced by psychologists working in industry asked to design tests for the purpose of maintaining racial segregation in the workforce. As different segments of the code were created, drafts were submitted to the membership for critique and revision. A final draft was adopted by APA in 1952 and published in 1953.

Revisions Preceding the 2002 Ethics Code

At the time of the adoption of the first Ethics Code, continual review and revision based on the experience and perspectives of members was seen as integral to maintaining the value of the Ethics Code for both the profession and the public (Adkins, 1952). As a result, the Ethics Code of the APA has undergone nine revisions since 1953. The 1953 version was more than 170 pages long and included case examples illustrating each ethical standard. The standards themselves were written broadly, using aspirational rather than narrow legalistic language. Subsequent revisions eliminated the cases from the text itself and moved toward more specific language.

From the beginning of its more than 50-year history, each revision of the APA's Ethical Principles of Psychologists and Code of Conduct has been guided by the following objectives (Hobbs, 1948):

♦ To express the best ethical practices in the field as judged by a large representative sample of members of the APA

♦ To reflect an explicit value system as well as clearly articulated decisional and behavioral rules

♦ To be applicable to the full range of activities and role relationships encountered in the work of psychologists

♦ To have the broadest possible participation among psychologists in its development and revisions

♦ To influence the ethical conduct of psychologists by meriting widespread identification and acceptance among members of the discipline

Aspirational Principles and Enforceable Standards

At its heart, an ethics code should reflect the moral principles underlying the values of the profession. For most professions, ethical behaviors are generally those that fulfill the fundamental moral obligations to do good, to do no harm, to respect others, and to treat all individuals honestly and fairly. For some, statements of general principles are sufficient to guide the ethical behavior of persons devoted to the ideals of their profession. For others, however, statements describing specific types of behaviors that meet these ideals are necessary to maximize the code's utility and to provide a means of evaluating its efficacy (Schur, 1982).

The form in which ethical guidelines are written will determine whether an ethics code is an aspirational or enforceable document. Although all codes should have a foundation in moral principles, the document can take one of three forms. An aspirational code is composed of statements of broadly worded ideals and principles that do not attempt to define with any precision right and wrong behaviors. An educational code combines ethical principles with more explicit interpretations that can help individual professionals make informed decisions in morally ambiguous contexts. An enforceable code includes a set of standards that specifically describes behaviors required and proscribed by the profession and is designed to serve as a basis for adjudicating grievances (Frankel, 1996).

Prior to the 1992 revision, the APA Ethics Code combined statements of aspirational principles with general guidelines and enforceable standards for ethical behavior (APA, 1981). By the late 1980s, the increasing legalistic reaction of consumers and psychologists involved in charges of ethical violations by psychologists raised concerns about the fairness of subjective interpretations of such broadly worded principles and standards. Moreover, a rise in the number of appeals to decisions made by the APA Ethics Committee and regulatory bodies (such as state licensing boards) that relied on the APA Ethics Code for their disciplinary procedures suggested that adjudicatory decisions based on this type of format would be increasingly difficult to enforce and thus a disservice to the APA membership (Bersoff, 1994). Accordingly, to strengthen both the enforceability and credibility of APA ethical guidelines, crafters of the 1992 APA Ethics Code separated the enforceable standards from the aspirational principles to make the standards simple, behaviorally focused, and representative of unitary concepts (Canter, Bennett, Jones, & Nagy, 1994).

During the revision process leading to the 1992 Ethics Code, some psychologists argued that adjudication based on specific ethical standards rather than general principles would diminish the moral foundation on which the APA Ethics Committee charged with adjudicating ethics complaints could base its decisions. Others supported the move toward separate enforceable standards arguing that in practice limiting the standards to legally and procedurally unenforceable wording would dilute the ethical goals intended by the foundational principles (Fisher & Younggren, 1997).

The 1992 Ethics Code represented a radical change from its predecessors in both structure and content. For the first time, clear distinctions were made between aspirational principles that articulated foundational values of the discipline and specific decision rules articulated in 180 distinct ethical standards that would be subject to enforcement by the APA, other organizations, and licensing boards that adopted them (Canter et al., 1994).

The Process of Developing the 2002 Ethics Code

In 1996, the APA Ethics Committee appointed the Ethics Code Task Force (ECTF), a 14-member committee whose membership reflected the scientific, educational, professional, gender, ethnic, and geographic diversity of the discipline. Over the 5-year period, members included Celia B. Fisher, Chair, Peter Appleby, Bruce Bennett, Laura Brown, Linda F. Campbell, Nabil El-Ghoroury, Dennis J. Grill, Jessica Henderson Daniel, Samuel J. Knapp, Gerald P. Koocher, Marcia Moody, Peter E. Nathan, Thomas D. Oakland, Mary H. Quigley, Julia M. Ramos-Grenier, Abigail Sivan, Steven N. Sparta, Elizabeth Swenson, Melba J. T. Vasquez, and Brian Wilcox.

The Purpose of an Ethics Code

The mission of the task force was to develop and implement a plan for revision of the 1992 Ethics Code. In its deliberations, the ECTF considered the importance of both the purpose and process of ethics code development, recognizing that such consideration would determine the content and format of the code, and ultimately whether psychologists will support it.

The many goals identified by the ECTF to guide the 2002 Ethics Code revision process included the professional, educational, public, and enforcement values of a code of ethics. These values guided decisions regarding inclusion and exclusion of ethical requirements and prohibitions and the language used to craft General Principles and Ethical Standards.

Establishing the integrity of a profession. One purpose of an ethics code is to help establish and maintain the viability of a profession. An ethics code reflects a collective decision that a profession is better off when ethical standards are not based solely on individual assessments of what is or is not morally acceptable. Adoption of a set of core values that reflect consensus among members of a discipline distinguishes psychology as a "community of common purpose" and enhances public confidence in individuals who have been trained to meet the profession's ethical standards (Callahan, 1982; Frankel, 1996, Seitz & O'Neill, 1996). Acceptance of an identified set of core values by individual psychologists across the broad spectrum of psychological activities also helps to protect the integrity of the profession by focusing the attention of individual psychologists on their responsibilities and duties to others and expectations that all members of the profession have a stake in behaving by the rules. A core value of the discipline of psychology as articulated in the Preamble of the 2002 Ethics Code is the welfare and protection of the individuals and groups with whom psychologists work.

Education and professional socialization. A second purpose of an ethics code is its professional socialization function. A document reflecting the profession's values and standards provides a guide to what psychologists should reasonably expect of themselves and one another. A code can be conceived as an enabling document that acts as a support and guide to individual psychologists in their efforts to resolve ethical dilemmas (Frankel, 1996; Sinclair, Poizner, Gilmour-Barrett, & Randall, 1987). A code of ethics also serves to deter psychologists from engaging in unethical conduct before a problem develops by specifically proscribing what the profession has identified as unethical behaviors (Fisher & Younggren, 1997). In addition, it assists faculty and supervisors in communicating the values of the profession to graduate students and to new Ph.D.s with limited professional experience.

Public trust. A third purpose of an ethics code is to gain public trust by demonstrating that psychologists are members of a responsible and substantial profession with high standards. A code can serve a public relations value by being seen as a contract with society to act in consumers' best interest. A professional ethics code also provides standards against which the public can hold psychologists accountable. It thus offers a means by which members of the public can draw on norms prescribed by the profession itself to evaluate the conduct of scientists, educators, consultants, and practitioners with whom they interact.

Enforcement value. A profession that demonstrates it can monitor itself is less vulnerable to external regulation. A fourth purpose of an ethics code is to provide a clear statement of the types of behaviors considered ethical violations to guide psychologists in avoiding such behaviors, assist consumers in making ethical complaints, and ensure that such complaints can be adjudicated clearly and fairly by the APA and other organizations (Fisher & Younggren, 1997). The APA Ethics Code also serves as a guide for licensing boards, courts, and other institutions for the evaluation of the responsible conduct of psychology and is thus a means of avoiding capricious standards set by nonpsychologists. The Ethics Code can also help psychologists defend their decisions to courts, institutions, or government agencies that would encourage them to go against the values of the profession.

The Revision Process

The ECTF was committed to an open and collaborative revision process that would be guided by the objectives articulated by the first ethics code committee (Hobbs, 1948). In response to the continually evolving legal landscape of ethics adjudication and federal regulation of science and health practices, the ECTF also concluded that although law should not dictate the content of the ethics code, sensitivity to law would protect the integrity of the document as a useful tool for the everyday ethical decisions of psychologists. The 2002 Ethics Code revision process involved the following:

♦ Collecting from psychologists engaged in a broad spectrum of scientific and professional activities critical incidents describing ethical challenges they had encountered, actual or ideal ethical approaches to these challenges, and the extent to which the existing Ethics Code could be applied to these challenges

♦ Establishing an open call for and review of comments from the membership, state psychological associations, licensing boards, and the public on the adequacy of the 1992 Ethics Code and on the content and format of each of seven drafts produced by the ECTF

♦ Opening ECTF meetings to observers from different APA constituencies so as to benefit from their insights and perspectives

♦ Ongoing legal review by APA General Counsel and outside defense, plaintiff, Federal Trade Commission, and federal regulatory attorneys

♦ Ongoing feedback from consumers, students, APA divisions and committees, the APA Ethics Committee, APA Board of Directors, and the APA Council of Representatives

As described previously, the crafters of the 1992 Ethics Code realized that earlier versions emphasizing aspirational principles were becoming increasingly difficult to enforce and more vulnerable to legal challenges based on behavioral vagueness and lack of due notice (Canter et al., 1994; Fisher & Younggren, 1997). As Bersoff (1994) pointed out, such indeterminacy resulted in a disservice to APA's members, whose ability to defend their ethical actions were increasingly compromised. Accordingly, a format dividing enforceable standards from aspirational principles in the 1992 Ethics Code strengthened the APA's success sustaining decisions by the APA Ethics Committee in court, thus strengthening both the enforceability and credibility of APA's ethical oversight procedures.

Based on a critical review of the 1992 document, comments received from APA members, and awareness of the continuing legal climate of ethics adjudication, the ECTF recommended and the APA Council of Representatives decided to retain the division of aspirational principles and enforceable standards in the 2002 Ethics Code.

In this format, the General Principles provide a conceptual framework that expresses the aspirational values of the common community of psychologists and the behavioral rules articulated in the standards flow from these principles.

Adoption of the Ethics Code by the APA Council of Representatives

After reviewing more than 1,300 comments and feedback on seven revisions, in August 2002, the APA Council of Representatives voted unanimously to adopt the final revision as the new Ethical Principles of Psychologists and Code of Conduct to go into effect in June 2003 (APA, 2002).

The remainder of this book explains the meaning and applications of the 2002 Ethics Code to the rightly conducted science and practice of psychology. Chapter 2 explains the Ethics Code's Introduction and Applicability section, Preamble, and General Principles. Chapter 3 provides a brief summary of significant differences between the 1992 and 2002 Ethics Code that readers may need to know right away to ensure their continued ethical compliance with the code. Chapters 4-13 provide in-depth analysis and examples of each of the 151 enforceable Ethical Standards. Chapter 14 concludes with models of ethical decision making for applying the Ethics Code in everyday activities and to emerging ethical challenges as the discipline of psychology continues to evolve.

CHAPTER 2

The Introduction and Applicability Section, Preamble, and General Principles

What Do They Mean?

> *Psychologists are committed to increasing scientific and professional knowledge of behavior and people's understanding of themselves and others and to the use of such knowledge to improve the condition of individuals, organizations, and society. Psychologists respect and protect civil and human rights and the central importance of freedom of inquiry and expression in research, teaching, and publication. They strive to help the public in developing informed judgments and choices concerning human behavior.*
>
> *—Ethical Principles of Psychologists and Code of Conduct, American Psychological Association (APA, 2002)*

The 2002 Ethics Code includes many of the innovations introduced in 1992. It begins with the Introduction and Applicability section, followed by the Preamble and a set of five General Principles reflecting the underlying values and ideals of the discipline. The remainder of the code is composed of 151 enforceable standards that describe required, prohibited, and permitted behaviors. This chapter highlights the implications for ethical conduct of the Introduction and Applicability section, Preamble, and General Principles. It also provides a special section explaining significant differences between standards in the 1992 and 2002 Ethics Code that readers may wish to peruse right away to ensure ethical compliance. Readers can refer to the appendix where the full text of the Ethics Code is provided.

Understanding the Introduction and Applicability Section and the Preamble

To Whom Does the Ethics Code Apply?

Membership in the APA commits members and student affiliates to comply with the standards of the ethics code.

To What Does the Ethics Code Apply?

The answer to this question is all activities, all persons, all settings, and all communication contexts that are conducted, encountered, or used in one's role as a psychologist. The Ethics Code applies only to psychologists' activities that are part of their scientific, educational, professional, or consulting roles. The code does not apply to the purely private conduct of psychologists; although the APA may take action against a member after his or her conviction of a felony whether or not it directly resulted from activities performed in the member's role as a psychologist.

♦ *Activities* include, but are not limited to, clinical, counseling, and school practice; research; teaching and supervision; public service and policy development; program design, implementation, and evaluation; construction, administration, and interpretation of assessment instruments; organizational consulting; forensic activities; and administration.

♦ *Persons* include individual clients/patients, research participants, and students; children and adults of all ages; individuals with or without mental disorders; individuals with disabilities; persons from diverse cultural and language backgrounds; individuals within families, groups, and organizations; attorneys; and other professionals.

♦ *Settings* include military bases, schools, research laboratories, universities, private or group practice offices, business organizations, hospitals, managed care companies, the courts, private and public social services programs, and government agencies.

♦ *Communication contexts* include research, consultation, and the delivery of services in person or through postal, telephone, fax, Internet, television and radio, and other electronic transmissions.

Psychologists should be aware that the Introduction and Applicability section clearly states that lack of awareness or misunderstanding of any part of the Ethics Code is not itself a defense to a charge of unethical conduct.

What Is the Relevance of Specific Language Used in the Ethics Code?

To fulfill the Ethics Code's professional, educational, public, and enforcement goals, the language of the Ethics Code needs to have the clarity necessary to provide adequate notice of behaviors that would be considered code violations, to be applicable across many multifaceted roles and responsibilities of psychologists, and to enhance and not impede good scientific and professional practice. The language of the Ethics Code must be specific enough to provide guidance and general enough to allow for critical thinking and professional judgment.

This section includes some general guidance for interpreting the language of the Ethics Code. The implications of specific terminology to specific standards are addressed in greater detail in relevant chapters.

Due notice. Adjudicatory decisions based on an ethics code remain vulnerable to overturn on appeal if defendants can argue they had no forewarning that specific behaviors were ethical violations (Bersoff, 1994). For example, language in enforceable standards requiring psychologists to be "alert to," "guard against," or "respect" certain factors are problematic because the behaviors expected by these terms remain undefined and are thus vulnerable to subjective interpretation by psychologists, consumers, and ethics committees. Accordingly, the language of the enforceable standards in the 2002 Ethics Code was crafted to describe the behaviors that are required and those that are proscribed in a manner that would be reasonably understood by readers.

Applicability across diverse roles and contexts. Psychologists teach, conduct research, provide therapy, administer and interpret psychological tests, consult to business, provide legal testimony, evaluate school programs, and serve in a multitude of different scientific and professional roles. An enforceable ethics code for psychologists must therefore be worded broadly enough to ensure that (1) standards apply across a broad range of activities in which psychologists are engaged; (2) role-specific standards are clearly presented as such; and (3) standards do not compromise scientific, practice, or consulting activities through inattention to or inconsistencies with the constantly changing realities of professional and legal responsibilities.

This requirement, viewed alongside the need for language providing due notice, means that some standards reflecting generally accepted ethical values in one work area were not included in the 2002 Ethics Code because they could not be worded in such a way as to prevent undue burden on psychologists working in another area. For example, the Ethics Code Task Force struggled with appropriate wording for a general "honesty" standard within the Human Relations section that would reflect the aspirational principle of Integrity. However, such a general standard had to be abandoned because it risked prohibiting ethically acceptable practices such as paradoxical therapy and deception research. The Ethics Code Task Force addressed issues of honesty through sanctions against specific types of fraudulent activities in standards on public statements, fees and financial arrangements, and data collection.

The use of modifiers. A modifier is a word or phrase that qualifies the meaning of an ethical rule. Modifiers in the Ethics Code include such terms as "appropriate," "potentially," "to the extent feasible," and "attempt to." An explanation for the use of "modifiers" is provided in the Introduction and Applicability section. The use of modifiers is necessary for standards that are written broadly to allow for professional judgment across a wide range of psychological activities and contexts. For example, the term "feasible" in a standard permits psychologists to evaluate whether factors within the specific context in which they are working justify delaying or not implementing behaviors required by a particular standard. Modifiers are also used to eliminate injustice or inequality that would occur without the modifier. For example, a modifier such as "appropriate" signals that the behaviors required to comply with a standard can vary with the psychological characteristics of the persons involved, psychologists' roles, or specific situational demands. A modifier such as the term "relevant" is used in standards to guard against language that would create a rigid rule that would be quickly outdated. Below are three examples of the use of modifiers:

♦ Standard 10.10a, Informed Consent to Therapy, requires psychologists to obtain informed consent from clients/patients as early as is feasible in the therapeutic relationship. The phrase "as early as is feasible" provides decisional latitude when fully informed consent during an initial therapy session may not be possible or clinically appropriate. A client/patient may be experiencing acute distress that requires immediate psychological intervention and for which informed consent procedures may be clinically contraindicated. Psychologists may need to wait for feedback from a client's/patient's health maintenance organization (HMO) before consent discussions regarding fees can be completed.

♦ Standard 3.10b, Informed Consent, requires that for persons who are legally incapable of giving informed consent, psychologists "provide an appropriate explanation." The term "appropriate" indicates that the nature of the explanation will vary depending on, among other factors, the person's developmental level, cognitive capacities, mental status, and language preferences and proficiencies.

♦ Under Standard 2.01c, Boundaries of Competence, psychologists planning to engage in activities new to them must undertake relevant education, training, supervised experience, consultation, or study. By including the term "relevant," this standard can continue to be applied to new roles, new techniques, and new technologies, as they emerge over time.

What is "reasonable"? In the Introduction and Applicability section, the term "reasonable" is defined as the "prevailing professional judgment of psychologists engaged in similar activities in similar circumstances, given the knowledge the psychologist had or should have had at the time." The use of this term serves two functions. It prohibits psychologists from exercising idiosyncratic ethical judgments inconsistent with the prevailing values and behaviors of members of the profession. In so doing it provides other psychologists and recipients of psychological services, students, and research participants a professional standard against which to judge psychologists' ethical behaviors. At the same time, by requiring that criteria for compliance or violation of an Ethical Standard be judged against the prevailing practices of peers, the use of the term "reasonable" guards against unrealistic or unfair expectations of responsible conduct. The wording enables psychologists to launch a legitimate defense of their actions based on current best practices in the field and documentation of efforts to resolve problems in an ethical manner. The examples below illustrate these two applications of the term "reasonable":

◆ Standard 4.07, Use of Confidential Information for Didactic or Other Purposes, prohibits psychologists from disclosing in public statements confidential and personally identifiable information about those with whom they work unless they have taken "reasonable steps to disguise the person or organization." The term "reasonable" recognizes that despite steps to protect confidentiality that would be considered ethically acceptable by other psychologists (i.e., the use of pseudonyms; disguising gender, ethnicity, age, setting, business products), persons to whom the statements refer may recognize (or erroneously attribute the description to) themselves or others may be privy to information not under the psychologist's control that leads to identification.

◆ Standard 2.05, Delegation of Work to Others, requires that psychologists who delegate work to employees, supervisees, research or teaching assistants, interpreters, or others take reasonable steps to authorize only those responsibilities that such persons can be expected to perform competently on the basis of their education, training, or experience, either independently or with the level of supervision being provided. In this case, a psychologist who asked a secretary who spoke the same language as a client/patient to serve as an interpreter during an assessment would not have taken steps considered reasonable in the prevailing view of the profession. On the other hand, a psychologist who hired an interpreter based on an impressive set of credentials in mental health evaluation would not be in violation if the interpreter had fabricated the credentials.

"Client/patient" and "organizational client." Throughout the Ethics Code, the combined term "client/patient" refers to individual persons to whom a psychologist is providing treatment, intervention, or assessment services. The term "organizational clients," "organizations," or "clients" refers to organizations, representatives of organizations, or other individuals for whom the psychologist is providing consultation, organization or personnel evaluations, test development, research, forensic expertise, or other services that do not involve a treatment, intervention, or diagnostic professional relationship with the person to whom services are provided. For example:

> A bank hired a psychologist to provide counseling services to employees who had experienced trauma during a recent robbery. In this context, the bank was the psychologist's "client" or "organizational client" and the employees who sought the psychologist's counseling services were the clients/patients. To further illustrate this distinction, readers can compare the use of the term "client" in Standard 3.11, Psychological Services Delivered To or Through Organizations, to the use of the term "client/patient" in Standard 10.01, Informed Consent to Therapy.

What Happened to References to Specific APA Guidelines?

The Introduction and Applicability section of the Ethics Code recommends that members refer to guidelines adopted or endorsed by scientific and professional psychological organizations as materials that may be useful in applying the Ethics Code to everyday activities. Unlike the 1992 Ethics Code, specific APA guidelines to which psychologists may refer are not listed. The reason for this decision was twofold: (1) APA guidelines are frequently revised or become outdated, and (2) some statements in the older guidelines are inconsistent with standards in the new Ethics Code and prevailing psychological science and practice.

How Is the Ethics Code Related to APA Ethics Enforcement?

The APA Ethics Committee investigates complaints against APA members alleging violations of the APA Ethics Code that was in effect at the time the conduct occurred. The APA Ethics Committee Rules and Procedures detail the ethics enforcement process and can be obtained online at http://www.apa.org/ethics/rules.html. Below is a brief summary of these rules and procedures.

Ethics complaints. Complaints to the Ethics Committee may be brought by APA members or nonmembers or initiated by members of the Ethics Committee (*sua sponte* complaints) within specified time periods. A complaint may be dismissed prior to review by the Ethics Committee if it does not meet jurisdictional criteria or if upon preliminary review the Ethics Office director and the Ethics Committee chair or their designees fail to find grounds for action. If the Ethics Committee does have jurisdiction and the complaint provides grounds for action, the case is opened, violations of specific Ethical Standards are charged, and an investigation is begun. The psychologist against whom the complaint is made receives a charge letter and is given an opportunity to provide the committee with comment and materials regarding the allegations.

Failure of the respondent to cooperate with the Ethics Committee is itself an ethical violation (APA Ethics Code Standard 1.06, Cooperating With Ethics Committees; see Chapter 4). However, in response to a request by a respondent, the committee may proceed or stay the ethics process if the respondent is involved in civil or criminal litigation or disciplinary proceedings in other jurisdictions. Psychologists who do not wish to contest the allegations may submit to the APA an offer of "resignation while under investigation."

Sanctions. The Ethics Committee reviews the materials and resolves to either dismiss the case or recommend one of the following actions:

- ♦ *Reprimand.* A reprimand is given when a violation was not of a kind likely to cause harm to another person or to cause substantial harm to the profession and was not otherwise of sufficient gravity as to warrant a more severe sanction.

♦ *Censure.* The Ethics Committee may issue a censure if the violation was of a kind likely to cause harm to another person, but the violation was not of a kind likely to cause substantial harm to another person or to the profession and was not otherwise of sufficient gravity as to warrant a more severe sanction.

♦ *Expulsion.* A member can be expelled from the APA when the violation was of a kind likely to cause substantial harm to another person or the profession or was otherwise of sufficient gravity as to warrant such action.

♦ *Stipulated resignation.* Contingent on execution of an acceptable affidavit and approval by the Board of Directors, members may be offered a stipulated resignation following a committee finding that they committed a violation of the Ethics Code or failed to show good cause why they should not be expelled.

The Ethics Committee may also issue directives requiring the respondent to (1) cease and desist an activity, (2) obtain supervision or additional training or education, (3) be evaluated for and obtain treatment if appropriate, or (4) agree to probationary monitoring.

A psychologist who has been found in violation of the Ethics Code may respond to the recommendation by requesting an independent case review or in the case of expulsion an in-person proceeding before a formal hearing committee.

Notification. The director of the Ethics Office informs the respondent and the complainant of the final disposition in a matter; provides to the APA membership on an annual basis the names of individuals who have been expelled from membership and those who resigned from membership while under investigation; and informs the APA Council of Representatives in confidence who received a stipulated resignation and who resigned from membership while under investigation. The Board of Directors or the Ethics Committee may also determine that additional notification is necessary to protect the APA or the public or to maintain APA standards. The Ethics Office director may also notify state boards, affiliated state and regional associations, the American Board of Professional Psychology, the Association of State and Provincial Psychology Boards, the Council for the National Register of Health Service Providers in Psychology, and other appropriate parties. In addition, the APA may provide such information to any person who submits a request about a former member who has lost membership because of an ethical violation.

Show cause procedure. The Ethics Committee can also take action against a member if a criminal court, licensing board, or state psychological association has already taken adverse action against the member. The rationale for such actions can go beyond a violation of the Ethics Code and can include conviction of a felony or revocation of state licensure.

How Is the Ethics Code
Related to Sanctions by Other Bodies?

The APA Ethics Code is widely used by other bodies regulating the ethical science and practice of psychology. It is intended to be applied by the APA Ethics Committee and by other bodies that choose to adopt specific standards. The Introduction and Applicability section states, "Actions that violate the standards of the Ethics Code may also lead to the imposition of sanctions on psychologists or students whether or not they are APA members by bodies other than APA, including state psychological associations, other professional groups, psychology boards, other state or federal agencies, and payors for health services." In contrast to the Ethical Standards, as stated in the General Principles section, the aspirational principles of the Ethics Code are not intended to represent specific obligations nor the basis for imposing sanctions.

Across the country, the Ethics Code is adopted in its entirety or in part in statute in more than half the state boards responsible for licensing the practice of psychology. Insurance companies regularly require psychologists applying or reapplying for professional liability policies to reveal whether they have been the recipient of an ethics complaint or found in ethical violation by a professional organization, state board, or state or federal agency, and many retain the right to raise rates or cancel policies depending on the nature of the violation. In addition, the APA Ethics Committee may notify other bodies and individuals of sanctions it imposes for ethical violations. For information on the procedures for filing, investigating, and resolving ethics complaints, readers should refer to the Rules and Procedures of the APA Ethics Committee at http://www.apa.org/ethics/rules.html.

How Is the APA Ethics Code Related to Law?

Civil litigation. The Introduction and Applicability section clearly states that the Ethics Code is not intended to be a basis of civil liability: "Whether a psychologist has violated the Ethics Code standards does not by itself determine whether the psychologist is legally liable in a court action, whether a contract is enforceable, or whether other legal consequences occur." However, psychologists should be aware that it seems highly unlikely that such a disclaimer would have any legally binding effect. Compliance with or violation of the Ethics Code may be admissible as evidence in some legal proceedings, depending on the circumstances. Similarly, although the Ethics Code states that using the General Principles as a representation of obligations or to apply sanctions distorts the meaning and purpose of the aspirational principles, attorneys may introduce into litigation the General Principles or Ethical Standards as evidence of the ethical values, requirements, or prohibitions of the discipline.

Compliance with law. Law does not dictate ethics, but sensitivity to law protects the integrity of the profession. Whereas few standards require psychologists to comply with law, many standards were written to minimize the possibility that compliance with the Ethics Code would be in conflict with state laws and federal regulations. Those standards that require compliance with the law include the following:

♦ Work-related discrimination, Standard 3.01, Unfair Discrimination

♦ Obtaining consent from legally authorized persons for individuals legally incapable of giving such consent, Standard 3.10b, Informed Consent

♦ Legal prohibitions against disclosure of confidential information, Standards 4.05a and b, Disclosures

♦ Creation, storage, and disposal of records, Standard 6.01, Documentation of Professional and Scientific Work and Maintenance of Records

♦ Fee practices, Standard 6.04a, Fees and Financial Arrangements

♦ Care and use of animals in research, Standard 8.09, Humane Care and Use of Animals in Research

♦ Legal and contractual obligations, Standard 9.11, Maintaining Test Security

Although there are no specific Ethical Standards for which a criminal conviction is a violation, the Introduction and Applicability section and the APA Rules and Regulations clearly state that the APA may take action against a member after his or her conviction of a felony, including expulsion from the organization.

Conflicts between ethics and law, regulations, or other governing legal authority. In applying the Ethics Code to their scientific and professional work, psychologists may find relevant laws, regulations, or other governing legal authority that conflict with the Ethical Standards. As articulated in the Introduction and Applicability section, psychologists must comply with the Ethics Code if it establishes a higher standard of conduct than is required by law. When an Ethical Standard is in direct conflict with law, regulations, or other governing legal authority, psychologists must make known their commitment to the Ethics Code and take steps to resolve the conflict in a responsible manner. If the conflict is unresolvable via such means, psychologists are permitted to adhere to the legal requirements. The Introduction and Applicability section of the Ethics Code urges psychologists to resolve such conflicts in keeping with basic principles of human rights; however, this latter obligation does not appear in the relevant enforceable standard, Standard 1.02, Conflicts Between Ethics and Law, Regulations, or Other Governing Authority.

General Principles

> *Ethics are principles of action based on a commonly accepted system of values, and agreement upon these principles and values must be reached before progress toward an acceptable code can be expected.*
>
> —*Bixler and Seeman (1946, p. 486)*

"A genuine and practical code of ethics . . . stems from a philosophy as well as a need" (Bixler & Seeman, 1946, p. 486). The moral values from which the APA Ethical Standards stem are articulated in five General Principles. These principles are aspirational, intended to inspire psychologists toward the highest ethical ideals of the profession. Unlike the Ethical Standards, they do not represent specific or enforceable behavioral rules of conduct. The General Principles articulate the moral vision of psychology's common community of purpose. The 2002 Ethics Code maintains the aspirational values articulated in the previous code, but defines them through the language of moral philosophy.

The principles are listed in alphabetical order and are not hierarchically organized. Although psychologists must strive to act in accordance with all the principles, the moral priority of any one principle will be determined by the specific ethical problem. The General Principles help guide psychologists' decision making by providing an analytic framework from which to identify those Ethical Standards that are appropriate to the situation at hand.

Principle A: Beneficence and Nonmaleficence. As articulated in the Preamble and in Principle A, psychologists strive to do good by promoting the welfare of others, treating animals humanely, increasing scientific and professional knowledge of behavior and people's understanding of themselves, and improving the condition of individuals, organizations, and society. Psychologists also strive to do no harm. In rightly practiced psychology, individuals may be harmed without being wronged. For example, disclosing confidential information to protect a client/patient, student, or research participant from self-harm or from harming others may have moral priority over protecting that individual's privacy rights. To preserve academic standards and ensure grading fairness, teaching psychologists may be obligated to give a student a poor or failing grade. Psychologists try to minimize such harms when they are unavoidable. To maximize good and minimize harm, Principle A also calls for psychologists to be alert to and guard against personal problems that could lead to exploitation or harm to individuals or organizations with whom they work.

Principle B: Fidelity and Responsibility. Fidelity reflects faithfulness of one human being to another (Ramsey, 2002). In psychology, such faithfulness includes promise keeping, the discharge and acceptance of fiduciary responsibilities, and the appropriate maintenance of scientific, professional, and teaching relationships. Psychologists recognize their responsibility to obtain and maintain high standards of competence in their own work and to be concerned about the ethical compliance of their colleagues. The nature of the competencies and responsibilities of psychologists to individuals, organizations, and communities will be determined by the specific scientific or professional relationship. As articulated in Principle B, psychologists seek to meet their responsibilities by consulting with other professionals when necessary and avoiding conflicts of interest that would jeopardize trust or lead to exploitation or harm.

Principle C: Integrity. Maintaining integrity in psychological activities involves honest communication, truth telling, promise keeping, and accuracy in the science, teaching, and practice of psychology. It involves refraining from making professional commitments that cannot be met and avoiding or correcting misrepresentations of one's work. In following Principle C, psychologists do not steal, cheat, or engage in fraud or subterfuge. In some scientific and professional relationships, deception may be justified to maximize knowledge gained or the welfare of individuals served. In each instance, psychologists have a serious obligation to evaluate whether deception is warranted, to decide whether negative consequences outweigh the benefits to individuals or society, and to correct any mistrust or harm that arises from the use of such techniques.

Principle D: Justice. Principle D calls for psychologists to strive to provide to all people fair, equitable, and appropriate access to treatment and to the benefits of scientific knowledge. Psychologists endeavor to be aware of and guard against their own biases and the prejudices of others that may condone or lead to unjust practices. They select procedures and services that meet the needs of those with whom they work, recognizing that existing social and economic inequities may require different but comparable scientific and professional techniques.

Principle E: Respect for People's Rights and Dignity. Principle E calls for psychologists to "respect the dignity and worth of all people, and the rights of individuals to privacy, confidentiality, and self-determination." Psychologists are attentive to the circumstances of individuals who may have limited capacity for autonomous decision making and take the extra precautions necessary to safeguard these individuals' rights and welfare. Psychologists are aware of and respect cultural, individual, and role differences, including those based on age, gender, gender identity, race, ethnicity, culture, national origin, religion, sexual orientation, disability, language, and socioeconomic status. They ensure that they are familiar with the scientific and professional knowledge relevant to these differences and acquire the competencies necessary to perform their roles effectively. Psychologists strive to be aware of and eliminate from their work the effect of their own and others' prejudices.

CHAPTER 3

Changes From
the 1992 Ethics Code
What You May Need to Know Right Now

If you are a seasoned psychologist who has been making ethical decisions guided by the 1992 Ethics Code or a graduate student or new Ph.D. whose training was on the previous code, this section identifies the significant differences between the 1992 and 2002 codes that you may need to know right away.

Since its inception in 1953, each revision of the American Psychological Association (APA) Ethics Code has been driven by the evolving roles and responsibilities of psychologists within a constantly changing sociocultural, economic, political, and legal landscape. Major trends influencing revisions leading to the 2002 Ethics Code included (1) the growth and influence of health maintenance organizations (HMOs) on the provision of health services; (2) the advent of Internet-mediated research and practice and the use of other electronic media; (3) greater sensitivity to the needs of culturally and language-diverse populations in research and practice; (4) increasing participation of psychologists in the legal system; and (5) the sea change from paternalistic to autonomy-based public attitudes and federal regulations affecting industries, organizations, health care, research, and educational institutions.

Revision of the enforceable standards of the 1992 Ethics Code ranged from (a) minor grammatical modifications to reworking of language that helped clarify but did not otherwise alter the meaning of an existing standard to (b) new language that expanded the scope of the standard to additional roles or activities to (c) major wording changes that significantly altered the meaning of the standard to (d) the inclusion of new rules for ethical conduct. As detailed in the Preface to this book, in the chapters explaining the enforceable standards, bracketed notations are placed at the end of each standard to help readers quickly identify the nature of these changes. A table comparing the 1992 and 2002 Ethics Code is also available on the APA Ethics Office Web site, www.apa.org/ethics/codecompare/html. This chapter highlights significant changes or additions in enforceable standards that psychologists may need to be immediately familiar with to ensure continued compliance to APA Ethical Standards. Each of these changes is discussed in greater detail in subsequent chapters of this book.

Where Did the Forensic Standards Go?

Among the significant format changes of the 1992 Ethics Code was the inclusion of a distinct section of the document devoted to forensic activities. Although the enforceable standards in that section were not uniquely related to forensic practice, crafters of the 1992 Ethics Code decided that ethical issues in forensic practice needed to be set out clearly and separately from other sections of the code in light of the increasing frequency of ethics complaints to the APA Ethics Office, licensing board actions, and civil litigation related to forensic activities (APA, 1995, 1996; Canter, Bennett, Jones, & Nagy, 1994). During the 1990s, formal training, credentialing, and practice guidelines in forensic psychology advanced along with an increase in the number of psychologists without formal forensic training who were expanding their services to the legal arena or were called on to serve as fact witnesses in litigation (Perrin & Sales, 1994). As a result, the Ethics Code Task Force (ECTF) charged with revising the 1992 code decided to eliminate the forensic section and incorporate standards relevant to court-related activities into other sections of the 2002 Ethics Code. This change in format was selected to better serve the educational function of the document by alerting psychologists without formal training in forensic psychology to the ethical issues they must consider in advance of taking on roles involving the legal system.

Forensic or court-related work activities are explicitly mentioned in Standards 2.01f, Boundaries of Competence; 3.05c, Multiple Relationships; 3.10c, Informed Consent; 9.01a, Bases for Assessments; 9.03c, Informed Consent in Assessments; 9.04b, Release of Test Data; 9.10, Explaining Assessment Results; and 10.02b, Therapy Involving Couples. The topical table of contents and the law icons ⚖ throughout the book will help readers quickly find discussions of these and other standards relevant to work within the legal system.

The Internet and Other
Electronically Mediated Research and Services

In reviewing the profession's evolving use of the Internet and other electronic media for behavioral telehealth, psychological assessment, consulting, video conferencing, public statements, and research, the ECTF concluded that throughout each section of the code most of the broadly worded enforceable standards were applicable to these activities and did not require specific reference to the medium in which research or services are conducted. Use of the Internet and other electronically mediated forms relevant to research or services are explicitly mentioned in four standards: 3.10a, Informed Consent; 4.02c, Discussing the Limits of Confidentiality; 5.01a, Avoidance of False or Deceptive Statements; and 5.04, Media Presentations. To quickly locate discussions in this book on how other standards should be applied to work using electronic media, readers can refer to the topical table of contents and look for this icon 🐾 in chapters on the enforceable standards.

Informed Consent for Research, Assessment, and Practice

In the 1992 Ethics Code, obtaining informed consent was only explicitly required for research and therapy. The 2002 Ethics Code (1) broadens this requirement to assessment and counseling services, (2) provides greater direction on the information that must be included in informed consent, (3) specifically details consent information required for intervention research, (4) requires additional consent safeguards for treatment for which generally recognized techniques and procedures have not been established, and (5) clarifies that informed consent requirements apply whether the activity is conducted in person or via electronic transmission (Standards 3.10, Informed Consent; 8.02, Informed Consent to Research; 9.03, Informed Consent in Assessments; and 10.01, Informed Consent to Therapy).

Dispensing with informed consent. Along with the expansion of informed consent obligations, the 2002 Ethics Code also provides more specific descriptions of situations in which the requirement for informed consent may be waived. These standards reflect enhanced sensitivity to neuropsychological, forensic, school, and industrial-organizational contexts in which psychologists provide services, conduct research, or administer assessments. Psychologists may dispense with informed consent:

> ". . . when conducting the psychological activities without consent is mandated by law or governmental regulation" (Standard 3.10a, Informed Consent)

> only ". . . where research would not reasonably be assumed to create distress or harm and involves (a) the study of normal educational practices, curricula, or classroom management methods conducted in educational settings; (b) only anonymous questionnaires, naturalistic observations, or archival research for which disclosure of responses would not place participants at risk of criminal or civil liability or damage their financial standing, employability, or reputation, and confidentiality is protected; or (c) the study of factors related to job or organization effectiveness conducted in organizational settings for which there is no risk to participants employability and confidentiality is protected or (2) where otherwise permitted by law or federal or institutional regulations" (Standard 8.05, Dispensing With Informed Consent for Research)

> ". . . when (1) testing is mandated by law or governmental regulations; (2) informed consent is implied because testing is conducted as a routine educational, institutional, or organizational activity (e.g., when participants

voluntarily agree to assessment when applying for a job); or (3) one purpose of the testing is to evaluate decisional capacity" (Standard 9.03a, Informed Consent in Assessments)

Information Provided To or Through Organizations

Psychologists working in industry, HMOs, or consulting or delivering services to other organizations should refer to Standard 3.11, Psychological Services Delivered To or Through Organizations. This standard expands on requirements of the older code with respect to information that must be provided to organizational clients beforehand and when appropriate to those directly affected by the services.

Teaching

The Ethics Code includes several modified or new standards designed to strengthen protections for students.

Program descriptions. Psychologists responsible for psychology programs must now include in program descriptions information regarding stipends and benefits and required course- or program-related counseling, psychotherapy, experiential groups, consulting projects, or community service (Standard 7.02, Descriptions of Education and Training Programs).

Student disclosures. Standard 7.04, Student Disclosure of Personal Information, prohibits teaching psychologists from requiring students or supervisees to disclose personal information regarding sexual history, history of child abuse or neglect, psychological treatment, or relationships with family or significant others unless such a requirement was clearly identified in the program description or the information is necessary to help a student or protect others from harm.

Therapy requirements. When therapy is a program or course requirement, students must be permitted to select a therapist unaffiliated with the program, and faculty who are likely to evaluate students are prohibited from providing that therapy (Standards 7.05a and b, Mandatory Individual or Group Therapy).

Student Authorship

Members of the academic community expressed concern in response to the 1992 Ethics Code Standard 6.23, Publication Credit, requiring student principal authorship on multiple-authored articles substantially based not only on student dissertations but on a student's "thesis." The concern was that for some undergraduate- and master's-level theses the rule was inconsistent with other standards requiring that publication credits accurately reflect an individual's relative contribution. Standard 8.12c, Publication Credit, maintains only the requirement for student first authorship on articles substantially based on dissertations. The revised standard affords student new protections by requiring that faculty advisors discuss publication credit with students as early as feasible and throughout the research and publication process as appropriate.

Research

Deception research. The 2002 Ethics Code provides more specific guidance on when the use of deceptive research methods are ethically prohibited and adds a new requirement that participants in deception studies must be permitted to withdraw their data following dehoaxing (Standard 8.07, Deception in Research).

Debriefing procedures. Researchers are now specifically required to take reasonable measures to alleviate psychological harm arising from experimental procedures when they are aware such harm has occurred (Standard 8.08c, Debriefing).

Data sharing. Standard 8.14b, Sharing Research Data for Verification, explicitly prohibits psychologists who request data from other psychologists to verify substantive claims through reanalysis, from using the data for any other purpose without prior written permission.

Assessment

With few exceptions, the 2002 Ethics Code now prohibits psychologists from providing opinions about the psychological characteristics of an individual they have not examined. The code explicitly permits record reviews, but requires psychologists conducting record reviews to explain why an individual examination was not warranted and the sources of information upon which their conclusions and recommendations are based (Standard 9.01, Bases for Assessment). The Ethics Code now includes specific requirements regarding the use of valid, reliable, and language-appropriate assessments (Standard 9.02b, Use of Assessments), and as noted above for the first time calls for informed consent prior to conducting assessments (Standard 9.03, Informed Consent in Assessments).

Release of Test Data

Perhaps the most notable change from the 1992 Ethics Code, and the standard that generated most comment and debate among the APA membership, is Standard 9.04,

Release of Test Data. The 1992 code prohibited psychologists "from releasing raw test results or raw data to persons, other than to patients and clients as appropriate, who are not qualified to use such information" (Standard 2.02b, Competence and Appropriate Use of Assessments and Interventions; APA, 1992). The wording of the 1992 standard created confusion about the definition of "raw test results," appropriate conditions for their release to clients/patients and qualified professionals, and how to respond to attorney requests, subpoenas, and court orders. In addition, the federal Health Insurance Portability and Accountability Act of 1996 (HIPAA) establishing the right of clients/patients to copies of their "designated record set" (medical or billing records maintained and used by the provider to make decisions about the patient) raised questions about the extent to which health care providers could withhold health records from clients/patients. (HIPAA is discussed in greater detail throughout relevant chapters of this book and introduced in the Preface in the section "A Word About HIPAA.")

New definition. Standard 9.04a defines "test data" as "raw and scaled scores, client/patient responses to test questions or stimuli, and psychologists' notes and recordings concerning client/patient statements and behavior during an examination." The definition of "test data" also includes the test materials or protocols if the psychologist wrote the client's/patient's responses, scores, or notes about behavior on the test protocol itself, and this information cannot be separated from the test materials in the client's/patient's record.

New duty to release test data. Standard 9.04a requires psychologists to provide test data "to the client/patient or other persons identified in a client/patient release." By contrast, the 1992 Ethics Code prohibited release of raw data to unqualified persons, except to the client/patient as appropriate. The rationale for reversing the 1992 prohibition was based on realities imposed by HIPAA regulations mandating release of health records to clients/patients, lack of APA member consensus on the definition of "qualified" professional, and shifting societal emphasis on client's/patient's rights to the discovery process and judicial scrutiny of psychological tests. Standard 9.04 does not preclude psychologists from discussing with a client/patient the potential for misuse of the information by individuals unqualified to interpret it.

Withholding test data. Standard 9.04a permits psychologists to withhold test data to protect the client/patient or another individual from substantial harm. At the same time, the standard includes the proviso that such decisions may be constrained by law. Under HIPAA, psychologists who are covered entities can deny client/patient access to designated record sets only if it is reasonably likely to endanger the life or physical safety of the individual or another person or cause equally substantial harm. Clients/patients also have the right to have the denial reviewed by a designated licensed health care professional. HIPAA regulations thus severely limit practicing psychologists' ability to exercise their professional judgment as to what constitutes substantial harm to clients/patients.

Standard 9.04a also permits withholding test data to protect misuse or misrepresentation of the data or the test. Before refusing to release test data under this clause, psychologists should carefully review relevant law. HIPAA does not recognize the protection of test materials as a legitimate reason to withhold designated record sets appropriately requested by a client/patient. There are instances, however, where HIPAA constraints are not at issue. HIPAA does not require release of records to clients/patients when information is compiled in reasonable anticipation of, or for use in, civil, criminal, or administrative actions or proceedings. In other instances, such as certain educational evaluations, the HIPAA Privacy Rule would not apply.

Release as required by law or court order. Subpart b of Standard 9.04 prohibits psychologists from releasing test data without client/patient permission, in response to a court order or other legal authority. This does not prevent psychologists from asking the court or other legal authority for a protective order to prevent the inappropriate disclosure of confidential information or suggest that the information be submitted to another psychologist for qualified review.

Test Security

Both the new Standard 9.11, Maintaining Test Security, and the 1992 Ethics Code Standard 2.10, Maintaining Test Security, require psychologists make reasonable efforts to protect the integrity and security of test materials and other assessment techniques. Under the new HIPAA regulations, pursuant to a patient's release, covered entities (providers) may not withhold a patient's designated record set. To protect psychologists who are covered entities from HIPAA noncompliance, Standard 9.11 defines "test materials" as "manuals, instruments, protocols, and test questions or stimuli that do not come under the definition of 'test data' as defined in Standard 9.04a, Release of Test Data." Thus, in contrast to the 1992 code, under Standard 9.11, psychologists are not obligated to protect test security when the materials include client/patient responses, the psychologist's contemporaneous notes regarding test performance, or individually identifiable information. Readers should refer to Chapter 12 for more detailed discussion and recommendations for complying with this standard.

Therapy

Group therapy. For the first time, the Ethics Code includes a standard that specifically addresses the responsibility of psychologists conducting group therapy to describe at the outset the roles and responsibilities of all parties and the limits of confidentiality (Standard 10.03, Group Therapy).

Sexual intimacies with relatives or significant others. Treatment is compromised when psychologists have a sexual relationship with a close relative or significant other of a current client/patient. Such relationships are now specifically prohibited (Standards 3.05, Multiple Relationships; 10.06, Sexual Intimacies With Relatives or Significant Others of Current Therapy Clients/Patients).

Terminating therapy. A noteworthy change in the 2002 Ethics Code is the elimination of the 1992 code's broadly worded prohibition against abandoning the client/patient. This change reflects the widely accepted view that termination based on reasonable professional judgment and proper pretermination counseling is ethically appropriate. The 2002 code also adds a standard that clarifies that it is permissible for psychologists to terminate therapy when they are threatened or otherwise endangered by a client/patient or another person with whom the client/patient has a relationship (Standard 10.10, Terminating Therapy).

Additional Changes That Might Require Immediate Attention

Reporting ethical violations. Standard 1.05, Reporting Ethical Violations, requires psychologists to formally report an ethical violation if it has or is likely to result in substantial harm, informal resolution is not appropriate, and the reporting would not violate confidentiality rights or when psychologists are retained to review another psychologist's ethical conduct.

Individuals involved in ethics complaints. Standard 1.08, Unfair Discrimination Against Complainants and Respondents, prohibits psychologists from penalizing persons based solely on their having made or being the subject of an ethics complaint. This standard is relevant to situations that arise in whistle-blowing and sexual harassment cases.

Emergency services. Standards 2.01d, Boundaries of Competence, and 2.02, Providing Services in Emergencies, for the first time provide decision rules for determining the competencies necessary to work with individuals for whom appropriate mental health services are not available.

Use of interpreters. For the first time, the Ethics Code includes enforceable standards that explicitly address the use of interpreters; see Standards 2.05, Delegation of Work to Others, and 9.03, Informed Consent in Assessments.

Conflict of interest. Standard 3.06, Conflict of Interest, prohibits psychologists from taking on a professional role when other interests or relationships could impair performing their functions or expose other persons or organizations to harm or exploitation.

PART II

Enforceable Standards

CHAPTER 4

Standards for Resolving Ethical Issues

1. RESOLVING ETHICAL ISSUES

1.01 Misuse of Psychologists' Work

If psychologists learn of misuse or misrepresentation of their work, they take reasonable steps to correct or minimize the misuse or misrepresentation. *[No Significant Change, 1992 Standard 1.16b, Misuse of Psychologists' Work]*

Psychologists have professional and scientific responsibilities to society and to the specific individuals, organizations, and communities with whom they work to ensure that their work products are not misused or misrepresented. Psychologists cannot reasonably be expected to anticipate all the ways in which their work can be wrongly used. Thus, Standard 1.01 of the American Psychological Association (APA) Ethics Code (2002) focuses on corrective action that must be taken when psychologists learn that others have misused or misrepresented their work. To remedy misuse, psychologists can write letters to or speak with interested parties, request retraction of misrepresentations, or discuss with appropriate persons corrective measures to be taken. Frequently, psychologists will not be aware that their work has been misrepresented, and inaction on their part would not be an ethical violation. However, when it is reasonable to expect that psychologists would be aware of misuse or misrepresentation of their work, a claim of ignorance would not be an acceptable defense against a charge of violation of this standard (Canter, Bennett, Jones, & Nagy, 1994).

☑ A school psychologist completed a report summarizing her assessment of a child whose test results did not clearly meet diagnostic criteria for serious emotional disturbance. Several days later, she learned that the principal of her school had forwarded to the superintendent of schools only those parts of the assessment report that supported the principal's desire to classify the student as emotionally disturbed to fill a special education quota. The psychologist asked the principal to send the entire report, explaining the ethical issues involved.

> ☑ A research psychologist learned that a special interest group had sent a listserv mailing for financial contributions that misquoted and misrepresented the psychologist's writings as supporting the group's cause. The psychologist contacted the group and asked it to cease sending this e-mail to other potential contributors and to e-mail a correction to the listserv recipients.
>
> ☑ A forensic psychologist learned that an attorney had submitted to the court a tampered version of the psychologist's written report. The psychologist, after consulting with an independent attorney, informed the court of the tampering.

The phrase "reasonable steps" recognizes that despite their best efforts in many instances psychologists may not be in a position to ensure their requests to correct misuse are followed. For example, if the research psychologist whose work had been misrepresented did not have access to the listserv, short of a civil suit, the psychologist would have few corrective options if the group refused requests for retraction. In other instances, it is not appropriate to actively seek a correction, For example, it is ethically appropriate for psychologists providing legal testimony in court who believe an attorney is misrepresenting the psychologist's work to rely on existing corrective mechanisms (i.e., cross-examination) or refrain from corrective actions when an attempt to remedy the misrepresentation would violate the rules of the court or the legal rights of a complainant or defendant. Psychologists should always document the corrective efforts made to remedy known misuse or misrepresentations.

1.02 Conflicts Between Ethics and Law, Regulations, or Other Governing Legal Authority

If psychologists' ethical responsibilities conflict with law, regulations, or other governing legal authority, psychologists make known their commitment to the Ethics Code and take steps to resolve the conflict. If the conflict is unresolvable via such means, psychologists may adhere to the requirements of the law, regulations, or other governing legal authority. *[Expanded, 1992 Standard 1.02, Relationship of Ethics and Law]*

This standard addresses instances in which the requirements of the Ethics Code may conflict with judicial authority, with state or federal laws, or with regulations governing the activities of psychologists working in the military, correctional facilities, or other areas of public service. For example, psychologists may be issued a court order for the release of confidential information that the client/patient or research participant does not want released.

Standard 1.02 requires psychologists take action when conflicts between the Ethics Code and laws, regulations, or governing legal authority arise. Psychologists must have sufficient understanding of the Ethics Code standards to identify such conflicts. Specific steps that may be taken include informing appropriate authorities of the conflict, explaining the rationale for the Ethics Code standard, and helping authorities develop alternative rules and procedures that will enable psychologists to fulfill their professional obligations as well as their obligations under the law.

☑ A psychologist who had received a court order for confidential information sent a letter to the judge explaining the relevant confidentiality standards in the Ethics Code and requesting judicial review to determine whether a limited release of information would meet legal requirements.

When a Conflict Cannot Be Resolved

Standard 1.02 also recognizes that legal and regulatory authorities may not always respond to specific steps taken by psychologists. When reasonable actions taken by psychologists do not resolve the conflict, they are permitted to make a conscientious decision regarding whether to adhere to the Ethics Code or the legal or regulatory authority.

For example, U.S. Department of Defense (DoD) regulations routinely require military psychologists to perform activities that place service to the military mission above those of the best interests of the individual client/patient, resulting in conflicts between DoD requirements and Ethical Standards involving confidentiality, maintenance of records, competence, and multiple relationships (Johnson, 1995).

Efforts by military psychologists to bridge the gap between APA Ethical Standards and DoD regulations regarding confidentiality, resulted in implementation of DoD Directive 6490.1 (DoD, 1997a) and DoD Instruction 6490.4 (DoD, 1997b), which protect the rights of active-duty servicemembers sent for commander-directed mental health evaluations (CDMHEs) to know why they were referred for evaluation and who will be conducting the evaluation, their right to obtain an evaluation summary and second opinion, and their right to speak with legal counsel, a chaplain, and a member of Congress regarding their situation (Orme & Doerman, 2001).

1.03 Conflicts Between Ethics and Organizational Demands

If the demands of an organization with which psychologists are affiliated or for whom they are working conflict with this Ethics Code, psychologists clarify the nature of the conflict, make known their commitment to the Ethics Code, and to the extent feasible, resolve the conflict in a way that permits adherence to the Ethics Code. *[Modified for Clarity, 1992 Standard 8.03, Conflicts Between Ethics and Organizational Demands]*

Psychologists working with organizations may encounter organizational policies, plans, or procedures that conflict with the Ethics Code. Standard 1.03 requires that psychologists inform the organization about the nature of the conflict and the ways in which policies or activities violate the Ethics Code, and take actions to resolve the conflict in a manner consistent with Ethics Code standards. The standard specifically requires psychologists to make known their commitment to the Ethics Code in communications with the organization.

> ☑ An industrial-organizational psychologist recently employed by an organization to handle employment testing discovered that the organization used a test for preemployment screening for which there was no applicable, documented validity evidence and that did not appear to be clearly job related (Standard 9.02b, Use of Assessments). The psychologist notified the employer of the problem and recommended that use of the test be suspended until a more suitable preemployment screening process could be identified and validated. The psychologist provided a specific, realistic plan for helping the employer move toward an ethical and legally defensible applicant screening process.
>
> ☑ A superintendent of schools wanted a psychologist whose job it was to evaluate and counsel students in the school district to take on an added role as the Title IX officer designated to evaluate and enforce school rules regarding student-student and faculty-student sexual harassment. The psychologist explained that the dual assignment could compromise his ability to effectively conduct either role because it was likely that some students who came to the psychologist for counseling about sexual harassment would need to appear before the psychologist in his Title IX role to press or defend against sexual harassment charges.

The phrase "to the extent feasible" recognizes that despite reasonable efforts by psychologists, an organization may refuse to change a policy that is inconsistent with the Ethics Code. This standard does not require psychologists to resign when their attempts at a resolution are unsuccessful (see Acuff et al., 1999, for excellent case examples).

> ☑ A psychologist was hired by a health maintenance organization (HMO) to *implement* preexisting company criteria for mental health services claims. During a utilization review, she noticed that company policy on the use of psychopharmacological medications in the absence of conjoint psychotherapy was counter to professional and scientific knowledge of the discipline for the particular disorder under review and believed the policy was potentially harmful to patients (Standards 1.06, Basis for Scientific and Professional Judgments, and 3.04, Avoiding Harm). The psychologist drew the company's attention to the problem and the relevant APA Ethical Standards, but the HMO management refused to change the policy. The psychologist agreed to use the preexisting criteria, while continuing her efforts to discuss with management ways in which they could improve the utilization criteria.

❌ A psychologist working for an HMO was asked to *develop* evidence-based utilization standards for a specific class of mental health disorders. Based on current research, he recommended that individuals diagnosed to have this class of disorders receive psychopharmacological medications and conjoint psychotherapy. During a review of the first draft of the psychologist's recommendations, his employer told him that conjoint psychotherapy would significantly diminish the profitability of plans covering the disorder and asked the psychologist to remove the recommendation from the final draft of the report. The psychologist did not attempt to discuss with his employer the ethical issues associated with approving for reimbursement what was known to be inadequate treatment (Standards 1.06, Basis for Scientific and Professional Judgments, and 3.04, Avoiding Harm) and simply agreed to change his recommendation in the final report.

Psychologists should not assume that Standard 1.03 waives their obligation to adhere to other standards in this Ethics Code. For example, a psychologist who implemented a health care organization's policy to increase revenue by providing unwarranted treatment to Medicaid patients could be charged with Medicaid fraud and a violation of Standards 6.04b, Fees and Financial Arrangements, and 9.01a, Bases for Assessment, even if the psychologist brought the unethical nature of the policy to the organization's attention (see Acuff et al., 1999).

1.04 Informal Resolution of Ethical Violations

When psychologists believe that there may have been an ethical violation by another psychologist, they attempt to resolve the issue by bringing it to the attention of that individual, if an informal resolution appears appropriate and the intervention does not violate any confidentiality rights that may be involved. (See also Standard 1.02, Conflicts Between Ethics and Law, Regulations, or Other Governing Legal Authority, and Standard 1.03, Conflicts Between Ethics and Organizational Demands.) *[No Significant Change, 1992 Standards 8.04, Informal Resolution of Ethical Violations]*

Professional and scientific misconduct by psychologists can harm coworkers, distort the public's ability to make decisions informed by knowledge generated by members of the profession, and harm the profession itself by instilling public distrust. When an ethical violation by another psychologist occurs, members of the profession are in the best position to recognize the violation and select a course of action that could ameliorate harm or prevent further violations. Standards 1.04 and 1.05 underscore the responsibility of psychologists to be concerned about and where appropriate address the scientific or professional misconduct of their colleagues (Principle B: Fidelity and Responsibility).

Standard 1.04 requires psychologists to attempt an informal resolution when they suspect an ethical violation has occurred that could be adequately addressed through discussion with and subsequent remedial actions by the violating psychologist. In such instances, psychologists should discuss the violation with the offending psychologist to confirm whether misconduct has actually occurred, and if appropriate recommend corrective steps and ways to prevent future ethical violations. Examples of misconduct psychologists might encounter in which an informal resolution is appropriate include the following:

☑ A psychologist with no prior education, training, or supervised experience in neuro-psychological assessment began to incorporate a number of such instruments into a battery of tests for elderly clients (Standard 2.01a, Boundaries of Competence). After a colleague brought this to her attention, an informal resolution was achieved when the psychologist agreed to obtain appropriate training in neuropsychological assessment before continuing to use such techniques.

☑ A psychologist working with a non-English-speaking psychotherapy client asked the client's son to serve as an interpreter during sessions (Standard 2.05, Delegation of Work to Others). After being approached by a colleague, the psychologist recognized the potential ethical risks involved in such procedures and agreed to use an independent translator in the future.

☑ A consulting psychologist hired to help management plan for a shift in organizational structure planned to take stock options in partial payment for the work (Standard 3.06, Conflict of Interest). When a colleague pointed out potential ethical problems involved, the psychologist agreed to discuss alternative compensation with the organization.

☑ In a job application, a psychologist claimed as a credential for health service delivery a degree earned from an educational institution that was neither regionally accredited nor a basis for state licensure (Standard 5.01c, Avoidance of False or Deceptive Statements). When the unethical nature of this behavior was pointed out, the psychologist agreed to send a letter to the potential employer clarifying the nature of the degree.

☑ A professor of psychology had not established a timely or specific process for providing feedback to and evaluating student performance (Standard 7.06, Assessing Student and Supervisee Performance). After discussions with the departmental chair, the professor agreed to develop such a system.

☑ An assistant professor of psychology began data collection without submitting a research proposal to the university's institutional review board (IRB) (Standard 8.01, Institutional Approval). After a senior faculty member brought this to the psychologist's attention, the researcher agreed to submit an IRB application and to cease data collection contingent on IRB approval.

☑ A psychologist working in a hospital had entered identifiable confidential information into a database available to other staff members (Standard 6.02b, Maintenance, Dissemination, and Disposal of Confidential Records of Professional and Scientific Work). When another psychologist working at the hospital pointed out the problem, the psychologist agreed to use a password and other procedures for protecting the information. In this last instance, psychologists should be aware that the Health Insurance Portability and Accountability Act (HIPAA) also requires that health care professionals take reasonable steps to mitigate any harmful effects of unlawful disclosure of protected health information (PHI) by an employee or business associate of which they are aware.

Standard 1.04 recognizes that in some instances an informal resolution may not be feasible. For example, previous attempts to discuss ethical problems with the offending psychologist may have been ineffective or the offending psychologist may have left the position in which he or she had committed the violation or is otherwise inaccessible. In addition, psychologists should not attempt an informal resolution if to do so would violate an individual's confidentiality rights.

☑ During a session at the university counseling center, a graduate student complained that her psychology professor required students to discuss their sexual history in a required experiential group (Standard 7.04, Student Disclosure of Personal Information). The student did not want anyone in the program to know she was receiving counseling. Although the counseling psychologist knew that the professor might be violating Standard 7.04, the psychologist did not attempt to resolve the issue because to do so might have placed the confidentiality of the counseling relationship at risk.

1.05 Reporting Ethical Violations

If an apparent ethical violation has substantially harmed or is likely to substantially harm a person or organization and is not appropriate for informal resolution under Standard 1.04, Informal Resolution of Ethical Violations, or is not resolved properly in that fashion, psychologists take further action appropriate to the situation. Such action might include referral to state or national committees on professional ethics, to state licensing boards, or to the appropriate institutional authorities. This standard does not apply when an intervention would violate confidentiality rights or when psychologists have been retained to review the work of another psychologist whose professional conduct is in question. (See also Standard 1.02, Conflicts Between Ethics and Law, Regulations, or Other Governing Legal Authority.) *[Modified for Clarity, 1992 Standard 8.05, Reporting Ethical Violations]*

Standard 1.05 requires psychologists to report ethical violations committed by another psychologist only if the violation has led to or has the potential to lead to substantial harm and informal resolution is unsuccessful or inappropriate. The extent to which most ethical violations have or are likely to cause substantial harm will depend on the professional or scientific context and the individuals involved. As a rule of thumb, behaviors likely to cause substantial harm are of a kind similar to sexual misconduct; insurance fraud; plagiarism; and blatant, intentional misrepresentation (APA, 2002, Section 5.3.5.1.1).

Standard 1.05 also offers nonbinding examples of available reporting options, including filing a complaint with the APA or one of its state affiliates if the offending psychologist is a member of that organization, referring the case to a state licensing board if the ethical violation also violates state law, or filing a complaint with the appropriate committee in the institution or organization at which the offending psychologist works. As in Standard 1.04, Standard 1.05 prioritizes the protection of confidentiality over the duty to report an ethical violation.

> ☑ A psychology professor reviewing an assistant professor's promotion application materials discovered that the faculty member had several publications that blatantly plagiarized articles written by a senior colleague. The psychologist presented the evidence to the chair of the department. The chair and the professor informed the faculty member that they had discovered the plagiarism and would be forwarding the information to the university committee on ethical conduct, and if the committee found that plagiarism had occurred, would inform the journal in which the articles were published.
>
> ☑ A client told a psychologist about the sexual misconduct of another psychologist with whom the client had previously been in psychotherapy (Standard 10.05, Sexual Intimacies With Current Therapy Clients/Patients). Judging that it was clinically appropriate, the psychologist discussed with the client the unethical nature of the previous therapist's behavior and the available reporting options. The psychologist, respecting the client's request to keep the sexual relationship confidential, did not pursue reporting the violation.

Psychologists may be retained to help an organization, the courts, or an individual evaluate whether the actions of a psychologist have violated the Ethics Code. Standard 1.05 preserves the ability of members of the discipline to provide expert opinion on the ethical conduct of their peers by exempting from the reporting requirement psychologists hired to review the ethical activities of another psychologist.

1.06 Cooperating With Ethics Committees

Psychologists cooperate in ethics investigations, proceedings, and resulting requirements of the APA or any affiliated state psychological association to which they belong. In doing so, they address any confidentiality issues. Failure to cooperate is itself an ethics violation. However, making a request for deferment of adjudication of an ethics complaint pending the outcome of litigation does not alone constitute noncooperation. *[Modified for Clarity, 1992 Standard 8.06, Cooperating With Ethics Committees]*

A profession that demonstrates it can monitor itself promotes public confidence in the services of its members. Thus, an ethics code must enable professional organizations to effectively adjudicate ethics complaints. Membership in the APA and its affiliated state psychological associations brings with it a commitment to adhere to the Ethical Standards of the profession. To ensure the validity and viability of APA ethics adjudication, Standard 1.06 requires that when called on to do so, psychologists cooperate with APA and state-affiliated ethics investigations, proceedings, and resulting requirements. During the comment phase of the Ethics Code revision, some members asked whether requiring cooperation with an ethics committee when a complaint has been brought against a psychologist raised Fifth Amendment issues regarding the right against self-incrimination. The answer to this question is no. Unlike state licensing boards and other government and judicial agencies, professional organizations are not bound by the Fifth Amendment.

Standard 1.06 recognizes that when a complaint is brought against a psychologist, the ability to respond in full to an ethics committee request for information may be limited by confidentiality responsibilities detailed in Section 4, Privacy and Confidentiality, of the Ethics Code.

☑ A patient submitted a complaint to the APA charging a psychologist with misinterpreting the results of an assessment battery leading to inaccurate diagnosis and denial of disability (Standards 3.04, Avoiding Harm, and 9.06, Interpreting Assessment Results). To fully respond to the complaint, the psychologist needed to obtain the patient's written release so that the psychologist could submit to the ethics committee the test report and other information about the patient relevant to the complaint. Despite reasonable efforts, the patient refused to sign the release. The psychologist informed the APA Ethics Committee about the confidentiality limitations on fully responding to the committee's request.

Standard 1.06 permits psychologists to request that an APA or affiliated state psychological association ethics committee delay adjudication of a complaint pending the outcome of litigation related to the complaint. If, however, the ethics committee declines such a request, failure to cooperate will be considered a violation of Standard 1.06.

1.07 Improper Complaints

Psychologists do not file or encourage the filing of ethics complaints that are made with reckless disregard for or willful ignorance of facts that would disprove the allegation. *[Modified for Clarity, 1992 Standard 8.07, Improper Complaints]*

The filing of frivolous complaints intended solely to harm the respondent undermines the educative, adjudicative, and public protection purposes of the Ethics Code. Unfounded and revengeful complaints can taint a scientific or professional career, lead to unfair denial of professional liability insurance or hospital privileges (because some insurers ask if a complaint has been made), incur costly legal fees for a respondent, and dilute public trust in the profession. Feelings of hostility and intent to do harm may accompany a valid complaint against psychologists who have acted unethically. Accordingly, the language of this standard was crafted to focus on the complaining psychologist's disregard for available information that would disprove the allegation rather than on the personal motives underlying the complaint.

Examples of improper complaints to the APA Ethics Committee often involve academic colleagues, business rivals, or psychologists with opposing forensic roles who attempt to misuse the ethics adjudication process as a means of defeating a competitor rather than addressing wrongful behavior; or who attempt to dilute a complaint against them through a counter-complaint. Standard 1.07 is violated if psychologists making a complaint had access to information refuting the accusation—whether or not they availed themselves of such information. The discipline of psychology and the public benefit from psychologists monitoring the ethical activities of other psychologists, but both are damaged when the Ethics Code is misused as a weapon to harass or otherwise harm members of the profession.

1.08 Unfair Discrimination Against Complainants and Respondents

Psychologists do not deny persons employment, advancement, admissions to academic or other programs, tenure, or promotion, based solely upon their having made or their being the subject of an ethics complaint. This does not preclude taking action based upon the outcome of such proceedings or considering other appropriate information. *[Significant Change, 1992 Standard 1.11b, Sexual Harassment]*

Situations arise in which employees, colleagues, students, or student applicants accuse others or are accused of sexual harassment or other forms of professional or scientific misconduct. Standard 1.08 protects the rights of individuals to make ethical complaints without suffering unfair punitive actions from psychologists responsible for their employ, academic admission, or training. The standard also protects the rights of those accused of unethical behaviors to pursue their career paths pending resolution of a complaint. As recent highly publicized cases of whistle-blowing have revealed (Lang, 1993; Needleman, 1993; Sprague, 1993), premature punitive actions against those who make complaints or those who are the subjects of complaints can hamper the ability of a profession or organization to monitor itself and can violate the rights of those accused to have a fair hearing. The Ethics Code makes clear that psychologists have a responsibility to be concerned about the ethical compliance of their colleagues' scientific and professional conduct (Principle B: Fidelity and Responsibility; Standard 1.04, Informal Resolution of Ethical Violations; and Standard 1.05, Reporting Ethical Violations).

Standard 1.08 supports the implementation of this obligation by prohibiting unfair discrimination against those who make ethics complaints.

> ❎ A psychology department voted to deny doctoral candidacy to a student in the department's master's program simply because she had filed a still pending sexual harassment complaint against a member of the faculty.

Standard 1.08 also recognizes that not all complaints have a basis in fact or rise to the threshold of an ethics violation. Therefore, the standard prohibits psychologists from unfair discrimination of individuals who have been accused of an ethical violation.

> ❎ A client accused a member of a group practice of misrepresenting the fee for psychotherapy. Fearful of additional litigation regardless of whether the psychologist was ultimately found innocent or guilty, the other group members asked the psychologist to leave the practice.

The use of the term "solely" in the first sentence of Standard 1.08 permits complainants or complainees to be denied employment, professional or academic advancement, or program admission for reasons unrelated to the complaint or for reasons based on the outcome of the complaint.

> ☑ An assistant professor accused of student sexual harassment had a documented history of poor student teaching evaluations, which, independent of the sexual harassment accusation, was sufficient to support a denial of promotion to associate professor.
>
> ☑ A psychologist who had accused a colleague of insurance fraud was found to have fabricated the evidence used against the colleague. The psychologist was fired from the group practice.

Chapter 5

Standards on Competence

2. COMPETENCE

2.01 Boundaries of Competence

(a) Psychologists provide services, teach, and conduct research with populations and in areas only within the boundaries of their competence, based on their education, training, supervised experience, consultation, study, or professional experience. *[Modified for Clarity, 1992 Standard 1.04, Boundaries of Competence]*

Psychologists benefit those with whom they work and avoid harm through the application of knowledge and techniques gained through education, training, supervised experience, consultation, study, or professional experience in the field. Competence is the lynchpin enabling psychologists to fulfill other ethical obligations required by the American Psychological Association (APA) Ethics Code (2002). Under Standard 2.01a, psychologists must refrain from providing services, teaching, or conducting research in areas in which they have not had the education, training, supervised experience, consultation, study, or professional experience recognized by the discipline as necessary to conduct their work competently.

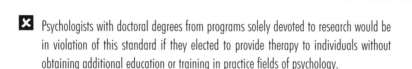

☒ Psychologists with doctoral degrees from programs solely devoted to research would be in violation of this standard if they elected to provide therapy to individuals without obtaining additional education or training in practice fields of psychology.

☒ Graduates of counseling, clinical, or school psychology programs should not conduct neuropsychological assessments unless their programs, internships, or postdoctoral experiences provided specialized training in those techniques.

☒ Psychologists should not offer courses or professional workshops if their graduate education, training, or continued study is insufficient to provide students with an adequate survey or explanation of the fundamental knowledge and concepts of the topics or areas to be taught.

☒ Psychologists without applicable training in counseling and job-related assessment should not offer executive coaching services.

Determinations regarding whether psychologists are engaged in activities outside the boundaries of their competence will vary with current and evolving criteria in the relevant field. As noted in the Introduction and Applicability section of the Ethics Code, psychologists are encouraged to refer to materials and guidelines that have been adopted or endorsed by scientific and professional psychological organizations to help identify competencies necessary for adherence to Standard 2.01a. For example:

☑ According to the Guidelines for Child Custody Evaluation in Divorce Proceedings (APA, 1994), custody evaluation requires specialized knowledge of psychological assessments for children, adults, and families; child and family development and psychopathology; the impact of divorce on children; applicable legal standards; and in some instances expertise on child abuse and neglect, domestic violence, or parental mental or physical illness.

☑ According to the Guidelines for the Evaluation of Dementia and Age-Related Cognitive Decline (see http://www.apa.org/practice/dementia.html), psychologists who perform evaluations for dementia and age-related cognitive decline must have education, training, experience, and supervision in clinical interviews and neuropsychological testing as well as in the areas of gerontology, neuropsychology, rehabilitation psychology, neuropathology, psychopharmacology, and psychopathology in older adults.

☑ The Guidelines for Ethical Conduct in the Care and Use of Animals (APA Committee on Animal Research and Ethics, 1996; http://www.apa.org/science/anguide.html) state that psychologists conducting research with animals must be knowledgeable about the normal and species-specific behavior characteristics of their animal subjects and unusual behaviors that could forewarn of health problems.

☑ According to the task force titled Ethical Practice in Organized Systems of Care convened by the APA Committee for the Advancement of Professional Practice (CAPP), psychologists who are contracted providers for health maintenance organizations (HMOs) should only accept clients/patients whom they have the expertise to benefit. (Acuff et al., 1999)

(b) Where scientific or professional knowledge in the discipline of psychology establishes that an understanding of factors associated with age, gender, gender identity, race, ethnicity, culture, national origin, religion, sexual orientation, disability, language, or socioeconomic status is essential for effective implementation of their services or research, psychologists have or obtain the training, experience, consultation, or supervision necessary to ensure the competence of their services, or they make appropriate referrals, except as provided in Standard 2.02, Providing Services in Emergencies. *[Modified for Clarity, 1992 Standard 1.08, Human Differences]*

An understanding of the ways in which individual differences relate to different psychological phenomena is essential to ensure the competent implementation of services and research. Insensitivity to factors associated with age, gender, gender identity, race, ethnicity, culture, national origin, religion, sexual orientation, disability, language, or socioeconomic status can result in underutilization of services, misdiagnosis, iatrogenic treatments, impairments in leadership effectiveness and member cohesion in group therapy, and methodologically unsound research designs (Bronstein & Quina, 2003; Chernin, Holden, & Chandler, 1997; Council of National Psychological Associations for the Advancement of Ethnic Minority Interests, 2000; Fisher, Hatashita-Wong, & Isman, 1999; Fisher et al., 2002; Fisher, Wallace, & Fenton, 2000; Glass, 1998; Ponterotto, Casas, Suzuki, & Alexander, 2001; Stefan, 2000).

Standard 2.01b requires psychologists to have or obtain special understanding and skills when the scientific and professional knowledge of the discipline establishes that an understanding of factors associated with these individual differences is essential to conduct work competently. According to this standard, the competencies required to work with the populations listed above are determined by the knowledge and skills identified by the scientific and professional knowledge base—not by personal differences or similarities between psychologists and those to whom they provide services or involve in research.

Under Standard 2.01b, psychologists have three sequentially related obligations:

Familiarity with professional and scientific knowledge. For each activity in which they engage, psychologists must be sufficiently familiar with current scientific and professional knowledge to determine whether an understanding of factors associated with the individual characteristics listed above is necessary for effective implementation of their services or research. For example:

☑ Research and professional guidelines suggest familiarity with the concept of cultural paranoia and with culturally equivalent norms on certain scales of psychopathology are required for competent clinical assessment of African American clients/patients with presenting symptoms of subclinical paranoia (APA, 1993a; Combs, Penn, & Fenigstein, 2002).

☑ Professional guidelines and research suggest that knowledge of the mental health risks of social stigmatization and individual differences in the developmental trajectories of gay and lesbian youths is required for psychologists treating or studying depression involving these populations (see APA's Guidelines for Psychotherapy With Lesbian, Gay, & Bisexual Clients, http://www.apa.org/pi/lgbc/guidelines.html; Savin-Williams & Diamond, 1999).

Appropriate skills. If current knowledge in the field indicates that an understanding of one or more of the factors cited in Standard 2.01b is essential to conduct activities competently, psychologists must have or obtain the training, experience, consultation, or supervision necessary. The type of knowledge and training required depends on the extent to which the individual difference factor is central or peripheral to the service required as well as the psychologist's prior training or experience.

Knowing when to refrain and refer. Under Standard 2.01b, psychologists who have not had or cannot obtain the knowledge or experience required must refrain from engaging in such activities and make referrals when appropriate, except when such services are needed, but unavailable (Standard 2.02, Providing Services in Emergencies; see also Standard 2.01d).

☑ A psychologist trained only in adult assessment was asked to assess a child for learning difficulties. The psychologist referred the family to another psychologist with the specialized knowledge and experience necessary to conduct child assessments in general and developmental disabilities assessments in particular (Childs & Eyde, 2002).

☒ A counseling psychologist agreed to provide career services to a client with profound bilateral deafness. The psychologist had no education or training in career skills and opportunities available to people who are hearing impaired, employment-relevant disability law, hearing loss-appropriate counseling techniques, the use of American Sign Language and other modes of communication, and the appropriate use of interpreters (Leigh, Corbett, Gutman, & Morere, 1996).

(c) Psychologists planning to provide services, teach, or conduct research involving populations, areas, techniques, or technologies new to them undertake relevant education, training, supervised experience, consultation, or study. *[Expanded, 1992 Standard 1.04b, Boundaries of Competence]*

Standard 2.01c applies when psychologists wish to expand the scope of their practice, teaching, or research to populations, areas, techniques, or technologies for which they have not obtained the necessary qualifications established by the field.

☑ Prior to offering rehabilitation services, a psychologist without previous training in this area obtained supervised experience with individuals with sensory impairments; burns; spinal cord, brain, and orthopedic injuries; catastrophic injury and illness; and chronically disabling conditions (Patterson & Hanson, 1995).

☑ A psychologist trained solely in individual psychotherapy obtained appropriate advanced education and training prior to extending his practice to group and family therapy work (Lakin, 1994).

☑ To deliver the short-term treatment required under the practice guidelines of the HMO for which she worked, a psychologist acquired additional supervised experience in the delivery of time-limited services (Haas & Cummings, 1991).

☑ A developmental psychologist who wished to test a theory of genetic and environmental influences on cognitive aging using an animal population obtained knowledge and supervised experience in animal models, animal care, and animal experimental techniques prior to conducting the research (APA Committee on Animal Research and Ethics, 1996).

☑ A teaching psychologist who planned to offer an interactive Internet course consulted with a specialist to ensure that the information would be presented accurately (e.g., Graham, 2001; Randsdell, 2002).

(d) When psychologists are asked to provide services to individuals for whom appropriate mental health services are not available and for which psychologists have not obtained the competence necessary, psychologists with closely related prior training or experience may provide such services in order to ensure that services are not denied if they make a reasonable effort to obtain the competence required by using relevant research, training, consultation, or study. *[New]*

Standard 2.01d applies to situations in which a psychologist without the appropriate training or experience is the only professional available to provide necessary mental health services. Such situations often arise in rural settings or small ethnocultural communities where a single psychologist serves a diverse needs population. The standard reflects the balance articulated in Principle A: Beneficence and Nonmaleficence, between the obligation to do good (to provide needed services) and the responsibility to do no harm (to avoid poor services provided by unqualified professionals). The standard also reflects the importance of providing fair access to services (Principle D: Justice).

Standard 2.01d stipulates two conditions under which it is permissible for psychologists to provide services for which they do not have the required education or experience: (1) Psychologists must have prior training or experience closely related to the service needed, and (2) having agreed to provide the service psychologists must make reasonable efforts to obtain the knowledge and skills necessary to conduct their work effectively.

A psychologist with expertise in culturally sensitive assessment of childhood personality and educational disorders was the only Spanish-speaking mental health professional with regularly scheduled appointments to a Mexican migrant worker community. A social worker serving the community asked the psychologist to evaluate a Spanish-speaking 80-year-old man for evidence of depression. The nearest mental health clinic was 500 miles away and the elder was too feeble to travel. The psychologist's expertise in multicultural assessment of mental disorders in children was related though not equivalent to the knowledge and expertise necessary for a culturally sensitive geropsychological diagnosis. The psychologist agreed to conduct the evaluation. Prior to evaluating the elder, she consulted by phone with a geropsychologist in another state. She also informed the elder, the elder's family, and the social worker that because she did not have sufficient training or experience in treating depression in elderly persons, if treatment was necessary it would have to be obtained from another provider.

(e) In those emerging areas in which generally recognized standards for preparatory training do not yet exist, psychologists nevertheless take reasonable steps to ensure the competence of their work and to protect clients/patients, students, supervisees, research participants, organizational clients, and others from harm. *[No Significant Change, 1992 Standard 1.04c, Boundaries of Competence]*

Standard 2.01e applies when psychologists wish to develop or implement new practice, teaching, or research techniques for which there are no generally agreed on scientific or professional training qualifications. The standard recognizes the value of innovative techniques as well as the added risks that such innovations may place on those with whom psychologists work.

Psychologists must take reasonable steps to ensure the competence and safety of their work in new areas. In using the term "competence" the standard reflects the assumption that all work conducted by psychologists in their role as a psychologist must draw on established scientific or professional knowledge of the discipline (see Standard 2.04, Bases for Scientific and Professional Judgments). Adherence to this standard thus requires that psychologists have the foundational knowledge and skills in psychology necessary to construct or implement novel approaches and to evaluate their effectiveness. For example:

 The growing literature in the field of executive coaching indicates that psychologists planning to offer new forms of these services must demonstrate a knowledge and expertise in, among other areas, (a) techniques for fostering and measuring change within business, government, not-for-profit, or educational organizations; (b) the nature of executive responsibility and leadership; (c) targeted goal setting within organizational cultures; (d) succession planning; and (e) relevant factors associated with executive challenges such as information technology and globalization (Brotman, Liberi, & Wasylyshyn, 1998; Kampa-Kokesch & Anderson, 2001; Kilberg, 1996).

☑ As states begin to give psychologists prescriptive authority, psychologists proposing to practice in this area will need to acquire the education and training outlined in the evolving practice guidelines for this field (Buelow & Chafetz, 1996; Chafetz & Buelow, 1994; Fox, Schwelitz, & Barclay, 1992). As training standards evolve in this area, psychologists who do *not* have prescription privileges but are knowledgeable about pharmacotherapy will need to be cautious about recommendations made to clients/patients regarding medications to ensure that they are not working outside newly established professional and legal boundaries of competence (DeLeon, Bennett, & Bricklin, 1997; Sechrest & Coan, 2002).

Standard 2.01e also requires that psychologists working in emerging areas take reasonable steps to protect those with whom they work from harm, recognizing that novel approaches may require greater vigilance when it comes to consumer or research protections.

For example, continuous advances in electronic and computer technology present new opportunities and ethical challenges for psychologists. Psychologists using e-mail or chat rooms to provide behavioral health services to clients/patients at a distance are venturing into relatively uncharted territories. Traditional psychotherapy techniques based on oral and nonverbal cues may not transfer to Internet communications through written text (Nickelson, 1998). Additional harm to Internet clients/patients may be incurred when psychologists fail to appropriately diagnose a disorder or to identify suicidal or homicidal ideation, or through the use of the Internet medium inadvertently reinforce maladaptive behavior (e.g., social phobia).

☑ Steps that psychologists using Internet-mediated assessment or therapeutic services might take to ensure the competence of their work and protect clients/patients from harm include (1) staying abreast of advances in the field, (2) requiring in-person initial consultation, and (3) identifying professionals and health and social service agencies in the locality in which the client/patient lives who can be called in crisis situations (Maheu, 2001).

(f) When assuming forensic roles, psychologists are or become reasonably familiar with the judicial or administrative rules governing their roles. *[Modified for Clarity, 1992 Standard 7.06, Competence With Law and Rules]*

Psychologists assume forensic roles when they engage in activities intended to provide psychological expertise to the legal system. According to the Specialty Guidelines for Forensic Psychologists (Committee on Ethical Guidelines for Forensic Psychologists, 1991), forensic roles include clinical forensic examiners, psychologists employed by correctional mental health systems, researchers who provide expert testimony on the relevance of psychological data to a psycholegal issue, trial behavior consultants, practitioners who are called to appear before the court as fact witnesses, forensic experts, or psychologists who otherwise consult with, or testify before, judicial, legislative, or administrative agencies acting in an adjudicative capacity.

The provision of competent forensic services requires not only education and training in a psychologist's specific area of expertise but also knowledge of the judicial or administrative rules governing various forensic roles.

☑ Scientific psychologists serving as expert witnesses should be familiar with federal rules of evidence regarding case law and expert testimony (e.g., *Daubert v. Merrell Dow Pharmaceuticals, Inc.,* 1993; *Kumho Tire Co., Ltd. v. Carmichael,* 1999).

☑ School or educational psychologists asked to serve as expert witnesses in due process hearings need to be familiar with the legal foundations for special education law such as *Brown v. Board of Education* (1954), Section 504 of the Rehabilitation Act, 1973; Education for All Handicapped Children Act, 1975; and the Individuals with Disabilities Education Act, 1990 (see Krivacska & Margolis, 1995).

☑ Psychologists conducting custody evaluations should have sufficient understanding of the hearsay rule and what the term "best interests of the child" means in legal proceedings.

☑ Psychologists conducting competency assessments should know that the term "insanity" has different meanings in different jurisdictions (Hess, 1998).

☑ Psychologists offering trial consultation services to organizations may need to have an understanding of change in venue motions, or sexual harassment or retaliation work policies and laws (Hellkamp & Lewis, 1995).

Sometimes psychologists who do not offer forensic services are called on to provide legal testimony as a fact witness. For example, an independent practitioner seeing a client for anxiety-related disorders might be called as a fact witness in a workers' compensation case involving the client. Under Standard 2.01f, even when psychologists have no advance knowledge that their work will be used in a legal or administrative setting, when called on to provide such a service they are nonetheless responsible for becoming reasonably familiar with the rules that will govern their forensic role.

☑ A licensed practitioner was called to testify as a fact witness regarding the diagnosis, treatment, and treatment progress of a child whom he was seeing in group therapy. Prior to going to court, the psychologist obtained consultation on rules governing privileged communications for children and for patients in group therapy in the state in which the psychologist practiced (Glosoff, Herlihy, Herlihy, & Spence, 1997; Knapp & VandeCreek, 1997).

2.02 Providing Services in Emergencies

In emergencies, when psychologists provide services to individuals for whom other mental health services are not available and for which psychologists have not obtained the necessary training, psychologists may provide such services in order to ensure that services are not denied. The services are discontinued as soon as the emergency has ended or appropriate services are available. *[New]*

The Oklahoma City bombing and the September 11, 2001, attack on the United States illustrate the important public role of psychological expertise during disasters. Standard 2.02 recognizes that when adequate mental health services are not available during emergencies psychologists without training in therapeutic services in general or in crisis intervention specifically nonetheless have knowledge and expertise that can benefit the public. The standard permits psychologists who do not have the necessary training to offer such services, but requires they limit their services to the immediate timeframe and to cease as soon as the emergency has ended or appropriate services become available.

In rare instances, psychologists who do not have education or training related to suicidality assessment or intervention may come in contact with an individual who appears imminently suicidal and for whom no mental health or other health services are immediately available. Under Standard 2.02, psychologists without the necessary competencies would be permitted to try to reduce the immediate risk of suicide. However, the psychologist should call for emergency services or attempt to obtain or refer the individual for appropriate services as soon as feasible. Unqualified psychologists should be wary of providing services in this type of situation recognizing the potentially harmful nature of uninformed interventions and the ethical inappropriateness of providing unqualified treatment if medical or other suicide crisis services are available.

2.03 Maintaining Competence

Psychologists undertake ongoing efforts to develop and maintain their competence. *[No Significant Change, 1992 Standard 1.05, Maintaining Expertise]*

The scientific and professional knowledge base of psychology is continually evolving, bringing with it new research methodologies, assessment procedures, and forms of service delivery. Information and techniques constituting the core curricula of psychologists' doctoral education and training are often outdated and replaced by new information and more effective practices as decades pass. Life-long learning is fundamental to ensure that teaching, research, and practice have an ongoing positive effect on those with whom psychologists work. Standard 2.03 requires that psychologists undertake ongoing efforts to ensure continued competence. The requirements of this standard can be met through independent study, continuing education courses, supervision, consultation, or formal postdoctoral study.

2.04 Bases for Scientific and Professional Judgments

Psychologists' work is based upon established scientific and professional knowledge of the discipline (See also Standards 2.01e, Boundaries of Competence, and 10.01b, Informed Consent to Therapy). *[Modified for Clarity, 1992 Standard 1.06, Basis for Scientific and Professional Judgments]*

Standard 2.04 requires psychologists to select methods and provide professional opinions that are firmly grounded in the knowledge base of scientific and professional psychology. Scientific knowledge refers to information generated according to accepted principles of research practice. Professional knowledge refers to widely accepted and reliable clinical reports, case studies, or observations.

Psychologists engaged in innovative activities that fail to draw on established knowledge of the field risk failing to anticipate or detect aspects of such procedures that could lead to substantial misrepresentation or harm. The standard permits the use of novel approaches, recognizing that new theories, concepts, and techniques are critical to the continued development of the field. It does, however, prohibit psychologists from applying idiosyncratic ideas and techniques that are not grounded in either accepted principles or the field's cumulative knowledge of psychological research or practice. Violations of this standard would be activities similar to the tragic use of extreme forms of "rebirthing therapy" to treat attachment disorder—a practice that resulted in a child's death. This therapy, loosely based on psychoanalytic theories of attachment, consisted of a physical restraining intervention (placing the child in suffocating and binding physical conditions to simulate birth) that had no substantial basis in either the scientific or practice literatures (Kreck, 2000).

2.05 Delegation of Work to Others

Psychologists who delegate work to employees, supervisees, or research or teaching assistants or who use the services of others, such as interpreters, take reasonable steps to (1) avoid delegating such work to persons who have a multiple relationship with those being served that would likely lead to exploitation or loss of objectivity; (2) authorize only those responsibilities that such persons can be expected to perform competently on the basis of their education, training, or experience, either independently or with the level of supervision being provided; and (3) see that such persons perform these services competently. (See also

Standards 2.02, Providing Services in Emergencies; 3.05, Multiple Relationships; 4.01, Maintaining Confidentiality; 9.01, Bases for Assessments; 9.02, Use of Assessments; 9.03, Informed Consent in Assessments; and 9.07, Assessment by Unqualified Persons.) *[Expanded, 1992 Standard 1.22, Delegation to and Supervision of Subordinates]*

In their obligation to protect the rights and welfare of those with whom they work, psychologists who delegate or use the services of others are responsible for ensuring that such work is competently performed. To be in compliance with Standard 2.05, psychologists should (a) evaluate whether employees, supervisees, assistants, or others whose services are used have the skills to independently or under appropriate supervision implement the task; (b) assign such individuals only those tasks for which they are qualified; and (c) monitor the activities to ensure that they are being competently implemented.

☑ Consulting and industrial-organizational psychologists who delegate employee assessments or organizational research responsibilities to others must ensure to the extent feasible that such individuals have adequate training in the testing or data collection skills necessary to proficiently implement the work.

☑ Psychologists in academia must take reasonable measures to ensure that research and teaching assistants have the knowledge and skills required to implement valid and ethical research procedures, teach or advise students, or grade exams.

☑ Psychologists in mental health settings who supervise psychologist and nonpsychologist staff (e.g., lay leaders for group work; see Glass, 1998) must take steps to determine that these individuals have the necessary training to perform or assist in therapeutic procedures.

Implications of HIPAA. Psychologists who are covered entities under Health Insurance Portability and Accountability Act (HIPAA) should be aware that HIPAA requires covered entities to train, document, and appropriately sanction employees regarding federal policies and procedures involving protected health information (DHHS 45 CFR 164.530[b][1]).

Use of interpreters. Standard 2.05 specifically draws attention to the appropriate delegation of work to interpreters who assist psychologists in providing services for individuals who use American Sign Language or who do not speak the same language as the psychologist. Psychologists must ensure that interpreters have adequate translation skills and sufficient understanding of the psychological nature and ethical responsibilities of the duties to be performed. Some individuals who are deaf or do not speak

English live, work, or socialize in close-knit communities in which those who serve as interpreters are known personally. In such settings, psychologists should avoid delegating work to such individuals when it will create a multiple relationship between the interpreter and the person receiving services or involved in research that could reasonably be expected to lead to breaches in confidentiality, exploitation, or loss of objectivity.

Reasonable steps. The phrase "take reasonable steps" recognizes that despite their best efforts, persons to whom work is delegated may fail to perform their duties appropriately. The phrase also recognizes that sometimes psychologists working in organizations, in the military and other public service positions, or at the bequest of the legal system may be assigned assistants, employees, or interpreters insufficiently qualified to perform their duties. Psychologists must at minimum discuss their concerns and ethical obligations with those responsible for such assignments (see Standards 1.02, Conflicts Between Ethics and Law, Regulations, or Other Governing Legal Authority, and 1.03, Conflicts Between Ethics and Organizational Demands).

2.06 Personal Problems and Conflicts

(a) Psychologists refrain from initiating an activity when they know or should know that there is a substantial likelihood that their personal problems will prevent them from performing their work-related activities in a competent manner. *[Modified for Clarity, 1992 Standard 1.13a, Personal Problems and Conflicts]*

There is a growing body of research indicating that emotional, social, health-related, and other personal problems can interfere with psychologists' ability to use their skills effectively. Substance abuse problems, acute depression or other mental disorders, chronic or life-threatening diseases, and other stressful life events such as divorce or the death of a loved one are situations that sometimes prevent psychologists from performing their work in a competent manner (O'Connor, 2001; Sherman & Thelen, 1998). Work-related stressors, such as social isolation in private practice, burn out, and vicarious traumatization encountered by some psychologists working with survivors of trauma, can lead to boundary violations and otherwise compromise effective job performance (Pearlman & Saakvitne, 1995; Skorupa & Agresiti, 1993). Clients/patients, students, employers, and employees suffer when personal problems prevent psychologists from competently implementing their work, and the misconduct that is often a product of these circumstances harms public perceptions of psychology.

Standard 2.06a requires psychologists to refrain from beginning an activity when there is a substantial likelihood that their personal problems may impair their ability to competently perform their work. The phrases "refrain from beginning" and "substantial likelihood" indicate that the intent of this standard is preemptive: It prohibits psychologists from taking on a professional or scientific role when their personal problems have the potential to impair their work. As signified by the phrase "or should know," psychologists suffering from problems that would reasonably be expected by members of the profession to cause work-related impairment will not avoid a finding of violation of this standard by claiming they did not know their problems could interfere with their work.

☑ A psychologist had just returned to independent practice following chemotherapy for a cancer that is now in remission. The psychologist believed that she had recovered from the fatigue and mental stress of the chemotherapy, but recognized that such symptoms may persist. She set up a weekly consultation meeting with a colleague to help monitor her work until she was confident that the symptoms had fully abated.

☒ An industrial-organizational psychologist responsible for preemployment screening for an organization had begun to drink heavily and found that he needed to have several beers before seeing candidates in the morning, and several more drinks periodically throughout the workday. In response to a complaint to the APA Ethics Committee filed by an applicant who was appalled by the psychologist's slurring of words during a screening, the psychologist claimed that his alcoholism prevented him from acknowledging he had a problem.

(b) When psychologists become aware of personal problems that may interfere with their performing work-related duties adequately, they take appropriate measures, such as obtaining professional consultation or assistance, and determine whether they should limit, suspend, or terminate their work-related duties. (See also Standard 10.10, Terminating Therapy.) *[No Significant Change, 1992 Standard 1.13c, Personal Problems and Conflicts]*

Standard 2.06b applies to situations in which psychologists already providing services, teaching, or conducting research become aware that their personal problems are interfering with their work. The standard calls for psychologists to take appropriate steps to remedy the problem and to determine whether such remedies are sufficient for them to continue work-related activities.

☑ A teaching psychologist who was undergoing outpatient treatment for a life-threatening medical disorder found it increasingly difficult to prepare lectures, grade papers, and mentor students effectively. The psychologist consulted with the chair of the department, who agreed to assign an experienced graduate teaching assistant for the lectures. The psychologist also asked a colleague to serve as a co-mentor on the two dissertations he was currently mentoring.

To comply with this standard, psychologists can also turn to the increasing number of state psychological association and other colleague-assistance programs that help psychologists deal proactively with and remediate impairment (Barnett & Hillard, 2001). If such steps are not adequate to ensure competence, Standard 2.06b requires that psychologists appropriately limit, suspend, or terminate work-related duties.

CHAPTER 6

Standards on Human Relations

3. HUMAN RELATIONS

3.01 Unfair Discrimination

In their work-related activities, psychologists do not engage in unfair discrimination based on age, gender, gender identity, race, ethnicity, culture, national origin, religion, sexual orientation, disability, socio-economic status, or any basis proscribed by law. *[Expanded, 1992 Standard 1.10, Nondiscrimination]*

Psychologists respect the dignity and worth of all people and in their work appropriately consider the relevance of personal characteristics based on such factors as age, gender, gender identity, race, ethnicity, culture, national origin, religion, sexual orientation, disability, or socioeconomic status (Principle E: Respect for People's Rights and Dignity). Much of the work of psychologists entails making valid discriminating judgments that best serve the people and organizations with whom they work and to fulfill their ethical obligations as teachers, researchers, organizational consultants, and practitioners. Standard 3.01 of the American Psychological Association (APA) Ethics Code (2002) does not prohibit such discriminations.

☑ The graduate faculty of a university used differences in standardized test scores, undergraduate grades, and professionally related experience as selection criteria for program admission.

☑ A researcher sampled individuals from specific age, gender, and cultural groups to test a specific hypothesis relevant to these groups.

☑ A psychologist working for a company designed assessments for employee screening and promotion to distinguish individuals with the requisite skills to perform tasks essential to the positions from individuals who did not have these skills.

☑ A school psychologist considered such factors as age, language, ethnicity, and disability to select educationally relevant assessment instruments whose validity and reliability had been established for populations with characteristics similar to the child tested.

☑ A psychologist in private practice regularly considered whether factors associated with gender, ethnicity, religion, sexual orientation, socioeconomic status, or other relevant factors were affecting the mental health of a client.

Psychologists must, however, exercise reasonable judgment and precautions to ensure that their work does not reflect personal or organizational biases or prejudices that can lead to injustice (Principle D: Justice). Standard 3.01 prohibits psychologists from making unfair discriminations based on the factors listed in the standard.

☒ The director of a graduate program in psychology rejected a candidate for program admission because the candidate had indicated that he was gay.

☒ A consulting psychologist agreed to a company's request to develop preemployment procedures that would screen out applicants from Spanish-speaking cultures.

☒ A psychologist decided not to include a cognitive component in a behavioral treatment based solely on the psychologist's belief that lower-income patients were in general incapable of responding to "talk therapies."

Discrimination proscribed by law. Standard 3.01 prohibits psychologists from discriminating among individuals on any basis proscribed by law. For example, industrial-organizational psychologists need to be aware of nondiscrimination laws that apply to companies with which they work (e.g., Americans with Disabilities Act of 1990 [ADA] and the Workforce Investment Act of 1988). In some instances, laws for small businesses stemming from the ADA also apply to psychologists in private practice. Therefore, psychologists in independent practice should familiarize themselves with relevant federal and state ADA compliance regulations, such as wheelchair accessibility. In addition, the Health Insurance Portability and Accountability Act (HIPAA) prohibits covered entities from discriminating against an individual for filing a complaint, participating in a compliance review or hearing, or opposing an act or practice that is unlawful under the regulation (45 CFR 164.530[g]).

3.02 Sexual Harassment

Psychologists do not engage in sexual harassment. Sexual harassment is sexual solicitation, physical advances, or verbal or nonverbal conduct that is sexual in nature, that occurs in connection with the psychologist's activities or roles as a psychologist, and that either (1) is unwelcome, is offensive, or creates a hostile workplace or educational environment, and the psychologist knows or is told this or (2) is sufficiently severe or intense to be abusive to a reasonable person in the context. Sexual harassment can consist of a single intense or severe act or of multiple persistent or pervasive acts. (See also Standard 1.08, Unfair Discrimination Against Complainants and Respondents.) *[Expanded, 1992 Standard 1.11, Sexual Harassment]*

It is always wise for psychologists to be familiar with and comply with applicable laws and institutional policies regarding sexual harassment. Laws on sexual harassment vary across jurisdictions, are often complex, and change over time. Standard 3.02 provides a clear definition of behaviors that are prohibited and considered sexual harassment under the Ethics Code. When this definition establishes a higher standard of conduct than is required by law, psychologists must comply with Standard 3.02.

According to Standard 3.02, sexual harassment can be verbal or nonverbal solicitation, advances, or sexual conduct that occurs in connection with the psychologist's activities or role as a psychologist. The wording of the definition was carefully crafted to prohibit sexual harassment without encouraging complaints against psychologists whose poor judgments or behaviors do not rise to the level of harassment. Thus, to meet the standard's threshold for sexual harassment, behaviors have to be either sufficiently severe or intense to be abusive to a reasonable person in that context, or psychologists have to be aware or have been told that less intense behaviors are unwelcome, are offensive, or are creating a hostile workplace or educational environment.

For example, a senior faculty member who places an arm around a student's shoulder during a discussion or who tells an off-color sexual joke that offends a number of junior faculty may not be in violation of this standard if such behavior is uncharacteristic of the faculty member's usual conduct, if a reasonable person might interpret the behavior as inoffensive, and if there is reason to assume that the psychologist is neither aware of nor has been told the behavior is offensive.

A hostile workplace or educational environment is one in which the sexual language or behaviors of the psychologist impair the ability of those who are the target of the sexual harassment to conduct their work or participate in classroom and educational experiences. The actions of the senior faculty member described above might be considered sexual harassment if the psychologist's behaviors reflected a consistent pattern of sexual conduct during class or office hours, if such behaviors had led students to withdraw from the psychologist's class, or if students or other faculty had repeatedly told the psychologist about the discomfort produced.

According to this standard, sexual harassment can also consist of a single intense or severe act that would be considered abusive to a reasonable person.

❌ A senior psychologist at a test company sexually fondled a junior colleague during an office party.

A violation of this standard applies to all psychologists irrespective of the status, sex, or sexual orientation of the psychologist or individual harassed.

> ❌ During clinical supervision, a trainee had an emotional discussion with her female supervisor about how her own experiences recognizing her lesbian sexual orientation during adolescence were helping her counsel the gay and lesbian youths she was working with. At the end of the session, the supervisor kissed the trainee on the lips.

3.03 Other Harassment

Psychologists do not knowingly engage in behavior that is harassing or demeaning to persons with whom they interact in their work based on factors such as those persons' age, gender, gender identity, race, ethnicity, culture, national origin, religion, sexual orientation, disability, language, or socioeconomic status. *[No Significant Change, 1992 Standard 1.12, Other Harassment]*

According to Principle E: Respect for People's Rights and Dignity, psychologists try to eliminate from their work the effect of bias and prejudice based on cultural, individual, and role differences including age, gender, gender identity, race, ethnicity, national origin, religion, sexual orientation, disability, language, and socioeconomic status. Standard 3.03 prohibits behaviors that draw on these categories to harass or demean individuals with whom psychologists work. Behaviors directed at lowering the status or reputation of a colleague or student based on these factors, ethnic slurs, or public statements attributing negative characteristics to a research participant, student, employee, or colleague based on that person's gender, sexual orientation, disability, or socioeconomic status would be in violation of this standard.

The term "knowingly" reflects the fact that evolving societal sensitivity to language and behaviors demeaning to different groups may result in psychologists unknowingly acting in a pejorative manner. The term "knowingly" also reflects awareness that interpretations of behaviors that are harassing or demeaning can often be subjective. Thus, a violation of this standard rests on an objective evaluation that a psychologist would have or should have been aware that his or her behavior would be perceived as harassing or demeaning.

This standard does not prohibit psychologists from critical comments about the work of students, colleagues, or others based on legitimate criteria. For example, professors can inform, and often have a duty to inform, students that their writing or clinical skills are below program standards or indicate when a student's classroom comment is incorrect or inappropriate. It is the responsibility of employers or chairs of academic departments to critically review, report on, and discuss both positive and negative evaluations of employees or faculty. Similarly, the standard does not prohibit psychologists conducting assessment or therapy from applying valid diagnostic classifications that a client/patient may find offensive.

3.04 Avoiding Harm

Psychologists take reasonable steps to avoid harming their clients/patients, students, supervisees, research participants, organizational clients, and others with whom they work, and to minimize harm where it is foreseeable and unavoidable. *[No Significant Change, 1992 Standard 1.14, Avoiding Harm]*

As articulated in Principle A: Beneficence and Nonmaleficence, psychologists seek to safeguard the welfare of those with whom they work and avoid or minimize harm when conflicts occur among professional obligations. In the rightly practiced profession and science of psychology, harm is not always unethical or avoidable. Legitimate activities that may lead to harm include (a) giving low grades to students who perform poorly on exams; (b) providing a valid diagnosis that prevents a client/patient from receiving disability insurance; (c) conducting personnel reviews that lead to an individual's termination of employment; (d) conducting a custody evaluation in a case in which the judge determines that one of the parents must relinquish custodial rights; (e) administering a survey on trauma, approved by an institutional review board, that elicits anxiety in a small percentage of research participants; or (d) disclosing confidential information to protect the physical welfare of another person.

Avoiding Harm

Recognizing that such harms are not always avoidable or inappropriate, Standard 3.04 requires that psychologists take reasonable steps to avoid harming those with whom they interact in their professional and scientific roles and to minimize harm where it is foreseeable and unavoidable.

Such steps often include complying with other standards in the Ethics Code, such as the following:

☑ Ensuring that informed consent procedures adequately disclose information about the risks and limits of confidentiality of any psychological activity in which a client/patient, organizational client, research participant, or others might be involved (Standards 3.10, Informed Consent; 8.02, Informed Consent to Research; 9.03, Informed Consent in Assessments; and 10.01, Informed Consent to Therapy)

☑ Selecting and using valid and reliable assessment techniques appropriate to the nature of the problem and characteristics of the individual assessed to avoid misdiagnosis and inappropriate services (Standards 9.01, Bases for Assessments, and 9.02, Use of Assessments)

☑ Acquiring adequate knowledge of relevant judicial or administrative rules prior to performing forensic roles to avoid violating the legal rights of individuals involved in litigation (Standard 2.01f, Boundaries of Competence)

☑ Terminating treatment when it becomes reasonably clear that the client is not benefiting or may be harmed by the therapy (Standard 10.10c, Terminating Therapy)

☑ Taking steps to minimize harm when during debriefing a psychologist becomes aware that a research procedure has created participant distress (Standard 8.08c, Debriefing)

Harm Caused by Violation of Other Standards

Often violation of Standard 3.04 will occur in connection with the violation of other standards in this code that detail the actions required to perform psychological activities in an ethically responsible manner. For example:

☒ Testifying on the poor parenting skills of an individual whom the psychologist has never personally examined, and the testimony contributes to that individual's loss of child custody (Standard 9.01b, Bases for Assessments)

☒ Engaging in a sexual relationship with a current therapy client/patient that contributes to the breakup of the client's/patient's marriage (Standard 10.05, Sexual Intimacies With Current Therapy Clients/Patients)

☒ Asking students to discuss their personal experience in psychotherapy in terms of past and current theories on mental health treatment when this requirement was not stipulated in admissions or program materials, causing some students to drop out of the program (Standard 7.04, Student Disclosure of Personal Information)

☒ Deceiving a research participant about procedures the investigator expected would cause a slight degree of physical pain (Standard 8.07b, Deception in Research)

Some work contexts require more stringent protections against harm. For example, psychologists working within institutions that use seclusion or physical or chemical restraint techniques to treat violent episodes or other potentially injurious behaviors must ensure that these extreme methods are used only when there is evidence of their effectiveness, when other treatment alternatives have failed, and when the use of such techniques are in the best interest of the patient and not for punishment, staff convenience or anxiety, or expense (Jerome, 1998).

Implications of HIPAA. Psychologists should be aware that HIPAA requires that covered entities take reasonable steps to mitigate any harmful effects of a violation of the Privacy Rule of which they are aware (45 CFR 164.530[f]).

3.05 Multiple Relationships

(a) A multiple relationship occurs when a psychologist is in a professional role with a person and (1) at the same time is in another role with the same person, (2) at the same time is in a relationship with a person closely associated with or related to the person with whom the psychologist has the professional relationship, or (3) promises to enter into another relationship in the future with the person or a person closely associated with or related to the person.

A psychologist refrains from entering into a multiple relationship if the multiple relationship could reasonably be expected to impair the psychologist's objectivity, competence, or effectiveness in performing his or her functions as a psychologist, or otherwise risks exploitation or harm to the person with whom the professional relationship exists.

Multiple relationships that would not reasonably be expected to cause impairment or risk exploitation or harm are not unethical. *[Modified for Clarity, 1992 Standard 1.17, Multiple Relationships]*

Individual psychologists may perform a variety of roles. For example, during the course of a year a psychologist might see clients/patients in private practice, teach at a university, provide consultation services to an organization, and conduct research.

Not All Multiple Relationships Are Unethical

Multiple relationships that would not reasonably be expected to cause impairment or risk exploitation or harm are not unethical. Standard 3.05 does not prohibit attendance at a client's/patient's, student's, employee's, or employer's family funeral, wedding, or graduation; the participation of a psychologist's child in an athletic team coached by a client/patient; gift giving or receiving with those with whom one has a professional role; or from entering into a social relationship with a colleague as long as these relationships would not reasonably be expected to lead to role impairment, exploitation, or harm. Similarly, psychologists can serve as clinical supervisors for students enrolled in one of their graduate classes because both supervision and teaching are educational roles.

Incidental encounters with clients/patients at religious services, school events, restaurants, health clubs, or similar places are not unethical. Nonetheless, psychologists should always consider whether the particular nature of a professional relationship might lead to misperceptions regarding the encounter. If so, it may be wise to keep a record of such encounters. For example:

 A client with a fluctuating sense of reality coupled with strong romantic transference feelings for a treating psychologist misinterpreted two incidental encounters with his psychologist as planned romantic meetings. The client subsequently raised these incidents in a sexual misconduct complaint against the psychologist. The psychologist's recorded notes made immediately following these encounters were effective evidence against the invalid accusations.

Posttermination nonsexual relationships. The standard does not have an absolute prohibition against posttermination *non*sexual relationships with persons with whom psychologists have had a previous professional relationship. However, such relationships are prohibited if the posttermination relationship was promised during the course of the original relationship or if the individual was exploited or harmed by the intent to have the posttermination relationship. Psychologists should be aware that posttermination relationships can become problematic when personal knowledge acquired during psychotherapy becomes relevant to the new relationship (see Anderson & Kitchener, 1996, for examples and discussion of nonromantic, nonsexual posttherapy relationships).

> ☒ A psychologist in independent practice abruptly terminated therapy with a patient who was an editor at a large publishing company so that the patient could review a book manuscript the psychologist had submitted to the company.

Clients in individual and group therapy. In most instances, treating clients/patients concurrently in individual and group therapy does not represent a multiple relationship because the practitioner is working in a therapeutic role in both contexts (Taylor & Gazda, 1991), and Standard 3.05 does not prohibit such practice. Psychologists providing individual and group therapy to the same clients/patients should consider instituting special protections against inadvertently revealing to a therapy group information shared by a client/patient in individual sessions. As in all types of professional practice, psychologists should avoid recommending an additional form of therapy based on the psychologist's financial interests rather than the client's/patient's mental health needs.

Potentially Unethical Multiple Relationships

Entering into another role. Psychologists may encounter situations in which the opportunity to enter a new relationship emerges with a person with whom they already have an established professional role. The following examples illustrate multiple relationships that with rare exception would be prohibited by Standard 3.05a because each situation could reasonably be expected to impair psychologists' ability to competently and objectively perform their roles or lead to exploitation or harm.

> ☒ A psychologist agreed to see a student in the psychologist's introductory psychology course for brief private counseling for test anxiety. At the end of the semester, to avoid jeopardizing the student's growing academic self-confidence, the psychologist refrained from giving the student a legitimate low grade for poor class performance; thus, the multiple relationship impaired the psychologist's objectivity and effectiveness as a teacher and created an unfair grading environment for other students in the class.

> ❌ A company hired a psychologist for consultation on how to prepare employees for a shift in management anticipated by the failing mental health of the chief executive officer (CEO). A few months later, the psychologist agreed to a request by the board of directors to counsel the CEO about retiring. The CEO did not want to retire and told the psychologist about the coercive tactics used by the board. The psychologist realized too late that this second role undermined both treatment and consultation effectiveness because the counseling role played by the psychologist would be viewed as either exploitative by the CEO or as disloyal by the board of directors.

Relationships with others. Psychologists may also encounter situations in which a person closely associated with someone with whom they have a professional role seeks to enter into a similar professional relationship. For example, the roommate of a psychotherapy client/patient might ask the psychologist for an appointment to begin psychotherapy. A CEO of a company that hires a psychologist to conduct personnel evaluations might ask the psychologist to administer a battery of psychological tests to the CEO's child to determine whether the child has a learning disability. With few exceptions, entering into such relationships would risk a violation of Standard 3.05a because it could reasonably be expected that the psychologist's ability to make appropriate and objective judgments would be impaired, which in turn would jeopardize the effectiveness of services provided and result in harm.

Preexisting personal relationships. Psychologists may also encounter situations in which they are asked to be in a professional role with someone with whom they have a preexisting personal relationship. These multiple relationships are frequently unethical because the preexisting relationship would reasonably be expected to impair the psychologist's objectivity and effectiveness.

> ❌ Relatives asked a psychologist to help his nephew overcome anxiety about going to school.
>
> ❌ A colleague asked a psychologist to administer a battery of tests to assess whether she had adult attention deficit disorder.

"Reasonably expected." It is important to note that the phrase "could reasonably be expected" indicates that violations of Standard 3.05a may be judged not only on the basis of whether actual impairment, harm, or exploitation has occurred but whether most psychologists engaged in similar activities in similar circumstances would determine that entering into the multiple relationship would be expected to lead to such harms.

☑ A judge asked a psychologist who had conducted a custody evaluation to provide 6-month mandated family counseling for the couple involved followed by a reevaluation for custody. The psychologist explained to the judge that providing family counseling to individuals whose parenting skills the psychologist would later have to evaluate could reasonably be expected to impair her ability to form an objective opinion independent of knowledge gained and the professional investment made in the counseling sessions. She also explained that such a multiple relationship would likely impair her effectiveness as a counselor if the parents refrained from honest engagement in the counseling sessions out of fear that comments made would be used against them during the custody assessment. The judge agreed to assign the family to another psychologist for counseling.

Unavoidable Multiple Relationships

In some situations, it may not be possible or reasonable to avoid multiple relationships. Psychologists working in rural communities, small towns, military bases, or American Indian reservations, or who are qualified to provide services to members of unique ethnic or language groups for which alternative psychological services are not available, would not be in violation of this standard if they took reasonable steps to protect their objectivity and effectiveness and the possibility of exploitation and harm. Such steps might include seeking consultation by phone from a colleague to help ensure objectivity; taking extra precautions to protect the confidentiality of each individual with whom the psychologist works; or explaining to individuals involved the ethical challenges of the multiple relationships, the steps the psychologist will take to mitigate these risks, and encouraging individuals to alert the psychologist to relational situations of which the psychologist might not be aware and that might place his or her effectiveness at risk.

(b) If a psychologist finds that, due to unforeseen factors, a potentially harmful multiple relationship has arisen, the psychologist takes reasonable steps to resolve it with due regard for the best interests of the affected person and maximal compliance with the Ethics Code. *[Modified for Clarity, 1992 Standard 1.17b, Multiple Relationships]*

There will be instances in which psychologists discover they are involved in a potentially harmful multiple relationship of which they had been unaware. Standard 3.05b requires that psychologists take reasonable steps to resolve the potential harms that might arise from such relationships, recognizing that in some instances the best interests of the affected person and maximal compliance with other standards in the Ethics Code may require psychologists to remain in the multiple roles.

☑ A psychologist responsible for conducting individual assessments of candidates for an executive-level position discovered that one of the candidates was a close friend's husband. Because information about this prior relationship was neither confidential nor harmful to the candidate, the psychologist explained the situation to company executives and worked with the organization to assign that particular promotion evaluation to another qualified professional.

☑ A psychologist working at a university counseling center discovered that a counseling client had enrolled in a large undergraduate class the psychologist was going to teach. The psychologist discussed the potential conflict with the client and attempted to help him enroll in a different class. However, the client was a senior and needed the class to complete his major requirements. In addition, there were no appropriate referrals for the student at the counseling center. Without revealing the student's identity, the psychologist discussed her options with the department chair. They concluded that because the class was very large, the psychologist could take the following steps to protect her objectivity and effectiveness as both a teacher and counselor: (1) A graduate teaching assistant would be responsible for grading exams and for calculating the final course grade based on the average of scores on the exams, and (2) the psychologist would monitor the situation during counseling sessions and seek consultation if problems arose.

☑ A psychologist in independent practice became aware that his neighbor had begun dating one of the psychologist's psychotherapy patients. The psychologist could not reveal to his neighbor that the patient was in therapy. Although telling the patient about the social relationship could cause some distress, it was likely the patient would find out about the relationship during conversations with the neighbor. The psychologist considered reducing his social exchanges with the neighbor but this proved infeasible. After seeking consultation from a colleague, the psychologist decided that he could not ensure therapeutic objectivity or effectiveness if the situation continued. He decided to explain the situation to the patient, provide a referral, and assist the transition to a new therapist during pretermination counseling.

(c) When psychologists are required by law, institutional policy, or extraordinary circumstances to serve in more than one role in judicial or administrative proceedings, at the outset they clarify role expectations and the extent of confidentiality and thereafter as changes occur. (See also Standards 3.04, Avoiding Harm, and 3.07, Third-Party Requests for Services.) *[Modified for Clarity, 1992 Standard 7.03, Clarification of Role]*

Standard 3.05c applies to instances when psychologists are required to serve in more than one role in judicial or administrative proceedings or because of extraordinary circumstances. This standard does *not* permit psychologists to take on these multiple roles if such a situation can be avoided. Standard 3.05c requires that when

such multiple roles cannot be avoided, as soon as possible and thereafter as changes occur, psychologists clarify to all parties involved the roles the psychologist is expected to perform and the extent and limits of confidentiality that can be anticipated by taking on these multiple roles.

☑ A military psychologist provided therapy to an enlisted officer who was ordered to enter treatment for difficulties in job-related performance. While the treatment was progressing, the client and psychologist were assigned to a field exercise in which the client would be under the psychologist's command. To reassign the client to a different officer for the exercise, the psychologist would need to speak with a superior who was not a mental health worker. Recognizing that the client's involvement in therapy would have to be revealed in such a discussion, the psychologist explained the situation to the enlisted member and asked permission to discuss the situation with her superiors. The client refused to give permission. The psychologist was the only mental health professional on the base, so transferring the client to another provider was not an option. The psychologist therefore developed a specific plan with the client for how they would relate to each other during the field exercise and how they would discuss in therapy issues that arose. (This case is adapted from one of four military cases provided by Staal & King, 2000.)

In most situations, psychologists are expected to avoid entering multiple relationships in forensically relevant situations or to resolve such relationships when they unexpectedly occur (Standards 3.05a and b). When such circumstances arise (e.g., performing a custody evaluation and then providing court-mandated family therapy for the couple involved), the conflict may sometimes be resolved by explaining to a judge or institutional administrator the problematic nature of the multiple relationship.

☑ A consulting psychologist developed a company's sexual harassment policy. After the policy had been approved and implemented, the psychologist agreed to counsel employees experiencing sexual harassment. One of the psychologist's clients then filed a sexual harassment suit against the company. The psychologist was called on by the defense to testify as an expert witness for the company's sexual harassment policy and by the plaintiff as a fact witness about the stress and anxiety observed during counseling sessions (see Hellkamp & Lewis, 1995, for further discussion of this type of dilemma). The psychologist (a) immediately told the company and the employee the nature of the multiple relationship, (b) described to both the problems that testifying might raise including the limits of maintaining the confidentiality of information acquired from either the consulting or counseling roles, and (c) ceased providing sexual harassment counseling services for employees. Neither party agreed to withdraw its request to the judge for the psychologist's testimony. The psychologist wrote a letter to the judge explaining the conflicting roles and asked to be recused from testifying.

3.06 Conflict of Interest

Psychologists refrain from taking on a professional role when personal, scientific, professional, legal, financial, or other interests or relationships could reasonably be expected to (1) impair their objectivity, competence, or effectiveness in performing their functions as psychologists or (2) expose the person or organization with whom the professional relationship exists to harm or exploitation. *[Significant Change in Meaning, 1992 Standard 1.17b, Multiple Relationships]*

Psychologists strive to benefit and establish relationships of trust with those with whom they work through the exercise of professional and scientific judgments based on their training and experience and established knowledge of the discipline. Standard 3.06 prohibits psychologists from taking on a professional role when competing professional, personal, financial, legal, or other interests or relationships could reasonably be expected to impair their objectivity, competence, or ability to effectively perform this role. Examples of conflicts of interest sufficient to appear to compromise the psychologist's judgments include the following:

☒ A psychologist had financial holdings in a company whose product the psychologist has been asked to professionally endorse.

☒ Irrespective of a patient's treatment needs, to save money a psychologist reduced the number of sessions for certain patients after he had exceeded his yearly compensation under a capitated contract with a health maintenance organization (HMO).

☒ A member of a faculty hiring committee refused to recuse herself from voting when a relative applied for the position under the committee's consideration.

☒ A psychologist in private practice agreed to be paid $1,000.00 for each patient he referred for participation in a treatment study.

☒ A research psychologist agreed to provide expert testimony on a contingent fee basis, thereby compromising her role as advocate for the scientific data.

☒ A psychologist failed to disclose on informed consent forms and in a subsequent publication that his research was funded by the company whose drug-related side effects the research was designed to evaluate.

☒ A prescribing psychologist failed to disclose to patients that she had a substantial financial investment in the company that manufactured the medication the psychologist frequently recommended.

☒ A psychologist used his professional Web site to recommend Internet mental health services in which he had an undisclosed financial interest.

☒ A school psychologist agreed to conduct a record review for the educational placement of the child of the president of a foundation that contributed heavily to the private school institution at which the psychologist was employed.

The standard also prohibits taking on a role that would expose a person or organization with whom a psychologist already works to harm or exploitation. For example:

☒ A psychologist accepted a position on the board of directors from a company for which she currently had been hired to conduct an independent evaluation of employee productivity.

☒ A psychologist took on as a psychotherapy client an individual who was a financial analyst at the brokerage company the psychologist used for his personal investments.

Many organizations, institutions, and federal agencies have conflict-of-interest policies.

♦ The APA Committee on Accreditation's Conflict of Interest Policy for Site Visitors includes prohibitions against even the appearance of conflict of interest of committee members and staff with a program being visited. Possible conflicts include former employment or enrollment in the program or a family connection or close friend or professional colleague in the program (http://www.apa.org/ed/accreditation/sitevstrconflict.html).

♦ The National Institutes of Health Office of Extramural Research requires every institution receiving research Public Health Service (PHS) grants to have written guidelines for the avoidance and institutional review of conflict of interest. These guidelines must reflect state and local laws and cover financial interests, gifts, gratuities and favors, nepotism, political participation, and bribery (http://grants.nih.gov/grants/policy/emprograms/overview/ep-coi.htm).

♦ PHS Regulations 42 CFR Part 50, Subpart F, and 45 CFR Part 94 provide conflict-of-interest guidelines for individual investigators (http://grants/guide/notice-files/not95–179.html). Many journals now require authors to submit an affidavit on conflict of interests prior to reviewing or publishing an article.

3.07 Third-Party Requests for Services

When psychologists agree to provide services to a person or entity at the request of a third party, psychologists attempt to clarify at the outset of the service the nature of the relationship with all individuals or organizations involved. This clarification includes the role of the psychologist (e.g., therapist, consultant, diagnostician, or expert witness), an identification of who is the client, the probable uses of the services provided or the information obtained, and the fact that there may be limits to confidentiality. (See also Standards 3.05, Multiple Relationships, and 4.02, Discussing the Limits of Confidentiality.) *[Modified for Clarity, 1992 Standard 1.21, Third-Party Requests for Services]*

Psychologists are often asked to conduct an assessment, provide psychotherapy, or testify in court by third parties who themselves will not be directly involved in the evaluation, treatment, or testimony.

In all these cases, Standard 3.07 requires that at the outset of the service, psychologists explain to both the third party and those individuals who will receive psychological services the nature of the relationship the psychologist will have with all individuals or organizations involved. This includes providing information about the role of the psychologist (i.e., therapist, consultant, diagnostician, expert witness), identifying whether the third party or the individual receiving the services is the client, who will receive information about the services, and probable uses of information gained or services provided.

> ☑ A company asked a psychologist to conduct preemployment evaluations of potential employees. The psychologist informed each applicant evaluated that she was working for the company, that the company would receive the test results, and that the information would be used in hiring decisions.
>
> ☑ A school district hired a psychologist to evaluate students for educational placement. The psychologist first clarified state and federal laws on parental rights regarding educational assessments, communicated this information to the school superintendent and the child's guardian(s), and explained the nature and use of the assessments and the confidentiality and reporting procedures the psychologist would use.
>
> ☑ A legal guardian requested behavioral treatment for her 30-year-old adult child with mental retardation because of difficulties he was having at the sheltered workshop where he worked. At the outset of services, using language compatible with the patient's

intellectual level, the psychologist informed the patient that the guardian had requested the treatment, explained the purpose of the treatment, and indicated the extent to which the guardian would have access to confidential information and how such information might be used.

☑ A defense attorney hired a psychologist to conduct an independent evaluation of a plaintiff who was claiming the attorney's client had caused her emotional harm. The plaintiff agreed to be evaluated. The psychologist first explained to the plaintiff that the defense attorney was the client and that all information would be shared with the attorney and possibly used by the attorney to refute the plaintiff's allegations in court. Once the evaluation commenced, the psychologist avoided using techniques that would encourage the plaintiff to respond to the psychologist as a psychotherapist (Hess, 1998).

☑ A judge ordered a convicted sex offender to receive therapy as a condition of parole. The psychologist assigned to provide the therapy explained to the parolee that all information revealed during therapy would be provided to the court and might be used to rescind parole.

Implications of HIPAA. Psychologists planning to share information with third parties should also carefully consider whether such information is included under the HIPAA definition of protected health information (PHI) and whether HIPAA regulations require prior patient authorization for such release or whether the authorization requirement can be waived by the legal prerogatives of the third party (45 CFR 164.508 and 164.512). Psychologists should then clarify beforehand to both the third party and recipient of services the HIPAA requirements for release of PHI.

3.08 Exploitative Relationships

Psychologists do not exploit persons over whom they have supervisory, evaluative, or other authority such as clients/patients, students, supervisees, research participants, and employees. (See also Standards 3.05, Multiple Relationships; 6.04, Fees and Financial Arrangements; 6.05, Barter With Clients/Patients; 7.07, Sexual Relationships With Students and Supervisees; 10.05, Sexual Intimacies With Current Therapy Clients/Patients; 10.06, Sexual Intimacies With Relatives or Significant Others of Current Therapy Clients/Patients; 10.07, Therapy With Former Sexual Partners; and 10.08, Sexual Intimacies With Former Therapy Clients/Patients.) *[No Significant Change, 1992 Standard 1.19, Exploitative Relationships]*

Standard 3.08 prohibits psychologists from taking unfair advantage of or manipulating for their own personal use or satisfaction students, supervisees, clients/patients, research participants, employees, or others over whom they have authority. Below are examples of actions that would violate this standard:

> ☒ Repeatedly requiring graduate assistants to work overtime without additional compensation
>
> ☒ Requiring employees to run a psychologist's personal errands
>
> ☒ Taking advantage of company billing loopholes to inflate rates for consulting services
>
> ☒ Encouraging expensive gifts from psychotherapy clients/patients
>
> ☒ Using "bait and switch" tactics to lure clients/patients into therapy with initial low rates that are hiked after a few sessions

Violations of Standard 3.08 often occur in connection with other violations of the Ethics Code. For example:

> ☒ Psychologists exploit the trust and vulnerability of individuals with whom they work when they have sexual relationships with current clients/patients or students (Standards 10.05, Sexual Intimacies With Current Therapy Clients/Patients, and 7.07, Sexual Relationships With Students and Supervisees).
>
> ☒ Exploitation occurs when a psychologist accepts nonmonetary remuneration from clients/patients the value of which is substantially higher than the psychological services rendered (Standard 6.05, Barter With Clients/Patients).
>
> ☒ Charging clients/patients for psychological assessments for which the client/patient had not initially agreed and that are unnecessary for the agreed on goals of the psychological evaluation is similarly exploitive (Standard 6.04a, Fees and Financial Arrangements).
>
> ☒ School psychologists exploit their students when in their private practice they provide fee-for-service psychological testing to students who could receive these services free of charge from the psychologist in the school district in which they work (Standard 3.05a, Multiple Relationships; see also the *Professional Conduct Manual for School Psychology*, National Association for School Psychologists, 2000, www.naspweb.org).

Standard 3.08 does not prohibit psychologists from having a sliding-fee scale or different payment plans for different types or amount of services, as long as the fee practices are fairly applied.

3.09 Cooperation With Other Professionals

When indicated and professionally appropriate, psychologists cooperate with other professionals in order to serve their clients/patients effectively and appropriately. (See also Standard 4.05, Disclosures.) *[No Significant Change, 1992 Standard 1.20, Consultation and Referrals]*

Individuals who come to psychologists for assessment, counseling, or therapy are often receiving or are in need of collateral medical, legal, educational, or social services. Collaboration and consultation with, and referral to, other professionals are thus often necessary to serve the best interests of clients/patients. Standard 3.09 requires that psychologists cooperate with other professionals when it is appropriate and will help serve the client/patient most effectively. For example, having obtained appropriate consent:

> ☑ With permission of the parent, a psychologist spoke with a child's teacher to help determine if behaviors suggestive of attention deficit disorder exhibited at home and in the psychologist's office were consistent with the child's classroom behavior.
>
> ☑ With consent from the parent, a school psychologist contacted a social worker who was helping a student's family apply for public assistance to help determine the availability of collateral services (e.g., substance abuse counseling).
>
> ☑ A psychologist with prescribing privileges referred patients to a physician for diagnosis of physical symptoms thought by the patient to be the result of a psychological disorder that were more suggestive of a medical condition.

Implications of HIPAA. Psychologists who are covered entities under HIPAA should be familiar with situations in which regulations requiring patient written authorization for release of PHI apply to communications with other professionals (45 CFR 164.510, 164.512). They should also be aware of rules governing patients' rights to know when such disclosures have been made (45 CFR 164.520, Notice of Privacy Practices, and 45 CFR 164.528, Accounting of Disclosures of Protected Health Information).

3.10 Informed Consent

(a) When psychologists conduct research or provide assessment, therapy, counseling, or consulting services in person or via electronic transmission or other forms of communication, they obtain the informed consent of the individual or individuals using language that is reasonably understandable to that person or persons except when conducting such activities without consent is mandated by law or governmental regulation or as otherwise provided in this Ethics Code. (See also Standards 8.02, Informed Consent to Research; 9.03, Informed Consent in Assessments; and 10.01, Informed Consent to Therapy.) *[Expanded, 1992 Standards 4.01d, Structuring the Relationship, and 4.02, Informed Consent to Therapy]*

Informed consent is seen by many as the primary means of protecting the self-governing and privacy rights of those with whom psychologists work. In the 1992 Ethics Code, the obligation to obtain informed consent was limited to research and therapy. In the 2002 Ethics Code, the broader informed consent requirement for most psychological activities reflects the societal sea change from a paternalistic to an autonomy-based view of professional and scientific ethics. Required elements of informed consent for specific areas of psychology are detailed in Standards 8.02, Informed Consent to Research; 9.03, Informed Consent in Assessments; and 10.01, Informed Consent to Therapy.

Language. The obligations described in Standard 3.10 apply to these other consent standards. In research, assessment, and therapy, psychologists must obtain informed consent using language that is reasonably understandable to the person who is asked to consent. For example, psychologists must use appropriate translations of consent information for individuals for whom English is not a preferred language or who use sign language. Psychologists should also adjust reading and language comprehension levels of consent procedures to an individual's developmental or educational level or reading or learning disability.

Consent via electronic transmission. Standard 3.10a requires informed consent be obtained when research, assessment, or therapy is conducted via electronic transmission, such as the telephone or the Internet. Psychologists need to take special steps to identify the language needs of those from whom they obtain consent via electronic media. In addition, psychologists conducting work via e-mail or other electronic communications should take precautions to ensure that the individual who gave consent is in fact the individual participating in the research or receiving the psychologist's services (i.e., use of a participant/client/patient password).

Exemptions. Some activities are exempt from the requirements of Standard 3.10. For example, psychologists conducting court-ordered assessments or evaluating military personnel may be prevented from obtaining consent by law or governmental regulation. In addition, there are several standards in the Ethics Code that detail conditions under which informed consent may be waived (Standard 8.03, Informed Consent for Recording Voices and Images in Research; Standard 8.05, Dispensing With Informed Consent for Research; Standard 8.07, Deception in Research). HIPAA also permits certain exemptions from patient authorization requirements relevant to research and practice, which are discussed in later chapters on standards for research, assessment, and therapy.

(b) For persons who are legally incapable of giving informed consent, psychologists nevertheless (1) provide an appropriate explanation, (2) seek the individual's assent, (3) consider such persons' preferences and best interests, and (4) obtain appropriate permission from a legally authorized person, if such substitute consent is permitted or required by law. When consent by a legally authorized person is not permitted or required by law, psychologists take reasonable steps to protect the individual's rights and welfare. *[Expanded, 1992 Standards 4.02b and 4.02c, Informed Consent to Therapy]*

Adults who have been declared legally incompetent and most children under age 18 do not have the legal right to provide independent consent to receive psychological services or participate in psychological research. In recognition of these individuals' rights as persons, Standard 3.10b requires psychologists obtain their affirmative agreement to participate in psychological activities after providing them with an explanation of the nature and purpose of the activities and their right to decline or withdraw from participation. The phrase "consider such persons' preferences and best interests" indicates that although in most instances psychologists respect a person's right to dissent from participation in psychological activities, this right can be superceded if the failure to participate would deprive persons of psychological services necessary to protect or promote their welfare.

For individuals who are legally incapable of giving informed consent, psychologists must also obtain permission from a legally authorized person, if such substitute consent is permitted or required by law. Psychologists working with children in the foster care system and in juvenile detention centers and those working with institutionalized adults with identified cognitive or mental disorders leading to decisional impairment must carefully determine who has legal responsibility for substitute decision making. Psychologists should be aware that in some instances, especially for children in foster care, legal guardianship might change over time.

Emancipated and mature minors. There are instances in which guardian permission for treatment or research for children under 18 is not required or possible. For example, *emancipated minor* is a legal status conferred on persons who have not yet attained the age of legal competency as defined by state law but are entitled to treatment as if they have such status by virtue of assuming adult responsibilities, such as self-support, marriage, or procreation. *Mature minor* is someone who has not reached adulthood (as defined by state law) but who according to state law may be treated as an adult for certain purposes (e.g., consenting to treatment for venereal disease, drug abuse, or emotional disorders). When a child is an emancipated or mature minor, informed consent procedures should follow Standard 3.10a.

Best interests of the child. The requirement for guardian permission may be inappropriate if there is serious doubt as to whether the guardian's interests adequately reflect the child's interests (e.g., cases of child abuse or neglect; genetic testing of a healthy child to assist in understanding the disorder of a sibling) or cannot reasonably be obtained (e.g., treatment or research involving runaways). In such cases, the appointment of a consent advocate can protect the child's rights and welfare by verifying the minor's understanding of assent procedures, supporting the child's preferences, ensuring participation is voluntary, and monitoring reactions to psychological procedures. Psychologists conducting research need to be familiar with federal regulations regarding waiver of parental permission (45 CFR 46.408c) and have such waivers approved by an institutional review board (Standard 8.01, Institutional Approval; Fisher, Hoagwood, & Jensen, 1996). Psychologists conducting therapy need to be familiar with their state laws regarding provision of therapy to children and adolescents without parental consent (Fisher, Hatashita-Wong, & Isman, 1999).

Adults with cognitive impairments who do not have legal guardians. There may be adults, such as those with Alzheimer's disease or developmental disabilities, who do not have a legal guardian but whose ability to fully understand consent relevant information is impaired. For example, clinical geropsychologists frequently work with older persons with progressive dementia living in nursing homes and assisted-living and residential care facilities where substitute decision making is typically handled informally by family members or others. In addition to obtaining consent from the individual, psychologists can seek additional protections for the individual by encouraging a shared decision-making process with or seeking additional permission from these informal caretakers (Fisher, 2002a, 2002b, 2003).

HIPAA Notice of Privacy Practices. Prior to beginning treatment or treatment relevant assessments, or randomized clinical trials in which health care is provided, HIPAA covered entities must provide patients with a Notice of Privacy Practices that describes the psychologist's policies for use and disclosure of PHI, the clients'/patients' rights regarding their PHI under HIPAA, and the provider's obligations under the Privacy Rule (45 CFR 164.520). In most instances, the notice will be given to prospective clients/patients at the same time as informed consent is obtained, since the notice provides information relevant to the scope and limits of confidentiality. HIPAA requires that if under applicable law a person has authority to act on behalf of an individual who is an adult, an emancipated minor, or an unemancipated minor in making decisions related to health care, a covered entity must treat such a person (called a personal representative) as the individual. Exceptions are permitted if there is reason to believe the patient has been abused or is endangered by the personal representative or that treating the individual as a personal representative would not be in the best interests of the client/patient (45 CFR 164.502g). This requirement refers to court-appointed guardians or holders of relevant power of attorney of adults with impaired capacities, parents who are generally recognized as personal representatives of their minor children, and individuals who have been designated as a representative by the patient. To comply with both Standard 3.10b and the HIPAA Notice of Privacy Practices, when working with persons who are legally incapable of giving consent, psychologists should provide the Notice of Privacy Practices to both the individual's legal guardian or personal representative and the client/patient.

(c) When psychological services are court ordered or otherwise mandated, psychologists inform the individual of the nature of the anticipated services, including whether the services are court ordered or mandated and any limits of confidentiality, before proceeding. *[New]*

In situations in which informed consent is prohibited by law or other governing authority, psychologists must nonetheless respect an individual's right to know the nature of anticipated services, whether the services were court ordered or mandated by another governing authority, and the limits of confidentiality before proceeding.

Military psychologists. When regulations permit, military psychologists should inform active-duty personnel of the psychologist's duty to report to appropriate military agencies violations of the Uniform Code of Military Justice revealed during assessment or therapy.

Court-ordered assessments. Psychologists conducting a court-ordered forensic assessment must inform the individual tested: why the assessment is being conducted; that the findings may be entered into evidence in court; and if known to the psychologist, the extent to which the individual and his or her attorney will have access to the information. The psychologist should not assume the role of legal advisor, but can advise the individual to speak with his or her attorney when asked about potential legal consequences of noncooperation.

(d) Psychologists appropriately document written or oral consent, permission, and assent. (See also Standards 8.02, Informed Consent to Research; 9.03, Informed Consent in Assessments; and 10.01, Informed Consent to Therapy.) *[Expanded, 1992 Standard 4.02a, Informed Consent to Therapy]*

Standard 3.10d requires psychologists conducting research or providing health or forensic services to document they have obtained consent or assent from an individual and permission by a legal guardian or substitute decision maker. In most instances, individuals will sign a consent, assent, or permission form. Sometimes oral consent is appropriate, such as when obtaining a young child's assent, when working with illiterate populations, or when there is concern that confidentially may be at risk (i.e., in war-torn countries where consent documents may be confiscated by local authorities). In these situations, documentation can be a note in the psychologist's records.

Implications of HIPAA. Appropriate documentation can also be related to legal requirements. For example, HIPAA requires that all valid client/patient authorizations for the use and disclosure of PHI must be signed and dated by the individual or the individual's personal representative (45 CFR 164.508[c][1][vi]).

3.11 Psychological Services Delivered To or Through Organizations

(a) Psychologists delivering services to or through organizations provide information beforehand to clients and when appropriate those directly affected by the services about (1) the nature and objectives of the services, (2) the intended recipients, (3) which of the individuals are clients, (4) the relationship the psychologist will have with each person and the organization, (5) the probable uses of services provided and information obtained, (6) who will have access to the information, and (7) limits of confidentiality. As soon as feasible, they provide information about the results and conclusions of such services to appropriate persons. *[Significant Change in Meaning, 1992 Standard 1.07a, Describing the Nature and Results of Psychological Services]*

The informed consent procedures described in Standard 3.10, Informed Consent, are often not appropriate or sufficient for consulting, program evaluation, job effectiveness, or other psychological services delivered to or through organizations. In such contexts, Standard 3.11 requires that the organizational client, employees, staff, or others that may be involved in the psychologists' activities be provided information about the nature, objectives, and intended recipients of the services; which individuals are clients and the relationship the psychologist will have with those involved; the probable uses of and who will have access to information gained; and the limits of confidentiality. Psychologists must also provide the results and conclusions of the services to appropriate persons as early as is feasible.

☑ An industrial-organizational psychologist was hired to evaluate whether a company's flexible-shift policy had lowered employee absentee rates. In addition to a review of employee records, the evaluation would include interviews with supervisors and employees on the value and limits of the policy. The psychologist prepared a document for all supervisors and employees explaining (a) the purpose of the evaluation, (b) the nature of and reason for employee record review and the interviews, (c) that the evaluation would be used to help the company decide if it should maintain or modify its current flexible shift policy, (d) that no one in the company would have access to the identities of the individuals interviewed, and (e) that the results and conclusions would be presented to the company's board of directors in a manner that protected confidentiality.

☑ A psychologist was hired by a school district to observe lunchroom and recess teacher management of student behavior to help the district determine how many teachers were required for such activities and whether additional staff training was needed for these responsibilities. The psychologist held a meeting for all teaching staff who would be involved in the observations. At the meeting, the psychologist explained why the school district was conducting the research, how long it would last, the ways in which notes on and summaries of observations would be written to protect the identities of individual teachers, that a detailed summary of findings would be presented to the school superintendent, and that with the district's permission teachers would receive a summary report.

(b) If psychologists will be precluded by law or by organizational roles from providing such information to particular individuals or groups, they so inform those individuals or groups at the outset of the service. *[No Significant Change, 1992 Standard 1.07b, Describing the Nature and Results of Psychological Services]*

Standard 3.11b pertains to situations in which psychological services not requiring informed consent are mandated by law or governmental regulations and the law or regulations restricts those affected by the services from receiving any aspect of the information listed in Standard 3.11a.

> ☑ A psychologist providing court-ordered therapy to a convicted pedophile submitted a report to the court regarding the therapy client's attendance and responsiveness to treatment. The therapist was prohibited from releasing the report to the client. At the beginning of therapy, the psychologist informed the client that such a report would be written and that the client would not have access to the report through the psychologist.
>
> ☑ A company stipulated that the results of a personality inventory conducted as part of an employee application and screening process would not be available to applicants. Psychologists informed applicants about these restrictions prior to administering the tests.

Implications of HIPAA. Standard 3.11b may also apply to health care settings in which institutional policy dictates that testing results are sent to another professional responsible for interpreting and communicating the results to the client/patient. However, the nature of such institutional policies may be changing in light of HIPAA regulations providing greater client/patient access to PHI and control of disclosures of PHI.

3.12 Interruption of Psychological Services

Unless otherwise covered by contract, psychologists make reasonable efforts to plan for facilitating services in the event that psychological services are interrupted by factors such as the psychologist's illness, death, unavailability, relocation, or retirement or by the client's/patient's relocation or financial limitations. (See also Standard 6.02c, Maintenance, Dissemination, and Disposal of Confidential Records of Professional and Scientific Work.) *[Modified, 1992 Standard 4.08, Interruption of Services]*

Planned and unplanned interruptions of psychological services often occur. For example, a psychologist can leave a job at a mental health care facility for a new position, take parental or family leave, interrupt services for a planned medical procedure, or retire from private practice. Clients/patients may move out of state or have a limited number of sessions covered by insurance.

When interruption of services can be anticipated, Standard 3.12 requires that psychologists make reasonable efforts to ensure that needed service is continued. Such efforts can include discussing the interruption of services with the clients/patients and responding to their concerns; conducting pretermination counseling; referring the client/patient to another mental health practitioner; and if feasible and clinically appropriate, working with the professional who will be responsible for the client's/patient's case (see also Standard 10.10, Terminating Therapy).

Standard 3.12 also requires psychologists to prepare for unplanned interruptions such as sudden illness or death. In most cases, it would be sufficient to have a trusted professional colleague prepared to contact clients/patients if such a situation arises. The phrase "reasonable efforts" reflects awareness that some events are unpredictable and even the best-laid plans may not be adequate when services are interrupted. The phrase "unless otherwise covered by contract" recognizes that there may be some instances in which psychologists are prohibited by contract with a commercial or health care organization from following through on plans to facilitate services.

CHAPTER 7

Standards on Privacy and Confidentiality

4. PRIVACY AND CONFIDENTIALITY

4.01 Maintaining Confidentiality

Psychologists have a primary obligation and take reasonable precautions to protect confidential information obtained through or stored in any medium, recognizing that the extent and limits of confidentiality may be regulated by law or established by institutional rules or professional or scientific relationship. (See also Standard 2.05, Delegation of Work to Others.) *[Modified, 1992 Standard 5.02, Maintaining Confidentiality]*

Psychologists respect the privacy and dignity of persons by protecting confidential information obtained from those with whom they work (Principle E: Respect for People's Rights and Dignity). Standard 4.01 of the American Psychological Association (APA) Ethics Code (2002) is broadly written and requires all psychologists to take reasonable precautions to maintain confidentiality. The nature of precautions required will differ with respect to the psychologist's role, the purpose of the psychological activity, the legal status of the person with whom the psychologist is working, federal regulations, state and local laws, and institutional and organizational policies. The term "reasonable precautions" recognizes both the responsibility to be familiar with appropriate methods of protecting confidentiality and the possibility that confidentiality may be broken despite a psychologist's best efforts. Below are general recommendations for maintaining confidentiality across a variety of psychological activities.

Use of the Internet and Other Electronic Media

When providing services, conducting distance learning, or collecting research data over the Internet, psychologists must become knowledgeable about or obtain technical assistance in employing appropriate methods for protecting confidential records concerning clients/patients, organizations, research participants, or students.

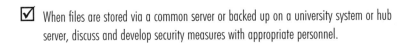

☑ When files are stored via a common server or backed up on a university system or hub server, discuss and develop security measures with appropriate personnel.

☑ Use encrypted data transmission, password-protected data storage, and firewall techniques.

☑ When confidential information is e-mailed, faxed, or otherwise electronically transmitted to scientists, professionals, or organizations, take reasonable steps to ensure that recipients of the information have an adequate confidentiality policy (see also discussion of the Health Insurance Portability and Accountability Act [HIPAA] below).

☑ Psychologists using the Internet for clinical supervision should instruct trainees on appropriate procedures to protect client/patient confidentiality.

☑ Avoid leaving telephone messages for clients/patients on answering machines. When such a message is unavoidable, take precautions to ensure that the message does not reveal to others that the client/patient is in treatment or any other confidential information.

Audio, Video, or Digital Recordings of Voices or Images

Protecting confidentiality when recording voice or images of clients/patients, research participants, employees, or others may require technical advice or assistance.

☑ Store recordings in safe locations or use passwords to protect computer access.

☑ Distort voice recordings or mask faces in visual images to protect confidentiality.

☑ Destroy recordings when they are no longer needed as long as their destruction does not conflict with other ethical obligations to maintain scientific or professional records.

Research

☑ Use participant codes on all data collection materials and data entered for analysis.

☑ Maintain records linking participant codes to personal identifiers in a secure file and destroy such records once they are no longer needed.

☑ Limit access to personally identifiable information and supervise research personnel in routine confidentiality precautions.

☑ Separate consent forms from coded materials to avoid participant identification.

☑ Apply for a Certificate of Confidentiality under 301d of the Public Health Service Act to obtain immunity from a subpoena to disclose identifying information when there is a possibility that data collected are of a sensitive nature that if released could result in stigmatization, discrimination, or legal action that could jeopardize an individual's financial standing, employment, or reputation (see http://ohrp.osophs.dhhs.gov/humansubjects/guidance/certconp).

☑ When publishing or otherwise disseminating research findings, consider special confidentiality protections for when unnamed, but small, unique samples can be identified through descriptions of demographic variables (e.g., persons with rare diseases from distinct communities).

☑ Ensure that recruitment and research procedures do not inadvertently reveal confidential information. For example, when studying addictions, mental disorders, sexually transmitted diseases, or other potentially stigmatizing conditions, approaching target populations for recruitment may result in public identification of the condition.

☑ Become familiar with and ensure HIPAA compliance when research involves the use of protected health information (PHI) obtained directly by the investigator or through a covered entity (see section on HIPAA below).

Assessment and Psychotherapy Records

☑ Store therapy notes or client/patient records in locked file cabinets or in password-protected computer files.

☑ When working with a health maintenance organization (HMO) or within an institution, do not assume without personally confirming that client/patient permission for sharing confidential information has been appropriately obtained through third-party contractual or institutional release forms.

☑ Protect the identity of clients/patients or other persons not covered by a health maintenance organization (HMO) when the HMO conducts a utilization review that includes inspection of noncovered clients' patients' records.

☑ Obtain appropriate written permission and/or signed HIPAA-compliant authorization (where appropriate) before releasing confidential information to third parties (see below).

Implications of HIPAA for Practice and Research

Practitioners and scientists whose work includes creating, using, disclosing, collecting, storing, or analyzing PHI should become familiar with requirements of the HIPAA Privacy Rule (45 CFR Parts 160-164). (See also "A Word About HIPAA" in the Preface of this book.) Under HIPAA, PHI is defined as information electronically transmitted or maintained in any form or medium relating to the past, present, or future physical or mental health condition, provision of care, or payment for provision of care for an individual that either identifies or can be used to identify the individual (see 45 CFR 160.103 and 164.501). The regulation applies to "covered entities" defined as a health plan, a health care clearinghouse, or a health care provider who transmits any health information in electronic form in connection with a transaction covered by the regulations (e.g., a transaction between two parties to carry out financial or administrative activities related to health care) (45 CFR 160.102[a] and 160.103).

Practice. Under HIPAA, "covered entities" must designate a "privacy officer" to oversee and ensure that HIPAA-compliant privacy procedures are developed and implemented. This requirement is "scalable," meaning that meeting the requirement will differ depending on whether a psychologist is in solo practice, directing a group practice, or administrating a large institutional program. Covered entities must implement security procedures that prevent unauthorized access to health records. They must also take steps to ensure that employees, business associates, individual contractors, consultants, collection agencies, third-party payors, and researchers with whom PHI is shared comply with HIPAA regulations. Psychologists transferring PHI files to or from HMOs or other companies are required to take steps to ensure that confidential records are transmitted in secure ways, for example, by means of a secured fax machine. Requirements for HIPAA compliance also vary with each state's privacy laws. The APA Insurance Trust and the APA Practice Directorate have excellent materials to guide practitioners in HIPAA compliance (see www.apait.org/resources/hipaa).

Research creating, using, or disclosing PHI. HIPAA defines research as "a systematic investigation, including research development, testing, and evaluation, designed to develop or contribute to generalizable knowledge" (45 CFR 164.501). Treatment is defined as "the provision, coordination, or management of health care and related services by one or more health care providers, including the coordination or management of health care by a health care provider with a third party; consultation between health care providers relating to a patient; or the referral of a patient for health care from one health care provider to another" (45 CFR 164.501). Psychologists who are health care providers or who employ health care providers to conduct research involving assessments or diagnoses that will be used for treatment decisions involving research participants should consider themselves or their research team covered entities under HIPAA. Investigators who are not themselves health care providers but conduct treatment research or quality improvement research for a health care facility or any other organization that is a covered entity must also ensure that their procedures are HIPAA compliant.

HIPAA permits covered entities to transmit PHI to researchers who are conducting nontherapeutic research if (1) a patient signs an authorization to release the information that is project specific and *not* a general authorization for use of PHI for future unspecified research; (2) an institutional review board (IRB) or privacy board approves in written form a waiver of the requirement for such authorization and the investigator provides the covered entity with written assurances that HIPAA-compliant procedures are in place to protect confidentiality; or (3) the records are de-identified, as specifically defined by HIPAA regulations.

HIPAA also permits covered entities to allow researchers to use PHI without patient authorization (1) for deceased patients; (2) for public health research; (3) when PHI will not leave the covered entity, will be used solely for reviews or protocol development, and the researcher represents to the covered entity that such access is essential and that the PHI will not be removed from the premises; or (4) when research involves the use of a "limited data set" (a partially de-identified data set specifically defined by HIPAA) and the investigator has signed a "data use agreement" assuring the covered entity PHI will be safeguarded and only used or disclosed for limited purposes (see 45 CFR 164.512[i]).

Implications of FERPA for Psychologists Working in Schools

The Family Educational Rights and Privacy Act (FERPA) (20 U.S.C. § 1232-34 CFR Part 99; http://www.ed.gov/offices/OM/fpco/ferpa/index.html) is a federal law that protects the privacy of student education records in all schools that receive funds under an applicable program of the U.S. Department of Education. FERPA gives certain rights to parents that transfer to the student at age 18 or beyond the high school level. A student's educational record may not be released without written permission from the parent or eligible student. FERPA does allow disclosure of records without consent (a) in cases of health and safety emergencies; (b) to comply with a judicial order or with state or local authorities within the juvenile justice system; (c) to school officials with legitimate educational interest; (d) to accrediting agencies, specified officials, or organizations in connection with auditing or certain studies on behalf of the school; (e) to schools to which the student is transferring; or (f) to parties in connection with student financial aid. HIPAA regulations do not apply to records that fall under FERPA regulations.

4.02 Discussing the Limits of Confidentiality

(a) Psychologists discuss with persons (including, to the extent feasible, persons who are legally incapable of giving informed consent and their legal representatives) and organizations with whom they establish a scientific or professional relationship (1) the relevant limits of confidentiality and (2) the foreseeable uses of the information generated through their psychological activities. (See also Standard 3.10, Informed Consent.) *[Expanded, 1992 Standard 5.01a, Discussing the Limits of Confidentiality]*

Legal, institutional, or professional obligations frequently place limits on the extent to which private information acquired during psychological activities can be kept confidential. Psychologists are often legally required to (a) report suspected child abuse or neglect to child protection agencies; (b) contact family members or other professionals to protect an individual from imminent self-harm; (c) warn a potential victim of a client's/patient's intent to harm him or her; (d) contact a law enforcement agency when they have foreknowledge of certain crimes; (e) assist in lawful military investigations; (f) provide companies, police departments, or military agencies psychological information to determine suitability for employment, promotion, or assignments; (g) provide treatment or assessment information in criminal or civil cases; or (h) provide information to third-party payors when mental health treatment is covered by a health plan.

Disclosure of such information can have serious material consequences for clients/patients, research participants, organizational clients, and others with whom psychologists work. Promising confidentiality, without revealing its known limitations, is a misrepresentation of fact that may violate a person's privacy and liberty (Bersoff, 1976). Release of confidential information poses risks to individuals and their families when disclosures lead to investigation by child protective services, arrest, conviction, institutionalization, loss of health or disability insurance, loss of child custody, or social stigmatization. Disclosures of confidential information can also lead to financial or legal risk for organizations.

Under Standard 4.02a, psychologists must discuss with persons and organizations with whom they work reporting obligations and other limits to the confidentiality of information that can be reasonably anticipated.

Persons legally incapable of consent. This requirement extends to persons who are legally incapable of giving informed consent and their legal representatives. For example, psychologists conducting research with children or adults with impaired cognitive capacity must inform legal guardians and to the extent possible the prospective participants themselves about any limitations in confidentiality. Such limitations might include reporting requirements if investigators are state-mandated child abuse or elder abuse reporters or protective policies if the investigators have elected to disclose to guardians or professionals information about participants with serious suicidal ideation (Fisher, Higgins-D'Alessandro, Rau, Kuther, & Belanger, 1996). Practitioner psychologists should inform clients/patients and their legal guardians about the nature of information that will be shared with guardians and with others based on law, institutional or organizational regulations, or the psychologist's policies regarding disclosure of child or adolescent health-compromising behaviors (Fisher, Hatashita-Wong, & Isman, 1999). School psychologists may need to inform students, guardians, and school personnel about laws governing the release of school records, for example, FERPA, which establishes the right of parents to obtain copies of their children's school records (20 U.S.C. § 1232G[a][1][A]; 34 C F R § 99.11b).

Third-party payors. When services will be covered by third-party payors, psychologists need to inform clients/patients about information that will be shared with the third party, including treatment plans, session notes, and diagnoses. Some contractual agreements with managed care companies (HMOs) permit utilization reviews that provide HMO access to information about clients/patients not covered under the policy. Clients/patients must be informed of such limits on confidentiality if records cannot be adequately de-identified. Psychologists who receive payment through credit cards should inform persons about the possible use of this information by credit card companies that may sell their client lists to organizations specializing in self-help or other related products.

Military. In the military, there is no psychologist-client confidentiality in the traditional sense. Military psychologists are required to release information on command to assist in the lawful conduct of investigations or to determine suitability of persons for service or assignments. One of the most noteworthy gains in confidentiality and respect for the rights of the individual was the implementation of U.S. Department of Defense (DoD) Directive 6490.1 (DoD, 1997a) and DoD Instruction 6490.4 (DoD, 1997b). Thanks to the efforts of military psychologists, active-duty servicemembers sent for commander-directed mental health evaluations now have the right to know why they were referred for the evaluation and who will be conducting that evaluation; an opportunity for a second opinion following receipt of a summary of the findings; and a right to speak with legal counsel, a chaplain, and a member of Congress regarding their situation (see Orme & Doerman, 2001).

Implications of HIPAA. Psychologists creating, transferring, analyzing, or storing PHI via electronic transmission, or working with a managed care company, bill collection agency, or other organization that does so, are required to provide individuals with a Notice of Privacy Practices that details the uses and disclosures of PHI and the individuals' privacy rights under relevant federal or state law (45 CFR 164.520). The APA

Insurance Trust and the APA Practice Directorate have available for purchase sample Notice of Privacy Practices compatible with laws governing practice in each state (see http://apait.org/hipaa, http://apa.org/practice).

(b) Unless it is not feasible or is contraindicated, the discussion of confidentiality occurs at the outset of the relationship and thereafter as new circumstances may warrant. *[No Significant Change, 1992 Standard 5.01b, Discussing the Limits of Confidentiality]*

Clients/patients, research participants, organizations, and others are entitled to know the limits of confidentiality and its potential consequences before deciding whether or how to engage in a scientific or professional relationship with a psychologist. Standard 4.02b requires that psychologists discuss the known extent and limits of confidentiality at the outset of the relationship. The phrase "unless it is not feasible or is contraindicated" permits psychologists to delay discussion of confidentiality in cases in which the treatment needs of a new client/patient, for example, acute trauma, must take priority. It also permits delays when the limits of confidentiality need to be further explored, for example, a therapist may need to call a client's/patient's health plan to determine its utilization review policies. In such situations, confidentiality is discussed as soon as the crisis has subsided or all information has been obtained.

In some instances, the scientific or professional relationship may change over time, requiring renewed discussion of confidentiality. For example, in longitudinal studies involving children that extend over several years, both participants and their guardians may need to be reminded of confidentiality policies, especially if a change in such policies is warranted as the child matures into adolescence.

Psychologists whose clients/patients ask them to testify as a fact witness on their behalf should carefully explain to the client/patient how this will change the nature of confidentiality and the implications of waiving client-therapist privilege.

(c) Psychologists who offer services, products, or information via electronic transmission inform clients/patients of the risks to privacy and limits of confidentiality. *[New]*

Psychological services or transmission of records conducted over the Internet and other electronic media are vulnerable to breaches in confidentiality that may be beyond the psychologist's individual control. Under Standard 4.02c, clients/patients must be made aware of the risks to privacy and limitations of protections the psychologist can institute to guard against violations of consumer confidentiality when information is transmitted electronically (see Standard 4.01, Maintaining Confidentiality).

 Psychologists conducting therapy or assessments via e-mail or through secure chat rooms need to inform clients/patients about the possibility of strangers hacking into secure sites, or when applicable, the extent to which institutional staff has access to secure sites on a hub server.

☑ Sometimes clients/patients may send unsolicited sensitive communications to a therapist's personal e-mail account. Once psychologists become aware that such an e-mail has been sent, they should inform such clients about the risks of others reading these e-mails, and discourage clients/patients from future e-mail communications if appropriate.

☑ Clients/patients who discuss sensitive information with psychologists over a cell phone should be warned about the limits of confidentiality when this medium is used.

☑ Psychologists transmitting health records to managed care companies or other health providers need to alert clients/patients to potential breaches that may occur when health information is passed through multiple systems including utilization reviewers, case managers, bookkeepers, and accountants.

☑ Psychologists providing services on a Web site should include a visible and easy-to-understand privacy statement whenever a consumer's personal information is requested. The privacy statement should advise consumers of how personal information will be used (e.g., sold to other sites, used to contact the consumer at a later date) and whether they can opt out of these uses. Psychologists can download a sample privacy policy statement from the APA's Web site at http://helping.apa.org/dotcomsense/privacy.html.

4.03 Recording

Before recording the voices or images of individuals to whom they provide services, psychologists obtain permission from all such persons or their legal representatives. (See also Standards 8.03, Informed Consent for Recording Voices and Images in Research; 8.05, Dispensing With Informed Consent for Research; and 8.07, Deception in Research.) *[Modified for Clarity, 1992 Standard 5.01c, Discussing the Limits of Confidentiality]*

Psychologists who use audio, visual, or digital recordings of voices or images to provide services to individuals must obtain permission from all such persons or their legal representatives before recording begins. Although there are exceptions for informed consent to recording voices and images in research (see Standards 8.03, 8.05, and 8.07), under Standard 4.03 no such exceptions are permissible for service providers. The following are examples of violations of this standard:

❌ A court-appointed forensic psychologist conducting a competency evaluation of a prisoner audiotaped the assessment without informing the prisoner or the prisoner's attorney.

> ☒ A clinical psychologist conducting behavior therapy with a 6-year-old diagnosed with attention deficit disorder decided to videotape the therapy sessions to better analyze the child's behavioral responses to different situations. The psychologist did not obtain permission from the child's parents to videotape the session.

4.04 Minimizing Intrusions on Privacy

(a) Psychologists include in written and oral reports and consultations, only information germane to the purpose for which the communication is made. *[No Significant Change, 1992 Standard 5.03a, Minimizing Intrusions on Privacy]*

Clients/patients, research participants, organizational clients, and students often share or unintentionally reveal private information to psychologists that may not be germane to the purpose of the psychological activities. Under Standard 4.04, psychologists are prohibited from including such information in their reports or consultations. Examples of potential violations of this standard include the following:

> ☒ A woman referred for a neuropsychological evaluation to assess the cause of a speech disorder immediately following a head injury was accompanied to the psychologist's office by an individual she identified as her long-time female domestic partner. The psychologist's report mentioned that the client was a lesbian, even though sexual orientation was not a relevant factor in the diagnosis.
>
> ☒ During a break in an assessment battery for a competency determination of an incarcerated young man, the forensic psychologist heard the man brag about the crime to another inmate. During the competency hearing, the psychologist's expert testimony included mention of the casual admission to the crime. (For further information, see Specialty Guidelines for Forensic Psychologists, VI. G. Methods and Procedures; Committee on Ethical Guidelines for Forensic Psychologists, 1991.)

Implications of HIPAA. Standard 4.04a is consistent with HIPAA regulations regarding the "minimum necessary." When disclosing or requesting PHI, a covered entity must make reasonable efforts to limit the information to the *minimum necessary* to accomplish the intended purpose of the use, disclosure, or request. This requirement does not apply to disclosures to another health care provider for treatment, disclosures to the individual client/patient, disclosures required by law, or for other purposes under the HIPAA regulation (45 CFR 164.502[b]).

(b) Psychologists discuss confidential information obtained in their work only for appropriate scientific or professional purposes and only with persons clearly concerned with such matters. *[No Significant Change, 1992 Standard 5.03b, Minimizing Intrusions on Privacy]*

With rare exception (see Standards 4.05, Disclosures, and 4.07, Use of Confidential Information for Didactic or Other Purposes), psychologists should never discuss confidential information obtained in their work without the permission of research participants, clients/patients, organizational clients, or others who have been promised confidentiality. In some instances, consent is implicit or refers to a category of individuals, such as when research participants and patients/clients consent to have confidential information shared with members of a research team or treatment staff. In other instances, clients/patients with psychological impairments may not have a legally appointed guardian but do have a family caregiver actively involved in their treatment with whom confidential information can be shared. Standard 4.04b requires that in such situations psychologists discuss confidential information only with persons who are clearly concerned with the matter and limit disclosures only to information that is pertinent to the scientific or professional issue at hand. The intent of the standard is to permit discussions with others necessary to competently conduct psychological activities, to prohibit unnecessary discussion of confidential information, and to avoid the use of such information as gossip among professionals.

☑ A graduate student told a psychology professor that she was recently the victim of a date rape and as a result was finding it difficult to concentrate and was in danger of failing several courses. She asked the psychologist to keep the information confidential. The professor agreed and urged her to see a rape counselor on campus. At a midyear student evaluation meeting, department faculty recommended the student be put on probation. Without revealing the nature of the incident, the psychologist with whom the student had spoken told the faculty that the student had disclosed confidential information that provided a credible reason for her recent academic performance. The psychologist volunteered to discuss the matter with the student and recommended that her midyear evaluation be deferred. The faculty concurred.

☑ A school psychologist evaluated a fourth-grade student for placement in a special education class. With permission of the child's parents, the psychologist discussed the need for such a placement with the school principal. However, the psychologist refused to discuss the child's diagnosis when questioned by several concerned teachers in the faculty dining room.

☑ A clinical gerontologist developed behavioral treatment plans for Alzheimer's patients at a long-term care facility. Although staff psychologists implemented the behavioral plans, it was often necessary to coordinate the patients' psychological services with staff and family members. The psychologist only provided nursing staff and family members with information they needed to ensure the consistency of the plan and carefully refrained from sharing with anyone who was not the patient's legal representative information about the patient's diagnosis or other personal information.

Implications of HIPAA. Under the HIPAA Privacy Rule, psychologists working in independent practice, group practices, or systems of health care are permitted to share PHI internally (45 CFR 164.502 and 165.506). The nature of information shared is not restricted when disclosure is with other health professionals for the purposes of providing treatment. However, psychologists must only disclose the minimum amount of information necessary to non-treatment personnel, such as staff responsible for scheduling appointments or billing, to enable them to perform their duties.

4.05 Disclosures

(a) Psychologists may disclose confidential information with the appropriate consent of the organizational client, the individual client/patient, or another legally authorized person on behalf of the client/patient unless prohibited by law. *[No Significant Change, 1992 Standard 5.05b, Disclosures]*

Standard 4.05a permits, but does not require, psychologists to disclose confidential information if appropriate consent has been obtained from the organizational client, the individual client/patient, or another legally authorized person. Psychologists should have persons or organizations provide a signed release, a signed authorization if HIPAA is applicable, or otherwise document the permission or request to have confidential information disclosed. Documentation should specifically identify the persons or organizations to whom confidential information may be released, should be time-limited, and where applicable HIPAA compliant. Psychologists should not ask individual or organizational clients to sign blanket releases for the disclosure of confidential information over an indeterminate period of time. Before releasing confidential information at the request of a hospital, organization, agency, or HMO, psychologists should confirm that the institution or organization obtained appropriate consent or authorization for the disclosure.

Implications of HIPAA. Standard 4.05a requires psychologists to be mindful of laws that prohibit disclosure. HIPAA requires that covered entities obtain written valid authorization from the individual or his or her personal representative prior to releasing PHI (45 CFR 164.508). The authorization must include a specific description of information to be disclosed, specific identification of the person or class of persons who can make the authorization and to whom information may be disclosed, a description of each purpose of the use of the disclosure, an expiration date, and signature (45 CFR 164.508[c]). In addition, when appropriate release and authorizations are obtained, the HIPAA Privacy Rule requires psychologists share only the minimum amount of information necessary for billing agencies and non-health provider internal staff to perform their roles (45 CFR 164.502[b]). The APA Insurance Trust and the APA Practice Directorate have available for purchase sample HIPAA-compliant authorization forms compatible with laws governing practice in each state (see http://apait.org/hipaa, http://apa.org/practice).

Declining requests. Under Standard 4.05a, psychologists may decline an appropriately obtained request to release confidential information if the psychologist believes that disclosure will cause harm. However, psychologists should be aware that certain federal and statutory laws limit providers' rights to withhold such information. Under the HIPAA Privacy Rule, covered entities have an obligation to agree to a patient's reasonable requests for release of PHI and can deny a request only if it is reasonably likely to endanger the life or physical safety of the individual or another person or is likely to cause equally substantial harm. In addition, psychologists must allow clients/ patients the right to have the denial reviewed by a designated licensed health care professional.

Research. An individual's access to PHI created or obtained in the course of treatment research may be temporarily suspended for as long as the research is in progress, provided the individual has agreed to the denial of access when consenting to the research and has been promised right of access upon completion of the research (45 CFR 164.524[a][2][iii]).

Psychotherapy notes and PHI compiled for legal or administrative action. HIPAA is highly protective of psychotherapy notes, defined as notes recorded by a health care provider who is a mental health professional documenting or analyzing the contents of conversation during a private counseling session or a group, joint, or family counseling session and that are separated from the rest of the individual's medical record (45 CFR 164.501). Patients do *not* have a right of access to psychotherapy notes, and a separate authorization is required for the release of psychotherapy notes when a covered entity agrees to their release. Psychologists who are or work for covered entities should also be aware that HMOs are prohibited from requiring patient authorization to disclose psychotherapy notes as a condition for evaluating eligibility.

Certain forensic records are also protected under HIPAA. Patients do not have the right of access to information compiled in reasonable anticipation of, or for use in, a civil, criminal, or administrative action or procedure (45 CFR 164.508 and 164.524[a][1]).

For information on other exceptions, see discussions of Standards 6.03, Withholding Records for Nonpayment, and 9.04, Release of Test Data.

(b) Psychologists disclose confidential information without the consent of the individual only as mandated by law, or where permitted by law for a valid purpose such as to (1) provide needed professional services; (2) obtain appropriate professional consultations; (3) protect the client/patient, psychologist, or others from harm; or (4) obtain payment for services from a client/patient, in which instance disclosure is limited to the minimum that is necessary to achieve the purpose. (See also Standard 6.04e, Fees and Financial Arrangements.) *[No Significant Change, 1992 Standard 5.05a, Disclosures]*

Standard 4.05b describes those situations in which it is ethically permissible to disclose identifiable confidential information without the consent of an individual or organization. The standard is permissive rather than mandatory, leaving the decision to disclose confidential information without consent under the above listed categories to the discretion of the psychologist. At the same time, the standard prohibits disclosure of confidential information without consent for any purpose other than those listed.

Clients/patients, research participants, organizational clients, and others with whom a psychologist works must be informed as early as feasible in the professional or scientific relationship about the potential for such disclosures when it is reasonable for the psychologist to anticipate that such disclosures may be necessary (see Standard 4.02, Discussing the Limits of Confidentiality).

Disclosures mandated by law. The standard permits psychologists to disclose confidential information without consent when the disclosure is mandated by law.

☑ Psychologists should be aware of the specific mandated child abuse reporting laws of their state. Following the 1976 Child Abuse Prevention and Treatment Act, all 50 states have enacted statutes mandating the reporting of suspected child abuse or neglect for mental health professionals and in at least 13 states to researchers, as members of the general citizenry (Liss, 1994). Some states have mandatory reporting laws for elder abuse and neglect and for knowledge of the intent to commit a criminal act. A number of states have adopted "duty to protect" laws following the landmark court case of *Tarasoff v. Regents of the University of California* (1976). Such laws require certain classes of health care providers to inform a third party of the prospect of being harmed by a client/patient if the provider has (1) a "special relationship" with the prospective assailant (i.e., a client-therapist relationship), (2) the ability to predict that violence will occur (e.g., the client/patient has made a credible threat against a third party), and (3) the ability to identify the potential victim (i.e., the client/patient has named the potential victim).

☑ Psychologists should remain up-to-date on controversies as to whether "duty to warn" laws apply to research or to situations involving a professional's knowledge of intentional or reckless HIV transmission to identified victims (Appelbaum & Rosenbaum, 1989; Chenneville, 2000; Webber, 1999).

☑ Psychologists working with persons with HIV and other sexually transmitted diseases should be aware of relevant partner notification laws (VandeCreek & Knapp, 1993).

☑ Psychologists providing services or conducting research over the Internet need to be familiar with state laws governing mandatory reporting in jurisdictions in which recipients of Internet services or Internet-administered research instruments reside.

Disclosures permitted by law. The standard also permits psychologists to disclose confidential information without consent if such disclosures are permitted by law *and* the disclosure is for a valid purpose. Valid purposes include those initiated to provide needed professional services; obtain appropriate professional consultation; protect the client/patient, psychologist, or others from harm; or obtain payment for services.

☑ It is ethically appropriate to disclose personally identifiable confidential information to another professional or family member if such notification is required to hospitalize or otherwise protect clients/patients, research participants, students, or others who have indicated credible suicidal intent or who psychologists believe to be engaged in activities that are likely to result in imminent and substantial harm.

☑ Irrespective of whether the jurisdiction in which a psychologist works has a duty-to-protect law, Standard 4.05b permits psychologists to disclose confidential information obtained by clients/patients or research participants to protect others from harm.

☑ Psychologists are permitted to report to appropriate law enforcement agencies credible threats to their welfare or to the welfare of their family or colleagues made by clients/patients, students, research participants, or others with whom they work.

☑ When a client/patient or organizational client fails to pay for a psychologist's services, the psychologist may disclose information to a bill collection agency to obtain payment. The information must be limited to the individual's or organization's name, contact information, amount of payments still outstanding, number of sessions or billable hours for which payment is due, and other factual information necessary to collect outstanding funds. Psychologists should not disclose to bill collection agencies a client's/patient's diagnosis, the nature of treatment, or other personal information. Nor should they disclose the purpose or nature of their work for a company or organization (see also Standard 6.04e, Fees and Financial Arrangements).

Military psychologists may disclose sensitive patient health information of military personnel without a client's/patient's signature for release to officers and employees in the DoD when the record is needed in the performance of their duties, such as referring military personnel for evaluation (see Jeffrey, Rankin, & Jeffrey, 1992).

Implications of HIPAA. Standard 4.05b is consistent with the HIPAA regulations under 45 CFR 164.512. The Privacy Rule permits disclosure of PHI without authorization (a) when required by law; (b) for public health activities such as for the purpose of preventing or controlling disease, injury, or disability; (c) for individuals the covered entity reasonably believes to be a victim of abuse, neglect, or domestic violence; (d) for health oversight activities such as audits, criminal investigations, or licensure or disciplinary actions; (e) for judicial or administrative hearings; and (f) for activities deemed necessary by appropriate military command to ensure the proper execution of the military mission. In some instances, HIPAA regulations may be more permissive of disclosure without client/patient consent than either state law or the Ethics Code. For example, HIPAA permits disclosure of information without consent for law enforcement purposes, such as reporting of wounds or other physical injuries or a court-ordered subpoena or when the information sought is relevant and material to a legitimate law enforcement inquiry. In such instances, psychologists should follow the Ethics Code as the more stringent standard.

4.06 Consultations

When consulting with colleagues, (1) psychologists do not disclose confidential information that reasonably could lead to the identification of a client/patient, research participant, or other person or organization with whom they have a confidential relationship unless they have obtained the prior consent of the person or organization or the disclosure cannot be avoided, and (2) they disclose information only to the extent necessary to achieve the purposes of the consultation. (See also Standard 4.01, Maintaining Confidentiality.) *[No Significant Change, 1992 Standard 5.06, Consultations]*

 Consultation with colleagues is an important means of ensuring and maintaining the competence of one's work and the ethical conduct of psychology. Standard 4.06 permits discussion of confidential information with colleagues without prior consent as long as the identity of the client/patient, research participant, organizational client, or other person with whom they have a confidential relationship can be adequately protected. In some instances, the obligation to provide the highest quality service or to address an ethical problem may require consultation that reveals a person's or organization's identity without prior consent. Standard 4.06 permits such actions only if the disclosure cannot be avoided and the psychologist discloses only information that is necessary to achieve the purposes of the consultation. The following is an example of how a psychologist might comply with this standard.

☑ A psychologist was hired by a bank to conduct crisis counseling for employees who had witnessed a recent armed robbery. During the course of counseling, the psychologist came across information that suggested that one of the employees helped plan the robbery. The psychologist consulted with a colleague and an attorney to help determine whether the psychologist was ethically or legally required to report this information to the company or law enforcement. Because the bank robbery had been highly publicized, the psychologist was unable to disguise the bank's identity. However, during each consultation the psychologist took specific steps to avoid mentioning the gender, job title, or any other details about the employee in question that could lead to personal identification.

4.07 Use of Confidential Information for Didactic or Other Purposes

Psychologists do not disclose in their writings, lectures, or other public media, confidential, personally identifiable information concerning their clients/patients, students, research participants, organizational clients, or other recipients of their services that they obtained during the course of their work, unless (1) they take reasonable steps to disguise the person or organization, (2) the person or organization has consented in writing, or (3) there is legal authorization for doing so. *[Modified for Clarity, 1992 Standard 5.08, Use of Confidential Information for Didactic or Other Purposes]*

Professionals, students, and the public benefit when psychologists use case material and other examples from their scientific or professional work to illustrate knowledge, concepts, challenges, and techniques in psychology. Psychologists must guard against harms that can occur when such materials contain confidential, personally identifiable information disseminated without the permission of the client/patient, student, research participant, organizational client, or other service recipients. Material relevant to this standard must be both confidential (the information was shared with the psychologist under expectations that it would not be released to others) and personally identifiable (the identity of the specific person or organization described could be recognized by others).

Disguising information. Psychologist are permitted to reveal confidential information if the person or organization has consented in writing or there is legal authorization for doing so, for example, the material has been authorized for release at a public hearing. When neither of these conditions is met, psychologists must take reasonable steps to adequately disguise the identity of the person or organization. When disguising information, simply using a pseudonym is often insufficient when other aspects of the case described contains details that make the individual or organization easily identifiable. Consider the following poorly disguised statements: "The patient, in her mid-twenties and the daughter of two national figures, had attended elite private schools in

Washington, D.C., and campaigned for her mother to become the first woman senator in her northeastern state"; "The energy company faced a management crisis when a divorce hearing revealed that the former CEO, who was a published expert on business, was receiving millions of dollars in retirement benefits."

The term "reasonable steps" recognizes that sometimes despite acceptable efforts to disguise information, an individual or organization might be recognized by others.

☑ A psychologist gave a public lecture on dream analysis that included a case example in which the occupation, family constellation, city of residence, and other patient characteristics were disguised. However, a friend of the patient who was in the audience was able to identify the patient because the patient had told the dream to her friend.

Privacy can also be violated when psychologists describe individuals living in small or distinct populations who can be readily identified by others in the community in which they live.

☒ A psychologist published ethnographic data on spiritual concerns, job stressors, and psychological distress facing gay and lesbian teachers working in religious schools. In the published report, the psychologist described the school where data were collected as a prestigious Catholic school affiliated with his university. The school was readily recognized by individuals who lived in the community, and many were able to correctly identify respondents from the specific narratives described in the report.

CHAPTER 8

Standards on Advertising and Other Public Statements

5. ADVERTISING AND OTHER PUBLIC STATEMENTS

5.01 Avoidance of False or Deceptive Statements

(a) Public statements include but are not limited to paid or unpaid advertising, product endorsements, grant applications, licensing applications, other credentialing applications, brochures, printed matter, directory listings, personal resumes or curricula vitae, or comments for use in media such as print or electronic transmission, statements in legal proceedings, lectures and public oral presentations, and published materials. Psychologists do not knowingly make public statements that are false, deceptive, or fraudulent concerning their research, practice, or other work activities or those of persons or organizations with which they are affiliated. *[Modified for Clarity, 1992 Standards 3.01, Definition of Public Statements, and 3.03a, Avoidance of False or Deceptive Statements]*

Psychologists aspire to promote accuracy, honesty, and truthfulness in the science, teaching, and practice of psychology and do not engage in subterfuge or intentional misrepresentation of fact (Principle C: Integrity). Standard 5.01a of the American Psychological Association (APA) Ethics Code (2002) prohibits false, deceptive, or fraudulent public statements regarding work activities or the activities of persons or organizations with which psychologists are affiliated.

The terms "avoidance" and "knowingly" excludes as violations statements that psychologists would reasonably be expected to believe are true but that they may later learn are false.

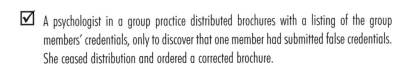
☑ A psychologist in a group practice distributed brochures with a listing of the group members' credentials, only to discover that one member had submitted false credentials. She ceased distribution and ordered a corrected brochure.

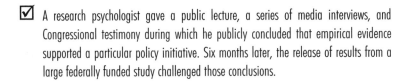
☑ A research psychologist gave a public lecture, a series of media interviews, and Congressional testimony during which he publicly concluded that empirical evidence supported a particular policy initiative. Six months later, the release of results from a large federally funded study challenged those conclusions.

Definition of public statements. This standard begins with a definition of public statements. This definition applies to the use of the terms "public statement" or "statement" in all standards under Section 5, Advertising and Other Public Statements. The definition refers only to statements made in the public domain. It does not apply to statements made during private professional or personal conversations with clients/patients, organizational clients, attorneys, students, colleagues, or others with whom psychologists have a professional or personal relationship.

Below are the types of statements included in this definition along with examples of false or deceptive statements that would be in violation of this standard:

☒ *Paid or unpaid advertising or product endorsements.* A toy company paid a school psychologist for her endorsement of the proven effectiveness of a tape-recorded language lesson for infants that would improve reading comprehension in elementary school. There was no empirical evidence supporting this claim.

☒ *Licensing, grant applications, and other credentialing applications.* In the Preliminary Studies section of a federal grant application, an experimental psychologist listed as completed a pilot study that was still in the data collection phase.

☒ *Brochures and printed matter.* A consulting psychologist distributed brochures to personnel departments of banks in major cities stating that he had developed a foolproof psychological technique for preemployment integrity screening to weed out applicants who were prone to dishonesty. The claim was based on undocumented consultations conducted by the psychologist over several years.

☒ *Directory listings, personal resumes, or curricula vitae.* A psychologist with a Ph.D. in social psychology and no specialized clinical or other practice-oriented postdoctoral training listed herself in the city directory under health care providers.

☒ *Comments for use in print, electronic, or other media.* In a television interview, a psychology professor claimed that his university refused to allow any faculty to teach courses that include discussion of human sexuality, when in fact the university catalogue listed several such courses.

☒ *Statements in legal proceedings, lectures, public oral presentations, and published materials.* A research psychologist was hired as an expert witness by a defense attorney. When asked by the prosecutor whether her research had produced findings inconsistent with the defense's position, she testified in court that no such data existed, despite the fact that her most recent investigations had yielded such data.

(b) Psychologists do not make false, deceptive, or fraudulent statements concerning (1) their training, experience, or competence; (2) their academic degrees; (3) their credentials; (4) their institutional or association affiliations; (5) their services; (6) the scientific or clinical basis for, or results or degree of success of, their services; (7) their fees; or (8) their publications or research findings. *[Modified for Clarity, 1992 Standard 3.03a, Avoidance of False or Deceptive Statements]*

In contrast to Standard 5.01a, 5.01b does not include the term "knowingly" because it is assumed that psychologists would have sufficient information about the facts listed to avoid false, deceptive, or fraudulent statements. Below are examples of violations of the eight types of statements listed.

> ❌ *Training, experience, or competence.* A clinical psychologist applying to the American Board of Professional Psychology (ABPP) for diplomate status in clinical neuropsychology falsely claimed he had received specialized training in neuropsychology during his postdoctoral internship.
>
> ❌ *Academic degrees.* On her personnel curriculum vitae, a psychologist claimed she had received her Ph.D. from an accredited university, when her actual degree was from an unaccredited school to which she had transferred.
>
> ❌ *Credentials.* On a professional liability insurance application, a psychologist stated that she obtained substance abuse certification from the APA College of Professional Psychology, when in fact she only attended a workshop on substance abuse treatment at an APA meeting.
>
> ❌ *Institutional or association affiliations.* A psychologist in independent practice who rented office space from a university created a letterhead on his stationery that suggested he was affiliated with the institution.
>
> ❌ *Services.* A psychology group practice Web site listed family therapy as one of the services offered, even though the only psychologist offering this service had left the group more than a year ago.
>
> ❌ *Scientific or clinical basis for, or results or degree of success of, their services.* A behavioral psychologist running a weight loss program for obese adolescents stated in the program brochure that "99% of clients maintain their weight loss after they leave the program." The statement did not include the fact that for most of these clients the maintenance of weight loss lasted for less than 3 weeks.
>
> ❌ *Fees.* A child clinical psychologist presented a talk on childhood disorders at a parents' association meeting. After the talk, she handed out printed information about her practice

---

that stated that she offered all clients a sliding scale of fees beginning at $40 a session. The handout did not mention that the $40 rate was only for clients specifically referred by the health maintenance organization with which the psychologist had a contract.

☒ *Publications or research findings.* A school psychologist on the faculty of a large university received a grant from an educational services company. The purpose of the funded project was to compare student academic achievement in city-administered public schools to those run by the educational services company. Data from schools in the eight cities studied indicated significant differences in favor of the city-run schools in two cities, in favor of the company-run schools in two cities, and no significant differences in the other four school districts. The psychologist published only data from the two cities in which a positive effect of company contracted schools was found and suggested in the conclusion of the article that these results could be generalized to other cities (see also Standard 3.06, Conflict of Interest).

(c) Psychologists claim degrees as credentials for their health services only if those degrees (1) were earned from a regionally accredited educational institution or (2) were the basis for psychology licensure by the state in which they practice. *[Modified for Clarity, 1992 Standard 3.03b, Avoidance of False or Deceptive Statements]*

Standard 5.01c specifically applies only to psychologists who are claiming degrees or credentials as evidence of their competence to provide health services. Unlike Standard 5.01b, this standard is not directed at whether a psychologist actually obtained the degree but whether the degree can be claimed as a basis for offering therapy or diagnostic or other types of health services. Psychologists may refer to only two types of degrees as evidence of education and training as a qualified health service provider. The first type is a degree in psychology (e.g., Ph.D., Ed.D., or Psy.D.) earned from a regionally accredited educational institution (e.g., the Commission on Higher Education of the Middle States Association of Colleges and Schools). The second type of degree is from a program in a nonaccredited institution, whose curriculum and training experiences have been approved by the state in which the psychologist practices as qualifying him or her for eligibility for licensure in psychology.

A psychologist who claims a degree as a credential for health services that does not meet the above criteria would be in violation of this standard:

☒ An individual licensed as a social worker in his state acquired a Ph.D. in counseling psychology from a nonaccredited university. He was unable to obtain licensure in psychology because the state in which he practices did not recognize his doctoral training as a basis for licensure in psychology. His business cards and professional letterhead included a Ph.D. after his name, the title Counseling Psychologist, and his social work licensure ID number. The letterhead did not indicate that his license was in social work and not psychology.

5.02 Statements by Others

(a) Psychologists who engage others to create or place public statements that promote their professional practice, products, or activities retain professional responsibility for such statements. *[No Significant Change, 1992 Standard 3.02, Statements by Others]*

Psychologists retain professional responsibility for false, deceptive, or fraudulent public statements by others whom they have engaged to promote their work or products. Failure to prevent or to correct such misstatements is a violation of Standard 5.02.

☑ A psychologist viewed the Web site of the company that was publishing a book she had just completed. She was surprised and pleased to see the company had started advertising the book as "forthcoming." She then noticed that she was wrongly listed on the Web site as Professor of Psychology at a university where she had taught as an adjunct several years ago. She called her editor at the company to notify him of the error and to ask him to take steps to correct the Web site. She followed up with a letter to him reiterating this request and carbon copied the chair of the psychology department at the university mentioned.

☒ A psychologist developed a program that enabled other psychologists to score a popular psychological test on their computers. The psychologist had not yet completed complimentary software that would provide narrative interpretations of the scores. The marketing staff at the distribution company he contracted with to sell his product advised him that the scoring software would sell better if it was advertised as providing both scoring and interpretation. They argued that even though this was not currently true, because he was already working on the new program, eventually those who bought the original software would be able to use the complimentary software for narrative interpretations. The psychologist agreed to the misleading advertisement.

(b) Psychologists do not compensate employees of press, radio, television, or other communication media in return for publicity in a news item. (See also Standard 1.01, Misuse of Psychologists' Work.) *[No Significant Change, 1992 Standard 3.02d, Statements by Others]*

Standard 5.02b underscores psychologists' obligations to avoid actions that might encourage others to make false or fraudulent statements about their work. It is reasonable for news media readers and audiences to assume that unless otherwise stated news reporters do not have a financial relationship with the individuals about whom they report. This standard prohibits psychologists from paying or otherwise compensating members of the media in return for news coverage of their work. The use of the term "compensate" rather than "pay" means that nonmonetary gifts or expensive dinners for journalists or others in the media in return for publicity in a news item may be considered a violation of this standard.

(c) A paid advertisement relating to psychologists' activities must be identified or clearly recognizable as such. *[No Significant Change, 1992 Standard 3.02e, Statements by Others]*

Standard 5.02c permits psychologists to run paid advertisements describing their services, publications, products, or other aspects of their work, as long as it is stated or otherwise clear to consumers that it is a paid advertisement. The standard applies to advertisements on the Internet, in print, or in other media. "Canned columns" are an example of a paid advertisement that often is presented in a way that can be deceptive to consumers. Canned columns written and paid for by psychologists are typically presented in news or advice column format intended to lead readers to believe that the psychologist has been invited or hired by the magazine or other media outlet to write the column because of his or her expertise. The "column" usually includes a description of the psychologist's services, the psychologist's picture, and contact information. Canned columns that do not include a clear statement that the column is a "paid advertisement" are in violation of this standard. In some instances, psychologists do not write the column themselves but purchase it from a writer who sells columns to psychologists nationwide. In such instances, the column must state that the psychologist is providing but has not written the column (see also Standard 5.01a, Avoidance of False or Deceptive Statements).

5.03 Descriptions of Workshops and Non-Degree-Granting Educational Programs

To the degree to which they exercise control, psychologists responsible for announcements, catalogs, brochures, or advertisements describing workshops, seminars, or other non-degree-granting educational programs ensure that they accurately describe the audience for which the program is intended, the educational objectives, the presenters, and the fees involved. *[No Significant Change, 1992 Standard 6.02, Descriptions of Education and Training Programs]*

Standard 5.03 applies to workshops, seminars, and non-degree-granting educational programs that are not part of the established degree-granting education and training programs covered under Standard 7.02, Descriptions of Education and Training

Programs. Psychologists who offer non-degree-granting programs are responsible for ensuring the accuracy of announcements, catalogs, brochures, or advertisements appearing in print, the Internet, or other media. Announcements must clearly specify the intended audience, educational objectives, presenters, and fees. The phrase "to the degree to which they exercise control" is included in the standard in acknowledgment that despite a psychologist's best efforts to control and monitor the process, errors or misrepresentations by others may occur during the production and distribution of materials. Psychologists should take reasonable steps to correct these errors.

❌ Registration for a 1-day workshop on projective assessment techniques given by a well-known psychologist was advertised in several psychology journals and newsletters. Individuals paid in advance to reserve a seat in the course. Registration money could be partially refunded up to 2 days prior to the workshop. Several registrants who arrived to take the workshop were surprised to learn that though they were permitted to attend, they would not be given a certificate of completion because they were not licensed psychologists. The registrants complained that the advertisement had not mentioned that a license was required to receive the certificate and asked for their money back. Stating the cancellation policy, the psychologist refused to return the fees.

❌ A psychologist offered a seminar on child abuse identification and reporting that was advertised as fulfilling the state licensing board requirement for child abuse reporting training. Attendees who later submitted their seminar completion certificate to the state board were told that the curriculum did not satisfy the state's educational requirement.

❌ A group of psychologists offered an 8-week certificate program on drug addictions counseling. Advertisements for the seminar listed the fee as $1,000. During the last week of the program, attendees were told that those who wished to obtain an official certificate documenting their participation must pay an additional $100.

5.04 Media Presentations

When psychologists provide public advice or comment via print, Internet, or other electronic transmission, they take precautions to ensure that statements (1) are based on their professional knowledge, training, or experience in accord with appropriate psychological literature and practice; (2) are otherwise consistent with this Ethics Code; and (3) do not indicate that a professional relationship has been established with the recipient. (See also Standard 2.04, Bases for Scientific and Professional Judgments.) *[Modified for Clarity, 1992 Standard 3.04, Media Presentations]*

Standard 5.04 applies to psychologists who issue public advice or comment via print, Internet, television, radio, or other media. The standard does not apply to comments made to individuals with whom psychologists have an established professional relationship, such as an Internet communication or videoconferencing with a client/patient, student, colleague, or organizational client.

Competence and basis for judgments. This standard prohibits psychologists from giving public advice or comment on radio, print media, television, the Internet, or other forms of communication on topics and issues that are outside the boundaries of their competence based on their education, training, supervised experience, or other accepted means of acquiring professional or scientific expertise (see Standard 2.01a, Boundaries of Competence). The standard also prohibits psychologists from giving public comment or advice that significantly deviates from or is otherwise inconsistent with established psychological literature and practice (see Standard 2.04, Bases for Scientific and Professional Judgments).

❌ A comparative psychologist who had spent her career specializing in language in primates appeared on several talk shows providing public advice on how parents could identify and correct child language disorders.

❌ In a television interview, a counseling psychologist advised college students to follow his 10-step cure for test anxiety. The steps included drinking green tea, taking vitamin supplements, studying in groups, and other recommendations not in accord with recent research or established counseling techniques for test anxiety.

Otherwise consistent with the Ethics Code. Providing public comment or advice through the media or the Internet does not immunize psychologists from complying with all relevant standards of the Ethics Code.

❌ After speaking with a listener for 3 minutes on a live radio talk show, a psychologist stated over the air that the listener showed definite signs of obsessive-compulsive disorder. Before going to a commercial break, the psychologist asked the listener to stay on the line "for a referral to a health care professional who can help you with this serious disorder" (violation of Standards 9.01a and b, Bases for Assessments).

❌ A developmental psychologist created a Web site on which he provided critiques and recommendations for age-appropriate children's products. The Web site did not include a statement informing visitors to the site that the psychologist was on the board of directors of a company whose toys he regularly reviewed favorably (violation of Standard 3.06, Conflict of Interest).

Do not indicate a professional relationship has been established. Psychologists providing public advice in response to questions over radio, television, the Internet, or published advice columns should clarify the educative versus therapeutic nature of their answers, avoid language that implies personal knowledge about the person asking the question, and take steps to avoid repeat communications with the person that may encourage the mistaken impression that a professional relationship has been established.

> ☒ A group of psychologists established a psychology advice e-mail service. The group's Web site included each participating psychologist's credentials and picture. The Web site described the service as one that provides advice for people suffering from "social anxiety." Individuals were charged by credit card for an answer to each e-mail question they submit. The site specifically stated that the service was not therapy. However, the psychologists' answers were written in a very individualized and personal manner rather than in broad educative statements, and individuals were encouraged to identify the psychologist they would like to answer their question. There was no limit to the number of questions that could be submitted, and some clients submitted daily questions to the same psychologist over several weeks or even months (see Shapiro & Schulman, 1996, for an excellent discussion of such a case and related issues).

5.05 Testimonials

Psychologists do not solicit testimonials from current therapy clients/patients or other persons who because of their particular circumstances are vulnerable to undue influence. *[No Significant Change, 1992 Standard 3.05, Testimonials]*

Psychologists are prohibited from asking individuals who are vulnerable to undue influence to provide commercial statements testifying to the benefits of the psychologist's services. Standard 5.05 specifically prohibits solicitation of testimonials from clients/patients currently in therapy with the psychologist. Clients/patients are particularly vulnerable to exploitation by a psychologist who seeks their public testimonials because of power inequities between therapist and client/patient, the psychological problems that brought clients/patients to therapy, the sharing of personal thoughts and feelings in therapy, and dependence on the psychologist for treatment.

Parents of children with learning disabilities, who depend on a school psychologist's yearly evaluation to qualify for special education services for their children, might because of their particular circumstances be considered vulnerable to undue influence. Former clients/patients who had been in therapy with a psychologist for court-ordered treatment would also be considered vulnerable to threat or exploitation if approached to give a testimonial.

The standard does not prohibit unsolicited testimonials or the solicitation of testimonials from former clients/patients who are not vulnerable. However, psychologists should be cautious about approaching former therapy clients/patients who may be vulnerable to undue influence based on their mental status, the duration and intensity of the therapy, the circumstances of termination, the amount of time that has passed since termination, or comments that the psychologist might have made during therapy inviting the possibility of a posttermination testimonial.

5.06 In-Person Solicitation

Psychologists do not engage, directly or through agents, in uninvited in-person solicitation of business from actual or potential therapy clients/patients or other persons who because of their particular circumstances are vulnerable to undue influence. However, this prohibition does not preclude (1) attempting to implement appropriate collateral contacts for the purpose of benefiting an already engaged therapy client/patient or (2) providing disaster or community outreach services. *[Expanded, 1992 Standard 3.06, In-Person Solicitation]*

Standard 5.06 prohibits psychologists from soliciting business from individuals who because of their particular circumstance are vulnerable to undue influence. The standard addresses business solicitation behaviors often characterized as "ambulance chasing." Individuals who are current or potential therapy clients/patients are specifically identified as vulnerable in this standard. Others who may be vulnerable to undue influence are individuals whose loved one has just committed suicide or a person who is abusing drugs or alcohol. Psychologists are prohibited from approaching these individuals either directly or through another person to solicit business if the psychologist has not been invited by the individual or a legally authorized representative to do so.

Permitted Behaviors

The standard does not prohibit psychologists from establishing a professional relationship with persons in therapy with another professional or otherwise vulnerable to undue influence if the person approaches the psychologist for services (see also Standard 10.04, Providing Therapy to Those Served by Others).

Collateral treatment. The standard does not preclude psychologists from approaching a family member or significant other to invite them to participate in collateral treatment to benefit a client/patient with whom a psychologist has a professional relationship.

> ☑ A psychologist treating an adult woman for bulimia, with the patient's permission, invited her husband to participate in family therapy sessions where the focus was on

the woman's health. Whether the husband was currently in therapy with another professional was not an issue because the reason he had been approached was to participate in therapy where the wife was the identified patient (see also Standard 10.02a, Therapy Involving Couples or Families).

Disaster and community outreach. The standard also explicitly permits psychologists to approach individuals to provide disaster or community outreach services. Psychologists may offer emergency services to individuals who are distraught or otherwise vulnerable as a result of a natural or other type of disaster. Within the mental health and aging field, it is generally recognized that older adults may not spontaneously self-refer for mental health services. A variety of outreach activities have been used in public and private services for older adults that involve approaching persons who are not thinking of seeking psychological interventions, educating them about the benefits of mental health intervention, and encouraging them to seek such help. Such outreach is permissible under Standard 5.06.

CHAPTER 9

Standards on
Record Keeping and Fees

6. RECORD KEEPING AND FEES

6.01 Documentation of Professional and
Scientific Work and Maintenance of Records

Psychologists create, and to the extent the records are under their control, maintain, disseminate, store, retain, and dispose of records and data relating to their professional and scientific work in order to (1) facilitate provision of services later by them or by other professionals, (2) allow for replication of research design and analyses, (3) meet institutional requirements, (4) ensure accuracy of billing and payments, and (5) ensure compliance with law. (See also Standard 4.01, Maintaining Confidentiality.) *[Modified for Clarity, 1992 Standards 1.23, Documentation of Professional and Scientific Work, and 1.24, Records and Data]*

Under Standard 6.01 of the American Psychological Association (APA) Ethics Code (2002), psychologists must create, maintain, disseminate, store, retain, and dispose of records and data in a manner that enables the records to be used effectively and appropriately by the psychologist or others and to benefit those with whom the psychologist works. Steps necessary to comply with this standard will vary with the purpose of the psychological activity and applicable state and federal regulations and institutional policies. The standard applies to written reports, computer files, audio- and videotapes, and reports in any other media in which information can be created and stored. Creating or maintaining records that are illegible to others would be a violation of this standard. The phrase "to the extent the records are under their control" recognizes that psychologists may have limited or no control over records once they are appropriately released to third parties or when they are the property of an organization, company, institution, or government agency for which a psychologist works or consults.

Record Keeping Guidelines and Retention of Records

The Record Keeping Guidelines developed by the APA Committee on Professional Practice and Standards, Board of Professional Affairs, recommends that such records minimally include "(a) identifying data; (b) dates of services; (c) types of services; (d) fees; (e) any assessment, plan for intervention, consultation, summary reports, and/or testing reports and supporting data as may be appropriate; and (f) any release of information obtained" (APA, 1993b, p. 985). Psychologists providing health care-related services need to be aware of the Health and Human Services (HHS) Transaction Rule requiring standard formatting of electronic patient records for health care claims and other purposes (see http://aspe.hhs.gov/admnsimp/).

Standard 6.01 requires accurate recording of billing and payments, and where relevant, barter, to ensure fair fee practices, to provide documentation when clients/patients have not paid for services, and for insurance claims (see also Standards 6.04, Fees and Financial Arrangements; 6.05, Barter With Clients/Patients; 6.06, Accuracy in Reports to Payors and Funding Sources; and 6.07, Referrals and Fees). Good record keeping can also serve as credible evidence of responsible conduct in malpractice suits. Soisson, VandeCreek, and Knapp (1987) recommend that psychologists keep a record of significant treatment decisions recorded along with the goal and rationale, risks and their justification, alternative treatments considered and why they were rejected, and subsequent service implementation.

The APA Record Keeping Guidelines (APA, 1993b) recommend that, in the absence of specific legal requirements for record retention, complete records are maintained for a minimum of 3 years after the last contact with the client/patient and records or a summary is maintained for an additional 12 years before disposal. If the client/patient is a minor, the guidelines recommend that the record period be extended until 3 years after the age of majority. At the writing of this book, these time limits follow the APA's Specialty Guidelines (APA Committee on Professional Standards, 1981). According to the Record Keeping Guidelines, if the Specialty Guidelines are revised, a simple 7-year requirement for the retention of the complete record, more stringent than any existing state statute, would be preferred.

Implications of HIPAA

Length of record retention. The number of years for retention of records varies with respect to state law, federal regulations, and institutional requirements. The Health Insurance Portability and Accountability Act (HIPAA) regulations require that policies and procedures used to comply with the Privacy Rule are documented and retained for 6 years from the date of creation or the last date in which it was in effect, whichever is later (45 CFR 164.530[j][2]). If state law establishes longer periods of record retention than HIPAA, psychologists who are covered entities must follow the state law (see "A Word About HIPAA" in the Preface to this book).

Access of individuals to protected health information. Clients/patients have the right to inspect and obtain a copy of their protected health information (PHI) records used by the psychologist to make diagnostic, treatment, and billing decisions (45 CFR 164.524). Where HIPAA regulations apply, psychologists' records must be created and stored in a manner that facilitates compliance with the following aspects of the Privacy Rule.

Right to amend. Clients/patients have the right to request their PHI be amended if they believe the information is incorrect (45 CFR 164.526). If a psychologist believes the amendment is justified, the amendment should be attached to the record; the psychologist should never alter the original record. Failure to keep an accurate record of such disclosures would be in violation of Standard 6.01.

Right to an accounting. Clients/patients have a "right to an accounting" of disclosures of PHI that entails a list of individuals or organizations to whom PHI has been disclosed in the last 6 years. Content of the accounting must include the date of the disclosure, the name of the entity or person who received the PHI and the address if known, a brief description of the PHI disclosed and the purpose of its disclosure (45 CFR 164.528).

Psychotherapy notes. Psychotherapy or personal notes are considered a work product privilege and are immune from subpoena (Mental and Developmental Disabilities Confidentiality Act, 1979, ¶ 802, § 2[4]; Soisson et al., 1987). Accordingly, psychotherapy notes can be disposed of at any time, unless state law provides otherwise.

HIPAA creates a separate category for "psychotherapy notes," defined as "notes recorded (in any medium) by a health care provider who is a mental health professional documenting or analyzing the contents of conversation during a private counseling session or a group, joint, or family counseling session and that are separated from the rest of the individual's medical record" (45 CFR 164.501). Patients do not have a right of access to psychotherapy notes. Psychologists may choose to provide patient access or agree to release psychotherapy notes to others with the appropriate authorization of the patient. Psychotherapy notes are exempted from HIPAA general provisions for sharing PHI for the treatment, payment, or health care operations of another entity. For example, health plan providers and other HIPAA-covered entities may *not* condition the provision of treatment, payment, enrollment in the health plan, or eligibility for benefits on a patient's authorization to have a psychologist release psychotherapy notes. For psychotherapy notes to meet HIPAA exemption criteria, psychologists *must* store the notes in a file separated from the client's/patient's other health records.

Educational Records

Psychologists working in the schools need to be familiar with the Family Educational Rights and Privacy Act (FERPA) (20 U.S.C. § 1232-34 CFR Part 99; http://www.ed.gov/offices/OM/fpco/ferpa/index.html) to ensure compliance with Standard 6.01. Under FERPA, parents and students over age 18 or attending school beyond college have the right to (a) inspect and review the student's education records maintained by the school; (b) request that a school correct records that they believe to be inaccurate or misleading; (c) call for a formal hearing if the school does not amend the record; and (d) if the school still does not decide to amend the report, place a statement with the record setting forth the parent or student views. Records that are kept in the sole possession of the school psychologist, that are used only as a personal memory aid, and are not accessible or revealed to any other person except a temporary substitute for the maker of the record are *not* considered part of a student's education record and therefore are not subject to parental or student inspection or amendment.

Forensic Records

Psychologists conducting forensically relevant activities need to be familiar with laws governing the creation, maintenance, and disposal of records. In the legal arena, the notes, test data, testing protocols, and research protocols are governed by the rules of evidence in the court's jurisdiction. For example, with the exception of relevant client/patient privilege, the entirety of the psychologist's records created or used in a case is subject to discovery. In addition, in deposition and court testimony, psychologists are often asked when certain facts became known and, if so, by whom and in what context. Sufficiently detailed records are essential when there is an extended period between relevant interviews or data collection and hearing of a case (Committee on Legal Issues, 1996; Hess, 1998). Under Standard 6.01, forensic records must be created and maintained in a manner that facilitates their appropriate use in the legal arena (see also Standard 2.01f, Boundaries of Competence).

Documentation of Scientific Work and Maintenance of Records

Psychologists conducting research must create and maintain records in a manner that allows for replication of the research design by the psychologist or others. This includes an adequate description of recruitment procedures, documentation of informed consent, relevant demographic characteristics of participants, data collection procedures, materials or equipment, and data analysis strategies. Raw data should be stored in a form accessible to analysis or reanalysis by the psychologist or other competent professionals who seek to verify substantive claims (see Standard 8.14, Sharing Research Data for Verification).

The number of years of retention of raw data for investigators will vary with state law, federal regulations, and institutional policies. Federal regulations (Office of Management and Budget Circular A-110) and Public Health Service (PHS) Grants Policy (National Institutes of Health [NIH] Grants Policy Statement, revised 03/01) require that data generated through federal support be maintained by institutions for at least a period of 3 years following the completion of the project and the filing of the final progress and financial reports. The number of years may be longer if a patent is involved. Specific record-keeping requirements for institutional review boards (IRBs) include maintenance of copies of the scientific proposal, the informed consent document, summaries of the project, financial reports, and reports of injuries or other serious adverse events. Authors of articles published in APA journals must have their raw data available for at least 5 years after the date of publication (APA, 2001).

Under Standard 6.01, principal investigators on federally funded grants must also create and maintain accurate records of costs associated with the research, including participant compensation, research assistant salaries, investigators' percent effort working on the grant, equipment, travel, and other supplies necessary to conduct the research. For federally funded projects, IRBs are subject to federal grants compliance and oversight. For each grant, the IRB must account for cost allocations/cost transfers, time and effort reporting, allowable grant charges, and unobligated balances (see http://grants.nih.gov/grants/compliance/compliance.htm).

6.02 Maintenance, Dissemination, and Disposal of Confidential Records of Professional and Scientific Work

(a) Psychologists maintain confidentiality in creating, storing, accessing, transferring, and disposing of records under their control, whether these are written, automated, or in any other medium. (See also Standards 4.01, Maintaining Confidentiality, and 6.01, Documentation of Professional and Scientific Work and Maintenance of Records.) *[No Significant Change, 1992 Standard 5.04, Maintenance of Records]*

Standard 6.02 requires that psychologists protect the confidentiality of professional or scientific information in all phases of record creation, maintenance, dissemination, and disposal. The standard refers to confidential records or data in the form of written and printed materials, automated scoring reports, audio and video recordings, Internet Web sites or e-mails, company computer networks, storage on hard drives or disks, and faxes. Steps that can be taken to protect confidentiality include (a) keeping records in a secure place, (b) limiting access to staff or team members who must use the record to competently perform their duties, (c) de-identifying records using code numbers or other methods, or (d) disposing of tapes and other identifiable records when they are no longer needed and their disposal is consistent with law.

Psychologists should be careful not to assume that their staff or employees of an institution or company with which they work are familiar with confidentiality requirements or appropriate confidentiality procedures. To the extent it is under their control, they must take steps to ensure that confidential records are kept secure from staff who do not have approved access. Consider the following example of a violation of Standard 6.02a.

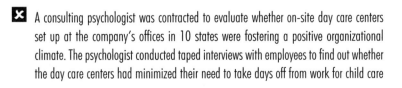

> ☒ A consulting psychologist was contracted to evaluate whether on-site day care centers set up at the company's offices in 10 states were fostering a positive organizational climate. The psychologist conducted taped interviews with employees to find out whether the day care centers had minimized their need to take days off from work for child care

> and their satisfaction with the plan. Each month, she traveled to a company's office in
> a different city to conduct the interviews. As she left, she usually asked one of the office
> secretaries to box up the tapes and UPS them to the company's main headquarters.

Implications of HIPAA. Psychologists creating or using PHI must comply with HIPAA regulations to protect the privacy rights of clients/patients. HIPAA compliance is required whenever PHI is transmitted in electronic form for health care claims, health plan premium payments, referral certification and authorization, injury reports, health care payment and remittance advice, and transfer of records to other professionals. HIPAA regulations require that client/patient authorization to transfer records of PHI to third parties should be different from and visually and organizationally separate from other permission forms, include a statement that the client/patient may revoke authorization in writing, and signed and dated (45 CFR 164.508).

The Final Rule of the HIPAA Security Standards establishes a minimum standard for security of PHI maintained in electronic form (45 CFR 160). These standards require measures to be taken to secure this information while in the custody of entities covered by HIPAA as well as in transit between covered entities and from covered entities to others. The Final Rule includes administrative procedures, physical safeguards, technical security services, and technical mechanisms covered entities must take to safeguard the integrity, confidentiality, and availability of electronic health information pertaining to individuals. The Security Standards require covered entities to implement basic safeguards to protect electronic PHI from unauthorized access, alteration, deletion, and transmission. Implementation depends on numerous factors including the configuration of the entity implementing it, the technology it employs, and the risks to and vulnerabilities of the information it must protect. Psychologists should be familiar with those standards that pertain to their specific practices (Department of Health and Human Services, 2003).

Practicing psychologists should remember that even if the specific files to be transmitted have never been electronically recorded by the psychologist, if any entity acting on behalf of the psychologists (e.g., a bill collection agency, a health maintenance organization) has electronically stored or transmitted PHI related to any other client/patient in the psychologist's practice, the HIPAA Privacy Rule is triggered for the entire practice. The APA Insurance Trust and the APA Practice Directorate (2002) recommend that all psychologists accepting third-party reimbursement, recording health information electronically, or employing a billing service make their confidentiality practices HIPAA compliant.

(b) If confidential information concerning recipients of psychological services is entered into databases or systems of records available to persons whose access has not been consented to by the recipient, psychologists use coding or other techniques to avoid the inclusion of personal identifiers. *[No Significant Change, 1992 Standard 5.07a, Confidential Information in Databases]*

Standard 6.02b draws attention to the need to take specific steps to protect confidential records when these records are stored in record systems or databases available to persons whose access has not been consented to by the recipient. To comply with this standard, practitioner and research psychologists storing data on institutional networks can use protected passwords, de-identify information, and discuss with institutional staff responsible for network maintenance and monitoring appropriate procedures for confidentiality protections. Psychologists working in group practices should be aware of and comply with HIPAA security rules governing office and other infrastructure PHI protections including access to offices, files, and secure transmission procedures (see the section "Implications of HIPAA" under Standard 6.02a above). When applicable, psychologists should identify limitations in efforts to protect confidentiality on databases and systems of records, and inform clients/patients, organizational clients, research participants, or others with whom they work about such limitations (see also Standard 4.02c, Discussing the Limits of Confidentiality).

(c) Psychologists make plans in advance to facilitate the appropriate transfer and to protect the confidentiality of records and data in the event of psychologists' withdrawal from positions or practice. (See also Standards 3.12, Interruption of Psychological Services, and 10.09, Interruption of Therapy.) *[Modified for Clarity, 1992 Standard 5.09, Preserving Records and Data]*

The obligation to maintain the confidentiality of professional or scientific records includes advance planning for the secure transfer of such records in the case of planned or unplanned withdrawals from a position or practice because of job termination, promotion, a new position, parental or family leave, retirement, illness, or death. Information may be transferred in person, by mail or by fax, through the Internet, or through private company networks. Psychologists planning in advance for the transfer of PHI need to be aware of the HHS Transaction Rule requiring standard formatting of electronic patient records for health care claims and other purposes.

Psychologists planning to transfer forensically relevant records should be familiar with laws in their state governing the extent to which licensed psychologists' privilege extends to their staff (Blau, 1984). Failure to take appropriate steps to protect the confidentiality of records or data transfer would be a violation of Standard 6.02c. Below are three examples of such violations.

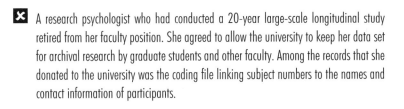

A research psychologist who had conducted a 20-year large-scale longitudinal study retired from her faculty position. She agreed to allow the university to keep her data set for archival research by graduate students and other faculty. Among the records that she donated to the university was the coding file linking subject numbers to the names and contact information of participants.

> ❌ After a 2-year postdoctoral fellowship in neuropsychology at a university hospital, a psychologist prepared to leave for a new position in a different state. The day before he left, he met the new postdoctoral fellow assigned to his office space. The psychologist apologized to the new fellow about leaving his patient records in the office file cabinets. He told her that the records were important to ensure continuity of care for patients that he had assessed but that the hospital administrators had not gotten back to him about where the records should be moved. He asked the new fellow to keep them in her office or to have one of the maintenance crew move the files to a temporary place in the basement.

> ❌ A psychologist in independent practice was told by the health maintenance organization (HMO) with which he had a contract that the HMO would not extend benefits for one of the psychologist's client's unless the psychologist provided the HMO with his psychotherapy notes. Knowing that his client needed and wanted to continue therapy, the psychologist reluctantly complied without getting written authorization from the client to release the notes. A week later, he attended a professional workshop on HIPAA regulations and learned that not only is a signed client/patient authorization required to release psychotherapy notes, but also managed care companies are prohibited from conditioning treatment benefits on the patient's authorization.

6.03 Withholding Records for Nonpayment

Psychologists may not withhold records under their control that are requested and needed for a client's/patient's emergency treatment solely because payment has not been received. *[Modified for Clarity, 1992 Standard 5.11, Withholding Records for Nonpayment]*

Psychologists, like other professionals, have the right to be paid for their services. However, the ideal of nonmaleficence, to do no harm, articulated in Principle A: Beneficence and Nonmaleficence, is a core value of the discipline that obligates psychologists to provide informational assistance, if not doing so would jeopardize the welfare of a current or former client/patient. Standard 6.03 prohibits psychologists from withholding records needed for a client's/patient's emergency treatment solely because payment for services has not been received. The term "solely" allows the psychologist to withhold such records if disclosure is prohibited by law or in the psychologist's judgment release of records would cause substantial harm to the client/patient or others.

The standard does not apply to nontreatment situations, such as when parents who have not paid for a completed psychological assessment of their child request the records for an application for special educational services. Similarly, the standard does not apply to treatments that are not an emergency, such as when a therapy client/patient who has not paid for services asks a psychologist to send treatment records to a new therapist.

Emergency treatment. The standard refers only to provision of records for treatment, and only when emergency treatment is needed. For example, a client's/patient's therapy or assessment records may be immediately needed to help other health professionals provide appropriate emergency treatment for a client/patient in an acute state of mental disorder such as a schizophrenic episode or a depression accompanied by frequent suicidal ideation. Records may also be required to help health professionals quickly determine whether an incapacitating cognitive or language disorder is the result of an injury, medical problem, or a symptom of a previous mental disorder. Under the Ethics Code, psychologists are not required to obtain the client's/patient's consent to release information if it is requested for emergency treatment (see Standard 4.05a, Disclosures). Similarly, the HIPAA Privacy Rule permits disclosure of PHI without patient authorization to avert a serious threat to health or safety (45 CFR 164.512[j]).

Control and requests. For the standard to apply, two other criteria must be met. The records must be under the psychologist's control. For example, Standard 6.03 would not apply if the health care system that a psychologist works for is legally responsible for the records and the institution refuses to release the records because of nonpayment. The records must also be requested, meaning that psychologists do not have to provide such records if they simply learn that a client/patient is receiving emergency treatment.

Regulatory and legal caveats. The HIPAA Privacy Rule establishing the rights of clients/patients to receive their PHI records does not distinguish between emergency and nonemergency requests nor does it consider failure to pay as a legitimate reason to refuse a patient request to release records. Thus, although ethically permissible under Standard 6.03, withholding records for nonpayment under nonemergency conditions may not be legally permissible. Psychologists should carefully review their contracts with HMOs to establish whether providers retain the right to withhold client/patient treatment records if the HMO has delayed or refused to reimburse for services.

6.04 Fees and Financial Arrangements

(a) As early as is feasible in a professional or scientific relationship, psychologists and recipients of psychological services reach an agreement specifying compensation and billing arrangements. *[No Significant Change, 1992 Standard 1.25a, Fees and Financial Arrangements]*

An individual's or organization's decision to enter into a professional or scientific relationship with a psychologist will depend in part on the costs and billing arrangements for the services. Failure to specify and agree on compensation and billing arrangements can lead to client/patient mistrust or financial exploitation. According to Standard 6.04a, psychologists providing counseling, therapy, assessment, consultation, forensic, scientific, or other services must reach an agreement about compensation and billing with the service recipient as early as is feasible in the professional or scientific relationship.

Specifying compensation. In specifying compensation, psychologists must include a description of all reasonably anticipated costs. For forensic, organizational, or research services this might include charges for telephone conversations; client, employee, or participant interviews; library or computer research; statistical analysis; court preparation time; travel; postage; or duplication. Psychologists arranging compensation for assessment services should provide information about fees for test administration, scoring, interpretation, and report writing. Financial agreements for therapy should include where appropriate discussion of (1) fees for therapy sessions, telephone sessions, sessions with family members or significant others, charges for consultation with other professionals and appointment cancellations, and (2) whether costs may be covered by health insurance, and time or costs limitations regarding third-party payors.

> **✗** A research psychologist agreed to provide expert testimony on developmental differences in the effect of divorce and stepparenting on child and adolescent development. The psychologist reached an agreement with the attorney stipulating a flat fee for reviewing the case material and writing a background paper relevant to her testimony. After receiving compensation for this work, the psychologist sent the attorney a bill for duplication and travel costs with a note saying that she would not be available to testify unless these costs were immediately reimbursed.

Billing arrangements. Standard 6.04a requires psychologists to reach an agreement about billing arrangements as early as is feasible in the professional relationship. Psychologist must notify and reach an agreement regarding when bills will be rendered and payments expected, for example, weekly or monthly. Billing arrangements may also include agreement on a series of scheduled prepayments or compensation for different phases of the psychologist's services.

> **☑** A research psychologist hired by a hospital to conduct a quality improvement study set up a payment schedule tied to completion of data collection, completion of a first draft of the report, and completion of a final draft.

To avoid billing disputes that may later arise between couples or family members, psychologists conducting couples therapy or child custody assessments may wish to consider reaching an agreement in advance regarding which member of the couple or which parent will assume responsibility for payments.

Timing. The use of the phrase "as early as is feasible" permits psychologists to delay finalizing a financial arrangement in order to obtain additional information about the client's/patient's service needs or health care benefits. Discussion of fees in the first session may be clinically contraindicated if a new client/patient is experiencing a crisis needing immediate therapeutic attention. In such situations, agreement on compensation and billing must be finalized as soon as all information is available or the crisis has subsided.

☑ A series of consultations with different company executives was required before a psychologist could develop a comprehensive plan for and pricing of services required.

☑ A psychologist was aware that a new patient's HMO frequently failed to provide timely feedback about the extent and limits of patient health care benefits. The psychologist discussed the possibility of this occurring during the initial consultation with the patient and discussed delaying additional sessions until the extent of coverage could be clarified.

☑ At his first session with a psychologist for treatment for alcoholism, the client was obviously intoxicated, evidencing speech impairment and a lack coherence in his remarks. The psychologist addressed clinical issues with the client relevant to the immediate situation and made an appointment with him to discuss fees and other issues regarding therapy at a time when he would be sober.

(b) Psychologists' fee practices are consistent with law. *[No Significant Change, 1992 Standard 1.25c, Fees and Financial Arrangements]*

This standard specifically requires psychologists' activities to be consistent with relevant laws. To comply with Standard 6.04b, psychologists must be familiar with and develop fee practices consistent with local, state, and federal laws governing fee practices. Below are examples of fee practices violating this standard.

❌ A group of psychologists started a mental health referral service. They charged psychologists to whom they referred patients a first-time fee for each referral and a fee for each subsequent session based on the patient's monthly bill. This method of reimbursement violated their state laws prohibiting kickbacks and fee splitting.

❌ The Medicaid system in the state in which a psychologist worked required professionals to have a preliminary meeting with a child to provide an initial diagnostic report that would then be used to request approval for a full battery of psychological testing. The psychologist routinely wrote the preliminary report without interviewing children to limit the loss of school time and to shorten the approval period.

☒ A couple began marriage counseling in the hopes of helping them meet the challenges of raising their severely autistic child and reduce arguments over family finances. The couple's health insurance company did not provide benefits for marriage counseling. The psychologist and the couple agreed to bill the sessions as individual therapy for the child.

☒ A psychologist charged a first-time fee when a client asked for a list of individuals to whom the psychologist had released the client's PHI over the past 2 years. The psychologist was unaware that under HIPAA, each year clients/patients have the right to receive one free accounting of all disclosures of PHI information made within the previous 6 years.

(c) Psychologists do not misrepresent their fees. *[No Significant Change, 1992 Standard 1.25d, Fees and Financial Arrangements]*

This standard requires that psychologists provide clients/patients, organizational clients, and others who will be charged for services an accurate statement of the costs of the services that will be offered. For example, under Standard 6.04c, psychologists are prohibited from the following:

☒ Listing in advertisements, brochures, or other public representations fees lower than what the psychologist actually charges (see also Standards 5.01a, Avoidance of False or Deceptive Statements, and 5.02, Statements by Others)

☒ Adding unnecessary tests to an assessment battery to raise the cost of services after reaching an agreement about fees with the client/patient

☒ Failing to disclose expectable costs of secretarial assistance or time devoted to telephone conversations, library reference work, or travel during fee negotiations for consulting or forensic work

☒ Using "bait and switch" tactics, such as offering low rates to lure a client/patient into therapy, only to raise the rates after a few sessions

☒ Inflating reports of hourly fees for noninsured patients to obtain a higher rate for covered services when submitting a provider application to an HMO

(d) If limitations to services can be anticipated because of limitations in financing, this is discussed with the recipient of services as early as is feasible. (See also Standards 10.09, Interruption of Therapy, and 10.10, Terminating Therapy.) *[No Significant Change, 1992 Standard 1.25e, Fees and Financial Arrangements]*

In some instances, financial limitations in providing services may be anticipated at the beginning or during the course of a professional or scientific relationship. This most frequently occurs when HMOs readily provide health care professionals with their policies on the type of mental health services and number of sessions that are covered by a client's/patient's health plan. When in a psychologist's professional judgment, clients/patients will require more therapy than their health plan covers, the psychologist must discuss this as early as is feasible in the professional relationship. Such discussion enables clients/patients to decide if they want to begin the treatment under the HMO's limitations and provides the psychologist the opportunity to inform clients/patients about other financial arrangements that can be made to ensure continued care. Alternative financial arrangements can include reduced fees, deferred payment, limited sessions, or referral to lower-cost services.

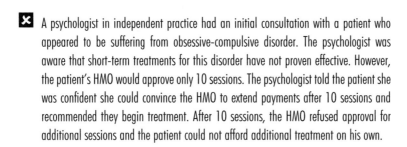

❌ A psychologist in independent practice had an initial consultation with a patient who appeared to be suffering from obsessive-compulsive disorder. The psychologist was aware that short-term treatments for this disorder have not proven effective. However, the patient's HMO would approve only 10 sessions. The psychologist told the patient she was confident she could convince the HMO to extend payments after 10 sessions and recommended they begin treatment. After 10 sessions, the HMO refused approval for additional sessions and the patient could not afford additional treatment on his own.

Standard 6.04d also applies to instances when during the course of a contractual agreement organizational, consulting, forensic, or research psychologists become aware that the actual costs of a project will exceed the agreed on costs. As soon as this becomes apparent, psychologists must discuss the limitations with the parties with whom they are contracted.

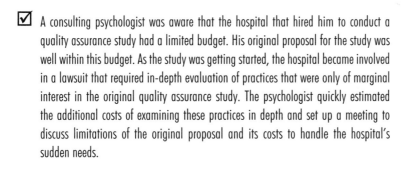

☑ A consulting psychologist was aware that the hospital that hired him to conduct a quality assurance study had a limited budget. His original proposal for the study was well within this budget. As the study was getting started, the hospital became involved in a lawsuit that required in-depth evaluation of practices that were only of marginal interest in the original quality assurance study. The psychologist quickly estimated the additional costs of examining these practices in depth and set up a meeting to discuss limitations of the original proposal and its costs to handle the hospital's sudden needs.

(e) If the recipient of services does not pay for services as agreed, and if psychologists intend to use collection agencies or legal measures to collect the fees, psychologists first inform the person that such measures will be taken and provide that person an opportunity to make prompt payment. (See also Standards 4.05, Disclosures; 6.03, Withholding Records for Nonpayment; and 10.01, Informed Consent to Therapy.) *[No Significant Change, 1992 Standard 1.25f, Fees and Financial Arrangements]*

Psychologists are permitted to use collection agencies or other legal measures to obtain compensation when the recipient of services has not made agreed on payments. Before using such services, under Standard 6.04e, psychologists must inform the client/patient or other service recipient that such measures will be taken and provide that person an opportunity to make prompt payment. The definition of prompt payment should be reasonable but need not extend beyond a month depending on the length of time that payments have been delinquent. As a rule of thumb, most businesses turn unpaid bills over to a collection agency after 60 to 90 days.

Standard 6.04e applies to psychologists providing therapy, assessment, consultation, forensic, and other services when the service recipient is an individual, couple, or family. The standard does not apply when psychologists choose to use a collection agency or legal measures to collect unpaid fees from companies, organizations, or institutions.

Implications of HIPAA. Several HIPAA regulations are relevant to Standard 6.04e. First, HIPAA permits covered entities to use and disclose PHI to carry out treatment, payment, or health care operations without specific authorization from the patient (45 CFR 164.506). Although specific requirements regarding consent were removed from the final HIPAA Privacy Rule, clients/patients must be aware of the covered entity's disclosure policies. Thus, covered entities who want the option of using collection agencies for nonpayment for health services must include this information in a Notice of Privacy Practices given to the client/patient at the onset of services (45 CFR 164.520). Psychologists should also include this information in their informed consent procedures (see Standards 4.02, Discussing the Limits of Confidentiality; 9.03, Informed Consent in Assessments; and 10.01, Informed Consent to Therapy). Psychologists who are HIPAA-covered entities should be aware that the Notice of Privacy Practices must be a separate document from the consent materials used for assessment or therapy. The APA Insurance Trust and APA Practice Directorate have available for purchase model Notice of Privacy Practices forms (see http://www.apait.org/hipaa).

Collection agencies hired by a psychologist may be considered a "business associate" under HIPAA (45 CFR 160.103). A business associate is an entity who acts on behalf of a covered entity, but not as an employee of the covered entity. An arrangement with a business associate must ensure that the business associate on behalf of the covered entity agrees to safeguard the use and disclosure of PHI in ways that are HIPAA compliant (45 CFR 164.504[e]).

What to disclose to collection agencies. HIPAA's "minimum necessary" standard (45 CFR 164.502[b]) as well as Standard 4.01, Maintaining Confidentiality, in the APA Ethics Code can be interpreted as requiring psychologists to limit the information provided to collection agencies to the minimum necessary to accomplish the intended purpose. Information to such agencies should be limited to (1) the client's/patient's name; (2) the dollar amount of the fee that is overdue; (3) the date of services for which the unpaid fee was billed; and (4) the client's/patient's address, telephone number, and other relevant contact information. Psychologists should never reveal a client's/patient's diagnosis or reason for seeking services. In most instances, psychologists do not need to mention the type of services provided (e.g., therapy) and can simply inform the collection agency that the overdue bill is for "services provided."

> ❎ A patient who had terminated therapy with a psychologist had failed to pay for sessions during the last 2 months of treatment. After sending the former patient several notices requesting payment and the psychologist's intention to use a collection agency if payment was not received, the psychologist turned the matter over to an agency. During the course of treatment, the psychologist had observed signs of sociopathy in the patient. Concerned that individuals at the collection agency might place themselves in danger if they angered the patient, the psychologist informed the head of the collection agency of the diagnostic reasons for these concerns.

6.05 Barter With Clients/Patients

Barter is the acceptance of goods, services, or other nonmonetary remuneration from clients/patients in return for psychological services. Psychologists may barter only if (1) it is not clinically contraindicated, and (2) the resulting arrangement is not exploitative. (See also Standards 3.05, Multiple Relationships, and 6.04, Fees and Financial Arrangements.) *[No Significant Change, 1992 Standard 1.18, Barter With Patients or Clients]*

This standard applies when psychologists accept from clients/patients nonmonetary remuneration for services. The issue of bartering often emerges in response to a client's/patient's financial limitations or lack of affordable health insurance. Providing services in return for bartered goods is ethically permissible in situations when to not do so would deprive clients/patients of needed services or run counter to community economic or cultural practices. Although barter is not a per se violation of the Ethics Code, psychologists need to be cautious about accepting bartered goods or services from clients/patients in lieu of monetary payments, because such arrangements have an inherent potential for client/patient harm, exploitation, and unethical multiple relationships (Standard 3.05a, Multiple Relationships). For example, it is often difficult to determine the extent to which a bartered good is equivalent in price to the dollar amount of a psychologist's fee, running the risk that clients/patients will be exploited or the psychologist underpaid. Bartering clerical or other (e.g., house painting, baby-sitting) services for psychological services risks creating potentially harmful multiple relationships resulting from interactions with the client/patient outside of a professional role or loss of professional objectivity in reaction to the quality of the client/-patient-bartered services.

Standard 6.05 specifically prohibits barter with clients/patients when it is clinically contraindicated or exploitative. Below is an example of a potential violation of this standard and an example of ethically permissible barter.

☒ A psychologist in independent practice in a wealthy suburban community saw clients in an office attached to her home. One of her clients, a landscaper, noticed that her driveway and landscaping in front of her home were in serious disrepair. He suggested that instead of paying fees for 2 months, he would relandscape her home. Although the cost of the landscaping would be greater than the psychologist's fees during this period, the psychologist agreed. The client was unable to complete the job in the 2-month period, leading to increased tension during the therapy sessions.

☑ A school psychologist worked 2 days a week at an isolated Alaskan Native fishing community providing parent and teacher consultations and behavior therapy for children diagnosed with attention deficit hyperactivity disorder and other learning problems. During the year, an oil spill created serious economic consequences for the village. It was estimated that it would take 2 months for normal fishing to resume. The tribal leader, on behalf of the parents and school, asked the psychologist if she would be willing to take free room, board, office space, and travel to the village donated by the tribe equivalent to her fees during this period. The psychologist agreed and set up a time-limited remuneration contract specifying the equivalent monetary value of the services. The psychologist reasoned that barter in this case would be ethically permissible because the barter did not directly affect her therapeutic relationships with the children or the parents or teachers with whom she consulted, and the exchange was a fair rate that was not exploitative. In addition, the psychologist's agreement to barter demonstrated her recognition and respect for the efforts and importance the tribe attributed to her services.

6.06 Accuracy in Reports to Payors and Funding Sources

In their reports to payors for services or sources of research funding, psychologists take reasonable steps to ensure the accurate reporting of the nature of the service provided or research conducted, the fees, charges, or payments, and where applicable, the identity of the provider, the findings, and the diagnosis. (See also Standards 4.01, Maintaining Confidentiality; 4.04, Minimizing Intrusions on Privacy; and 4.05, Disclosures.) *[Modified for Clarity, 1992 Standard 1.26, Accuracy in Reports to Payors and Funding]*

This standard requires accuracy in reports to payors and funding sources and reflects the values of honesty and truthfulness articulated in Principle C: Integrity. The standard applies when psychologists bill insurance companies for client/patient therapy or assessments, charge companies for consulting fees or forensic clients for services, or document grant-related research expenses. The phrase "take reasonable steps" recognizes that in some instances psychologists may have limited control over financial reports sent to third-party payors (i.e., psychologists working in group practices or in health delivery systems) or to funding sources (i.e., research psychologists working in academic institutions through which reports to external funders must be made).

Research and Industrial-Organizational and Forensic Services

Psychologists receiving research support from their institution, private foundations, or federal programs must provide accurate reports of charges for and the research-related purpose of equipment and supplies, travel, and payments to research participants, investigators, and research assistants. Psychologists billing companies or forensic clients for services should provide an accurate accounting of the number of hours worked on the particular project, the nature of and work product produced during those hours, and any other legitimate expenses (i.e., additional staff, travel, duplication or postage costs) associated with the work contracted for.

Therapy

Accurate diagnosis. Psychologists conducting therapy must provide an accurate diagnosis to third-party payors. Psychologists who provide an incorrect diagnosis in order to obtain reimbursement from a client's/patient's health plan would be in violation of this standard. In addition, such practices would represent insurance fraud and violation of Standard 6.04b, Fees and Financial Arrangements.

Billing for missed appointments. Some psychologists have a policy of charging for sessions missed when a client/patient cancels a therapy appointment. Health insurers will not reimburse for these charges, because no mental health services were provided. In their report to third-party payors, psychologists must clearly identify sessions for which charges are for a client/patient cancellation. Psychologists must also make any missed-appointment policies clear to clients/patients at the outset of the professional relationship (Standards 6.04a, Fees and Financial Arrangements, and 10.01, Informed Consent to Therapy).

Accurate representation of billing practices. Some HMOs calculate reimbursement for provider services on a percentage of the psychologist's fee scale. Psychologists must provide these organizations with an accurate representation of their billing practices for all clients/patients for the period requested by the HMO, including use of a sliding-fee scale if relevant. In some instances, licensed psychologists may supervise therapy or assessments conducted by unlicensed trainees or employees. When reimbursement for such therapy or assessment is sought from third-party payors, the licensed psychologist must clearly identify the actual provider of the services.

6.07 Referrals and Fees

When psychologists pay, receive payment from, or divide fees with another professional, other than in an employer-employee relationship, the payment to each is based on the services provided (clinical, consultative, administrative, or other) and is not based on the referral itself. (See also Standard 3.09, Cooperation With Other Professionals.) *[No Significant Change, 1992 Standard 1.27, Referrals and Fees]*

This standard is meant to ensure that client/patient referrals among professionals are based on the expertise of the professional to whom the referral is being made and the appropriateness of the service for the client/patient, and not on the basis of the referral itself. Standard 6.07 prohibits psychologists from charging other professionals for client/patient referrals, or conversely for paying another professional for a referral. Such payments place psychologists in a potential conflict of interest if the referral is based on the financial remuneration rather than on the needs of the client/patient (see Standard 3.06, Conflict of Interest).

Standard 6.07 is also meant to ensure that fees charged to clients/patients reflect the services provided. A psychologist may divide fees with another professional only if both have contributed to the service.

> ☑ A clinical geropsychologist regularly consulted with a neurologist when conducting cognitive assessments of patients with Parkinson's disease and other neurological disorders. The patient fee included the amount of money the psychologist paid the neurologist for the consultation. These billing arrangements were described to the patient or his or her legal guardian in advance, and the psychologist accurately described the arrangement in billing statements to patients and third-party payors (see Standards 6.06, Accuracy in Reports to Payors and Funding Sources; 9.03, Informed Consent in Assessments; and 10.01, Informed Consent to Therapy).

Referral services. The standard does not prohibit psychologists who are members of a psychotherapy referral service from paying a percentage of a referred client's/patient's fee to support the administrative costs of the service including the intake interview as long as (1) the service follows a policy of making referrals only to those members who have expertise appropriate to a client's/patient's treatment needs, and (2) the costs of the administrative and professional services are spread over the membership so that no individual psychologist is treated as a preferred referral solely because of his or her financial contribution to the service. However, psychologists need to be familiar with their state regulations regarding kickbacks and fee-splitting to ensure these activities are consistent with law.

Other permissible payments. The standard does not prohibit psychologists from (1) charging another psychologist payment for office space, (2) paying professionals who are employees a percentage of a client/patient fee, (3) paying an institution for referrals, or (4) membership in an HMO (Canter, Bennett, Jones, & Nagy, 1994).

CHAPTER 10

Standards on
Education and Training

7. EDUCATION AND TRAINING

7.01 Design of Education and Training Programs

Psychologists responsible for education and training programs take reasonable steps to ensure that the programs are designed to provide the appropriate knowledge and proper experiences, and to meet the requirements for licensure, certification, or other goals for which claims are made by the program. (See also Standard 5.03, Descriptions of Workshops and Non-Degree-Granting Educational Programs.) *[Modified for Clarity, 1992 Standard 6.02a, Descriptions of Education and Training Program]*

Psychologists responsible for education and training programs have an obligation to establish relationships of loyalty and trust with their institutions, students, and members of society who rely on academic institutions to provide the knowledge, skills, and career opportunities claimed by the specific degree program. Psychologists responsible for administering academic programs must ensure that course requirements meet recognized standards in the relevant field.

☑ Department chairs and other faculty responsible for undergraduate curricula development need to ensure that course requirements expose undergraduate psychology majors, minors, and individuals taking survey courses to the knowledge and skills considered fundamental to the discipline.

☑ Chairs or directors of doctoral programs claiming to produce graduates competent to conduct psychological research need to ensure that students receive education and training in the theoretical, methodological, and statistical skills required to competently conduct psychological science in the specific fields emphasized by the program.

☑ Psychologists responsible for professional degree programs need to ensure that course requirements and field experiences meet those required by potential employers, relevant state or professional organizations for program accreditation, internship placements where relevant, and applicable individual licensure and credentialing bodies.

 Psychologists administering internship programs must ensure that supervisory and training experiences meet the standards of the specific areas of psychological practice claimed, appropriate state and professional accreditation criteria, and state licensing board requirements.

The phrase "reasonable steps" reflects recognition that despite a program administrator's best efforts, there may be periods during which curriculum adjustments must be made in reaction to changes in faculty composition, departmental reorganizations, institutional demands, modifications in accreditation or licensure regulations, or evolving disciplinary standards.

7.02 Descriptions of Education and Training Programs

Psychologists responsible for education and training programs take reasonable steps to ensure that there is a current and accurate description of the program content (including participation in required course- or program-related counseling, psychotherapy, experiential groups, consulting projects, or community service), training goals and objectives, stipends and benefits, and requirements that must be met for satisfactory completion of the program. This information must be made readily available to all interested parties. *[Expanded, 1992 Standard 6.02b, Descriptions of Education and Training Programs]*

 Department and program chairs and psychologists responsible for internship training programs must also ensure that prospective and current students have an accurate description of the nature of the academic and training programs to which they may apply or have been admitted. This standard of the American Psychological Association (APA) Ethics Code (2002) requires psychologists responsible for these programs to keep program descriptions up-to-date regarding (a) the required coursework and field experiences; (b) the educational and career objectives supported by the program; (c) the current faculty or supervisory staff; (d) currently offered courses; and (e) the dollar amount of available student stipends and benefits, the process of applying for these, and the obligations incurred by students, interns, or postdoctoral fellows who receive stipends or benefits.

Standard 7.02 specifically obligates teaching psychologists to ensure that prospective and current students, externs, or interns are aware of program requirements to participate in personal psychotherapy or counseling, experiential groups, or any other courses or activities that require them to reveal personal thoughts or feelings. Many program descriptions now appear on university or institutional Web sites. Psychologists need to ensure to the extent possible that these Web sites are appropriately updated. The

term "reasonable steps" recognizes that efforts to ensure up-to-date information may be constrained by publication schedules for course catalogues, Webmasters not directly under the auspices of the department or program, and other institutional functions over which psychologists may have limited control.

 A psychology graduate department described itself as offering an industrial-organizational track that included paid summer placements at companies in the city in which the university is located. The required curriculum included only one class in industrial-organizational psychology taught by an adjunct professor. Other required courses for the industrial-organization track consisted of traditional intelligence and personality test administration classes, test construction, and statistics courses offered by faculty in the department's clinical and psychometric programs. For the past 2 years, the department had been able to place only one or two students in paid summer internships.

7.03 Accuracy in Teaching

(a) Psychologists take reasonable steps to ensure that course syllabi are accurate regarding the subject matter to be covered, bases for evaluating progress, and the nature of course experiences. This standard does not preclude an instructor from modifying course content or requirements when the instructor considers it pedagogically necessary or desirable, so long as students are made aware of these modifications in a manner that enables them to fulfill course requirements. (See also Standard 5.01, Avoidance of False or Deceptive Statements.) *[Modified for Clarity, 1992 Standard 602b, Descriptions of Education and Training Programs]*

Standard 7.03a requires that teaching psychologists provide students with accurate and timely information regarding course content; required and recommended readings; exams, required papers, or other forms of evaluation; and extra-classroom experiences if required. Psychologists who provide their syllabi via the Internet or who require students to use Web-based references need to keep these Web sites accurate and appropriately updated.

Modifying course content or requirements. This standard also recognizes that syllabi may sometimes include an unintentional error, required readings may become unavailable, changes in institutional scheduling sometimes create conflicts in dates set for exams, and many times psychologists have valid pedagogical reasons for changing course content or requirements at the beginning or middle of a semester. For example, a professor may find that assigned readings are too difficult or not sufficiently advanced for the academic level of students in the class. In such instances, it would be appropriate for professors to modify course reading requirements as long as materials are available to students and they are given sufficient time to obtain and read them. Similarly, in response to constraints imposed by publishers, bookstores, other professors, or the institution, psychologists may rightly need to modify required texts or exam schedules.

Modifications to course content or requirements do not violate this standard as long as students are made aware of such modifications in a clear and timely manner that enables them to fulfill course requirements without undue hardship. However, a professor who has neither discussed nor specified how students will be evaluated until the last week of class or one who fails to update an old syllabi that does not reflect the current content of the course would be in violation of this standard.

☑ In his first year of teaching, an assistant professor prepared a syllabus for an undergraduate developmental psychology course that drew largely on required readings from books by well-known developmental theorists. He carefully planned weekly quizzes, a midterm exam, and a term paper requiring a critique of several journal articles. Students performed very poorly on the first two quizzes and did not seem to be involved in class discussions. The professor learned that for reasons unknown to the department chair, the dean's office had assigned this class as a "non-major" section. The students were therefore not as prepared as had been anticipated because introductory psychology was not a prerequisite for enrollment for non-psychology majors. The psychologist decided to modify the curriculum to ensure that students received a basic foundation in developmental psychology. He rush-ordered a basic developmental psychology text, extended the date of the midterm, and changed the topic of the term paper to a review of sections of the originally assigned books. He distributed a revised syllabus detailing the changes and gave the students the option of using the first two quizzes as extra credit.

(b) When engaged in teaching or training, psychologists present psychological information accurately. (See also Standard 2.03, Maintaining Competence.) *[Modified for Clarity, 1992 Standard 6.03, Accuracy and Objectivity in Teaching]*

Standards prescribing the nature of information teachers should provide raise legitimate concerns about academic freedom. At the same time, in many ways teaching is a "process of persuasion" where instructors are in the unique socially sanctioned and desired role of systematically influencing the knowledge base and belief systems of students (Friedrich & Douglass, 1998). Standard 7.03b reflects the pedagogical obligation of psychologists to share with students their scholarly judgment and expertise along with the right of students to receive an accurate representation of the subject matter enabling them to evaluate where a professor's views fit within the larger discipline.

The narrowness or breadth of information required to fulfill this standard will depend on the nature of the course. For example, a psychologist who presented readings and lectures only on psychodynamic theories of personality would be presenting accurate information in a course by that name, but inaccurate information if teaching a general survey course on theories of personality. A professor who was teaching the same material for 20 years when such material was considered obsolete in terms of recognized standards of the discipline would be providing students inaccurate information about the current state of the subject matter.

7.04 Student Disclosure of Personal Information

Psychologists do not require students or supervisees to disclose personal information in course- or program-related activities, either orally or in writing, regarding sexual history, history of abuse and neglect, psychological treatment, and relationships with parents, peers, and spouses or significant others except if (1) the program or training facility has clearly identified this requirement in its admissions and program materials or (2) the information is necessary to evaluate or obtain assistance for students whose personal problems could reasonably be judged to be preventing them from performing their training- or professionally related activities in a competent manner or posing a threat to the students or others. *[New]*

This standard requires psychologists to respect the privacy rights of students and supervisees. In many instances, information about students' or supervisees' sexual history, personal experience of abuse or neglect, whether they have or are currently receiving psychotherapy, and their relationships with relatives, friends, or significant others is outside the legitimate boundaries of academic or supervisory program inquiry.

With two exceptions, Standard 7.04 prohibits psychologists from requiring students or supervisees to disclose such information:

Clear identification of requirements. Teaching and supervisory psychologists may require disclosure of information about sexual experiences, history of abuse, psychological treatment, or relationships with significant others only if the admissions and program materials have clearly identified that students or supervisees will be expected to reveal such information if admitted into the program. The requirement for advance notification includes programs that explore counter-transference reactions during supervisory sessions, if questions about such reactions will tap into any of the categories listed above. Clear and advance notification about the types of disclosures that programs require will allow potential students to elect not to apply to a program if they find such a requirement intrusive or otherwise discomforting.

Interference with academic performance or self- or other harm. The standard also recognizes that there are times when students' personal problems may interfere with their ability to competently perform professionally related activities or pose a threat of self-harm or harm to others. In such instances, psychologists are permitted to require students or supervisees to disclose the personal information necessary to help evaluate the nature of the problem, to obtain assistance for the student or supervisee, or to protect others' welfare.

☑ A psychologist supervising a third-year clinical student's work at the university counseling center was growing increasingly concerned about the sexual nature of verbal exchanges the student reported having with one of her undergraduate clients. The psychologist also suspected from one of the student's comments that she had been meeting with the client outside of the counseling sessions. The supervisor asked the student whether she had been seeing the client socially. When she responded yes, the psychologist probed further to find out if she was having a romantic relationship with the client.

❌ A student came to see a professor during office hours to discuss his poor grade on the midterm exam in a graduate course on human sexuality. The professor asked the student if he might be doing poorly in the course because of anxieties about his own sexuality.

7.05 Mandatory Individual or Group Therapy

(a) When individual or group therapy is a program or course requirement, psychologists responsible for that program allow students in undergraduate and graduate programs the option of selecting such therapy from practitioners unaffiliated with the program. (See also Standard 7.02, Descriptions of Education and Training Programs.) *[New]*

Standard 7.05a addresses the privacy rights of undergraduate and graduate students enrolled in programs that require individual or group psychotherapy. During the commenting period for the revision of the 2002 APA Ethics Code, a number of graduate students raised concerns about revealing personal information (1) in the presence of other students in required group therapy or experiential courses and (2) to therapists in required individual psychotherapy, if the therapist was closely affiliated with their graduate program. In response to these concerns, this standard requires programs that have such requirements to allow students to select a therapist unaffiliated with the program.

Standard 7.05a does not prevent programs from instituting a screening and approval process for practitioners outside the program whom students may see for required psychotherapy. It is sound policy for programs to ensure that required individual or group therapy is conducted by a qualified mental health professional. In addition, in some programs the therapeutic experience may be seen as one facet of training about a particular form of psychotherapy; and the program is entitled to require students to select a private therapist who conducts treatment consistent with the program's training goals.

Postdoctoral training. This standard does not apply to postdoctoral programs, such as postgraduate psychoanalytic programs, that require a training analysis with a member of the faculty. These advanced programs are optional for individuals who seek specialized training beyond a graduate degree in psychology, and unlike such requirements at the graduate level, a decision not to enroll in such programs because of therapy requirements does not restrict opportunities to pursue a career in professional psychology.

(b) Faculty who are or are likely to be responsible for evaluating students' academic performance do not themselves provide that therapy. (See also Standard 3.05, Multiple Relationships.) *[New]*

This standard is designed to protect the integrity and fairness of evaluations of student academic performance. Whereas, Standard 7.05a protects a student's right to keep personal information private from program-affiliated practitioners, Standard 7.05b protects the student from grading or performance evaluation biases that might arise if a faculty member who serves as the student's psychotherapist is also involved in judging his or her academic performance. This standard pertains not only to faculty that might teach a course in which a student who is in therapy with them might enroll but also to faculty that may be involved in decisions regarding passing or failing of comprehensive exams, advancement from master's- to doctoral-level status, training supervision, and dissertation committees. As indicated by the cross-reference to Standard 3.05, Multiple Relationships, serving in the dual roles of therapist and academic evaluator can impair the therapist's objectivity when knowledge gained from one role is applied to the other; or undermine treatment effectiveness when students are afraid to reveal personal information that might negatively affect their academic evaluations.

> ✗ A clinical psychology program required first-year students to participate in group therapy led by a member of the faculty. During one group therapy session, there was a heated discussion among students about cheating on exams. At a faculty meeting a year later, a professor who proctored the comprehensive exam mentioned that he suspected one of the students had cheated. The psychologist who conducted the group therapy did not mention the specific comments made by this student during group therapy, but suggested that on the basis of the students' disclosures in the group therapy class the department strongly consider investigating the cheating incident in greater detail.

7.06 Assessing Student and Supervisee Performance

(a) In academic and supervisory relationships, psychologists establish a timely and specific process for providing feedback to students and supervisees. Information regarding the process is provided to the student at the beginning of supervision. *[Expanded, 1992 Standard 6.05a, Assessing Student and Supervisee Performance]*

Psychologists establish academic and supervisory relationships of trust with students and supervisees based on fair processes of evaluation that provide students and supervisees with the opportunity to learn from positive and negative feedback of their work. Under Standard 7.06a, psychologists must inform students and supervisees (a) when and how often they will be evaluated, (b) the basis for evaluation (e.g., performance on exams, attendance, summaries of client/patient sessions, administration and interpretation of psychological assessments), and (c) the timing and manner in which feedback will be provided.

> ❌ A psychology professor teaching a graduate course in statistics used a midterm and final exam to evaluate students. The professor delayed returning the midterm, telling the students they should not worry because most of them would do very well. When she returned the graded midterms during the last week of class, students were shocked to discover that most had received Cs and Ds on the exam. Many felt the delay caused them to miss opportunities to learn what aspects of course material they had misunderstood and to adequately prepare for the final.

Providing specific information about student evaluation at the beginning of the process is especially important for the supervision of clinical work, psychological assessment, or research because these supervisory activities are often less uniformly structured than classroom teaching.

> ❌ A clinical psychology student had a second-year externship in an anxiety disorders clinic. Each time the student asked her supervisor for guidelines on how her clinical work would be evaluated, the psychologist would discuss these concerns only within the context of how the student's personal anxiety about her own performance could shed light on the anxiety experienced by the clinic's clients. The student felt increasingly frustrated and anxious about the lack of specific feedback. At the end of the year, the supervisor gave her a poor evaluation, stating that the student's anxieties interfered with her ability to take direction.

(b) Psychologists evaluate students and supervisees on the basis of their actual performance on relevant and established program requirements. *[No Significant Change, 1992 Standard 6.05b, Assessing Student and Supervisee Performance]*

Fairness and justice require that academic and supervisory evaluations should never be based on student personal characteristics that have not been observed to affect their performance or that are outside the established bounds of program requirements.

> ✖ A psychologist learned from a member of the clinic staff that one of her supervisees had expressed harsh, racially prejudiced attitudes at a staff party. Over the course of the supervisory period, there was no evidence that the supervisee treated clients in a racially biased manner. However, in the final written evaluation, the psychologist reported that the supervisee appeared to have difficulty working with clients from other racial backgrounds.

7.07 Sexual Relationships With Students and Supervisees

Psychologists do not engage in sexual relationships with students or supervisees who are in their department, agency, or training center or over whom psychologists have or are likely to have evaluative authority. (See also Standard 3.05, Multiple Relationships.) *[Expanded, 1992 Standard 1.19b, Exploitative Relationships]*

Sexual relationships with students or supervisees are specifically prohibited by Standard 7.07. The student-professor/supervisor role is inherently asymmetrical in terms of power. Teachers and supervisors have the power to affect student careers through grading, research and professional opportunities, letters of recommendation, scholarships and stipends, and reputation among other faculty or staff. Using this power to coerce or otherwise unduly influence a student to enter a sexual relationship is exploitative (Standard 3.08, Exploitative Relationships). The prohibition against sex with students and supervisees applies not only to those over whom the psychologist has evaluative or direct authority but also to anyone who is a student or supervisee in the psychologist's department, agency, or training center or over whom they might be likely to have evaluative authority while the student is in the program or supervised setting.

Sexual relationships with students and supervisees is a specific example of an unethical multiple relationship (Standard 3.05, Multiple Relationships). When psychologists enter into a sexual relationship with a student or supervisee their ability to judge the student's/supervisee's academic, professional, or scientific performance objectively is impaired. In addition, when other students learn about such relationships it can jeopardize the psychologist's ability to maintain an impression of professional impartiality and provides students with a model of unethical conduct that jeopardizes the psychologist's effectiveness as a teacher or supervisor. Such relationships also risk compromising psychologists' ability to exert appropriate authority or evaluations regarding the student/supervisee and others with whom they work if the sexual partner can manipulate the psychologist through threats of exposure or complaints of misconduct.

CHAPTER 11

Standards on
Research and Publication

8. RESEARCH AND PUBLICATION

8.01 Institutional Approval

When institutional approval is required, psychologists provide accurate information about their research proposals and obtain approval prior to conducting the research. They conduct the research in accordance with the approved research protocol. *[Modified for Clarity, 1992 Standard 6.09, Institutional Approval]*

This standard of the American Psychological Association (APA) Ethics Code (2002) has four basic requirements. First, psychologists must know if and from whom institutional approval is required. All institutions receiving federal funding for bio-medical or behavioral research are required to establish institutional review boards (IRBs) to protect the rights and safety of research participants. Institutions must also follow federal, state, and local laws requiring the review and regulation of research involving animal subjects. In addition, many social welfare agencies, health care facilities, schools, correctional facilities, businesses, and other public and private organizations have their own internal review requirements for research. Federal guidelines list activities that are exempt from institutional review; however, the exempt status of any specific project must be approved by an institution's IRB (Department of Health and Human Services [DHHS], 2001). Depending on institutional policy, psychology laboratory course experiments may not require review.

Applications for institutional review must be accurate and approval obtained before the research is conducted, and research procedures must follow the approved protocol. Failure to meet any of these conditions violates this standard. It is not unusual for methods to be modified during different phases of research. Any changes in participant informed consent language or procedures, compensation, confidentiality protections, or methods that increase human or animal participant risk or safety should be resubmitted for institutional approval prior to implementation. Psychologists should consult the appropriate IRB about the need to provide an informative memo or to resubmit proposals for minor changes unrelated to participant protections or welfare.

Implications of HIPAA. Investigators conducting program evaluation or archival research involving "protected (identifiable) health information" (PHI) as defined under the new Health Insurance Portability and Accountability Act (HIPAA; 45 CFR 160-164) should be aware that institutions, health plans, or providers who have obtained the information in many instances must have a waiver from either an IRB or a "privacy board" before they may provide such information to an investigator without specific written patient authorization. The next section provides an expanded discussion of HIPAA as it relates to informed consent to research. Readers may also refer to the section "A Word About HIPAA" in the Preface of this book.

8.02 Informed Consent to Research

(a) When obtaining informed consent as required in Standard 3.10, Informed Consent, psychologists inform participants about (1) the purpose of the research, expected duration, and procedures; (2) their right to decline to participate and to withdraw from the research once participation has begun; (3) the foreseeable consequences of declining or withdrawing; (4) reasonably foreseeable factors that may be expected to influence their willingness to participate such as potential risks, discomfort, or adverse effects; (5) any prospective research benefits; (6) limits of confidentiality; (7) incentives for participation; and (8) whom to contact for questions about the research and research participants' rights. They provide opportunity for the prospective participants to ask questions and receive answers. (See also Standards 8.03, Informed Consent for Recording Voices and Images in Research; 8.05, Dispensing With Informed Consent for Research; and 8.07, Deception in Research.) *[Expanded, 1992 Standard 6.11b, Informed Consent to Research]*

Ensuring Consent Is Informed, Rational, and Voluntary

To comply with this standard, psychologists must obtain and document written or oral consent in the manner set forth in Standard 3.10, Informed Consent. This includes providing information in a language and at a language level understood by prospective participants and where applicable their legally authorized representative. When conducting research involving children or adults with impaired consent capacity from diverse language populations, psychologists should be alert to the possibility that prospective participants and their legal guardians have different language preferences and proficiencies (Council of National Psychological Associations for the Advancement of Ethnic Minority Interests, 2000; Fisher et al., 2002).

Describing the nature of participation. Prospective participants, and when appropriate their legal guardians, must be given information and the opportunity to ask questions about the purpose, duration, procedures, foreseeable risks, potential benefits, and compensation involved in participation sufficient to make an informed decision. The Office for Protection From Research Risks (OPRR, 1993) has interpreted federal regulations as prohibiting investigators from describing participant compensation as a benefit when obtaining informed consent.

The voluntary nature of participation. Consent procedures must directly inform participants they will not be penalized for declining participation, especially when the prospective participant has reason to believe that dissent may result in adverse consequences (see Standard 8.04, Client/Patient, Student, and Subordinate Research Participants). The conditions under which individuals will qualify for full compensation for participation or continuation of experimental interventions if they withdraw from the study must also be fully described (see Standard 8.06, Offering Inducements for Research Participation).

Confidentiality. Disclosure of confidential information can result in criminal or civil liability or financial or social damage. Informed consent procedures must provide a clear explanation of the extent and limits of confidentiality, including (1) whether investigators must comply with reporting requirements such as mandated child abuse reporting, elder abuse, or duty-to-warn laws; (2) the investigator's confidentiality and disclosure policy for responses indicating a participant or another person is in immediate danger or otherwise at a high level of risk; (3) if the method of data collection itself may limit the extent of confidentiality protections as may be the case when research is conducted via the Internet; or (4) if the investigator has applied for and received a DHHS Certificate of Confidentiality that protects research records from most types of subpeonas (see http://ohrp.osophs.dhhs.gov/humansubjects/guidance/certconp and discussions of confidentiality in research in Chapter 7 under Standards 4.01, Maintaining Confidentiality, and 4.02, Discussing the Limits of Confidentiality).

Investigators conducting research in schools or studies involving children or adults with questionable consent capacities should familiarize themselves with evolving federal and state laws governing guardians' rights of access to health- or school-related records created, used, or disclosed by a researcher (e.g., HIPAA, PPRA; see below), and disclose such information to guardians and children during informed consent.

❌ A psychologist decided to conduct a survey study on marital conflict over the Internet. She posted an explanation of the study on a university Web site. Those who wished to participate were asked to download the questionnaire into their personal computers and to e-mail their responses back to the psychologist. The explanation on the Web site claimed that participant responses were anonymous and thus there were no risks to confidentiality. However, the psychologist's university did not have the technology necessary to de-identify respondent e-mail addresses, so in fact there was a chance that an e-mail address might be recognized by the psychologist, a research assistant, or others. In addition, the Web site explanation did not warn participants to password protect the completed file saved on their personal computer.

Persons legally incapable of giving informed consent. As required in Standard 3.10b, Informed Consent, psychologists must (1) provide appropriate explanations and obtain assent for research participation from persons legally incapable of informed consent, such as children or adults with severely impaired cognitive capacities, and (2) obtain appropriate permission from a legally authorized person, if such substitute consent is permitted or required by law. Psychologists who do not obtain the active permission of guardians or who use passive consent procedures (sending guardians forms asking for a response only if they do *not* wish their child to participate in the research) violate this standard except when the research meets the conditions for Standard 8.05, Dispensing With Informed Consent for Research, or when an IRB has followed federal guidelines for waiving parental permission. Research psychologists conducting longitudinal studies with minors should also consider re-consent procedures appropriate to children's changing developmental maturity.

☑ A psychologist was conducting a study on language skills involving adults with mild levels of mental retardation and developmental disabilities (MR/DD) living in community group residences. Some of the prospective participants had a parent or sibling who was their legal guardian. Other prospective participants had maintained the legal right to consent to decisions affecting their lives, but such decisions were often made in collaboration with residence staff and family. The psychologist obtained signed permission from all legal guardians followed by the signed assent of individuals who wished to participate. The psychologist obtained signed consent from all adults with MR/DD who had the legal right to consent. However, information forms were also sent in advance to the family members with whom these individuals relied on for decision making. In all situations, the psychologist did not attempt to obtain consent from a prospective participant until after a resident staff member had confirmed that the individual wanted to be approached.

Implications of HIPAA

Under HIPAA, protected health information (PHI) is defined as any information transmitted or maintained in any form or medium relating to the past, present, or future physical or mental health condition, provision of care, or payment for provision of care for an individual that either identifies or can be used to identify the individual. HIPAA requires that all providers who are covered entities under HIPAA (a health plan, a health care clearinghouse, or a health care provider who transmits any health information in electronic form relevant to carry out financial or administrative activities related to health care) comply with the regulations (45 CFR 160.102). Whether or not an individual investigator is providing the service or is a health care provider, if the research is conducted in an organized system of health care or implemented by a provider, HIPAA will apply (see http://www.hhs.gov/ocr/hipaa/finalreg.html and discussions of the implications of HIPAA for confidentiality in research in Chapter 7 under Standards 4.01, Maintaining Confidentiality, and 4.02a, Discussing the Limits of Confidentiality).

Authorization to use PHI for research. HIPAA requires that in order for a covered entity to create, use, or disclose PHI for research purposes, the covered entity must receive a signed authorization from the prospective participant or a legal guardian limited to the specific research project (45 CFR 164.508[c]). Research is one of the few activities for which HIPAA permits authorization for the use or disclosure of PHI to be combined with informed consent information and other types of written permission for the same research (45 CFR 164.508[b][3][i]). Under HIPAA, a valid authorization must contain the following:

- A description of the information to be used or disclosed written in clear language.
- Specific identification of the person(s) who will be involved in the request for, use, and disclosure of PHI.
- A description of each purpose of the requested use or disclosure.
- An expiration date.
- Signature and date of signature.
- A statement regarding the individual's right to revoke the authorization in writing.
- Exceptions to the right to revocation (e.g., if the PHI has already been obtained and used on the basis of the original authorization the investigator may maintain data analyses based on the information, although no additional information may be used or disclosed following revocation).
- The consequences to the individual of a refusal to sign the authorization. Research is one of the few conditions in which HIPAA permits treatment to be conditioned upon authorization (45 CFR 164.508[b][4][i]).
- The participant must receive a copy of the authorization.

The HIPAA transition provision. So as not to unnecessarily impede research, HIPAA has a transition provision that permits the use of PHI obtained with appropriate IRB-approved informed consent prior to the April 14, 2003, compliance date. However, individuals who are participating in longitudinal studies must be re-consented with appropriate HIPAA authorization if they are retested or otherwise reinvolved in the research after April 14 (45 CFR 164.532).

Health records research. HIPAA is also relevant for research psychologists conducting records research on PHI collected by social services agencies, hospitals, or other health or service provider institutions. With some exceptions, covered entities can allow investigators access to PHI only if the covered entity obtains authorization by the client/patient or a legally authorized representative to release PHI for the specific research purposes and to the specific investigator or investigative team. Whenever a covered entity releases PHI to an investigator, the covered entity is required to disclose only the "minimum necessary" to reasonably achieve the purpose of the disclosure (45 CFR 164.514[3]). Under the HIPAA Privacy Rule, covered entities are permitted to use and disclose PHI for research without a client's/patient's authorization under specific conditions described below in the discussion of Standard 8.05, Dispensing With Informed Consent for Research.

Parental Consent in School-Based Research

Implications of PPRA for U.S. Department of Education-funded research. The Protection of Pupil Rights Amendment (PPRA) (20 U.S.C. § 1232-34 CFR Part 98; http://www.ed.gov/offices/OM/fpco/ppra/index.html) seeks to ensure that certain instructional materials used in connection with a federally funded survey, analysis, or evaluation of students are available for inspection by parents and that written parental consent is obtained before minor students participate in such research. The types of materials to which PPRA applies include the following:

1. Political affiliations

2. Mental and psychological problems potentially embarrassing to the student and his or her family

3. Sexual behaviors and attitudes

4. Illegal, antisocial, self-incriminating, and demeaning behaviors

5. Critical appraisals of other individuals with whom respondents have close family relationships

6. Legally recognized privileged or analogous relationships, such as those of lawyers, physicians, and ministers

7. Income (other than that required by law to determine eligibility for participation in a program or for receiving financial assistance under such programs)

Evolving law. Psychologists conducting research in the schools should also keep up-to-date on the implementation of the Hutchinson Amendment to the Reauthorization of the Elementary and Secondary Education Act (ESEA) directing state and local education agencies that receive funds under ESEA to develop guidelines to protect student privacy in dealings with public and private entities that are not schools.

(b) Psychologists conducting intervention research involving the use of experimental treatments clarify to participants at the outset of the research (1) the experimental nature of the treatment; (2) the services that will or will not be available to the control group(s) if appropriate; (3) the means by which assignment to treatment and control groups will be made; (4) available treatment alternatives if an individual does not wish to participate in the research or wishes to withdraw once a study has begun; and (5) compensation for or monetary costs of participating including, if appropriate, whether reimbursement from the participant or a third-party payor will be sought. (See also Standard 8.02a, Informed Consent to Research.) *[New]*

This new standard governs research on behavioral, psychosocial, biomedical, psychopharmacological, or other interventions involving individuals, families, groups, or communities.

Addressing the "therapeutic misconception." The first provision, clarifying the experimental nature of the treatment, requires that informed consent procedures address the general misconception that "experimental" treatment means "better" treatment with known direct benefits for participants. The primary goal of intervention research is to provide generalizable information on whether a particular type of intervention is successful. Depending on the stage of research, an untested experimental treatment may place participants at greater risk than a no-treatment or treatment-as-usual condition. Most important, psychologists must take reasonable steps to communicate to prospective participants that the purpose of conducting treatment research is to determine whether or not a treatment works or how it works in comparison to another treatment.

This standard does not prevent psychologists from describing direct benefits that may be derived from participation, such as (a) access to new treatments not yet available for general use; (b) benefits of the experimental treatment if it proves effective during or following the conclusion of the study; (c) comprehensive psychological assessment and monitoring; (d) treatment referrals; or (e) upon participant-signed authorization, forwarding a summary of the participant's response to the treatment conditions to a qualified mental health professional.

> ☑ A team of psychologists and psychiatrists at a medical school received IRB approval to assess the behavioral, cognitive, and physical side effects of a medication recently approved by the Food and Drug Administration (FDA) as an alternative to methylphenidate (Ritalin) in hyperactive children. Using Latin square assignment, each child would be given 2 weeks of each of five experimental conditions (placebo, three different dose levels of medication, and one dose of methylphenidate). Although no long-lasting negative effects had been observed in adult studies for more than two decades, there was some controversy in the literature about whether animal studies demonstrating some negative effects were replicable or applicable to humans. The researchers included a paragraph in the parental permission forms describing the animal results and stating that there was some unknown risk that the drug could

cause permanent neurological damage in participating children. Many of the parents had children who had failed to be helped by traditional treatment with methylphenidate. To avoid inadvertently implying to these parents that the animal data suggested that the medication was a powerfully effective drug, the investigators were also careful to clarify in the parental permission information that the reason the study was being conducted was because there was as yet no empirical evidence indicating that the agent would be more effective than methylphenidate for hyperactive children. On entry to the study, parents were also informed that at the end of the child's participation in the study, the investigators would prepare a summary letter for the parent and with signed parental permission and authorization the child's primary physician would receive the child's diagnosis, a summary of the nature of the treatment conditions, observed behavioral changes in reaction to the different experimental conditions, and any recommendations for treatment that emerged from the child's responses to different conditions (adapted from Fisher, Hoagwood, & Jensen, 1996).

Explanation about control groups and methods of assignment to treatment conditions. The principles of good scientific design often require investigators to (1) assign some participants to control group conditions as a point of comparison for the experimental treatment (between-group designs) or (2) vary the treatment and control conditions for individual participants (within-group designs). Control conditions may consist of participants receiving different levels of the investigational intervention, a treatment of documented effectiveness, currently available services (treatment-as-usual), a placebo, or no treatment. Provision No. 2 and No. 3 of Standard 8.02b require that informed consent adequately describes the nature, potential risks, and probable benefits of control group assignment as well as how assignment to experimental and control group conditions will be made. When appropriate, the nature of random assignment should be explained in language that can be understood by individuals unfamiliar with the scientific method. Informed consent for studies using single- or double-blind procedures should describe the extent to which participants and members of the treatment and research teams will know the group to which the participant has been assigned, and steps that will be taken to determine if and how the blind will be broken.

❌ A developmental psychologist designed a substance abuse prevention study to determine whether providing a program to junior high school students would yield more effective results than previous studies examining programs initiated during high school when students have had more exposure to or experience with illicit drugs. Students would be surveyed through 12th grade to evaluate the effect of the program on drug attitudes and use. The psychologist received permission from the school district to implement the prevention program in five schools and use five additional schools as controls. Parents and students in the schools receiving the experimental program were given full information about the project. However, the psychologist decided that there was no reason to tell the control group parents and students that they would be taking part in an intervention study, because they might feel angry or deprived that they were not getting the program. The informed consent for these schools simply said that the purpose of the study was to use questionnaires to examine students' drug use and attitudes across 7th through 12th grades.

The voluntary nature of participation. Provision No. 4 addresses the need to ensure that research participation is voluntary. Individuals who apply for or who already receive nonexperimental services at the study site may fear that failure to participate will result in deterioration or removal of existing services (see also Standard 8.04, Client/Patient, Student, and Subordinate Research Participants). Informed consent procedures must assure clients/patients currently receiving services that dissent will not disrupt their ongoing treatment and inform individuals new to the treatment facility of available alternative services. This standard does not require psychologists to describe or provide treatment alternatives when they are not otherwise available.

Costs and compensation. The cost of treatments provided in intervention research may be provided at no cost to the participant through federal or private funding of the research, charged to the participant, or billed through a participant's health plan. Understanding the financial costs and the extent to which third-party payors will be aware of diagnoses and services received during a research study is essential for informed decision making. In some cases, participants may be provided monetary compensation for participation. Provision No. 5 requires that prospective participants are given sufficient information about the nature of such financial arrangements to make an informed decision about participation (see also Standard 6.04, Fees and Financial Arrangements).

Implications of HIPAA. Psychologists creating, using, or disclosing PHI during the conduct of research evaluating health interventions such as different therapeutic techniques will under almost all circumstances have to comply with HIPAA regulations. For specific discussion of the relevance of HIPAA to such research, see "A Word About HIPAA" in the Preface of this book; discussions in other chapters of Standards 3.10, Informed Consent; 4.01, Maintaining Confidentiality; 4.02, Discussing the Limits of Confidentiality; 8.02a, Informed Consent to Research; 9.03, Informed Consent in Assessments; and 10.01, Informed Consent to Therapy; and other sections in this book identified by the HIPAA icon .

8.03 Informed Consent for
Recording Voices and Images in Research

Psychologists obtain informed consent from research participants prior to recording their voices or images for data collection unless (1) the research consists solely of naturalistic observations in public places, and it is not anticipated that the recording will be used in a manner that could cause personal identification or harm, or (2) the research design includes deception, and consent for the use of the recording is obtained during debriefing. (See also Standard 8.07, Deception in Research.) *[Expanded, 1992 Standard 6.13, Informed Consent in Research Filming or Recording]*

Psychologists must obtain informed consent to electronically record research participation before beginning data collection. Stored auditory and visual records pose a greater risk of personal identification over time than other data formats, and therefore consent procedures must allow persons to evaluate the personal consequences of such risks prior to research participation. Restricting data access to the research team best protects personal identification. If recordings will also be used for training purposes or presentation at professional meetings, consent must be obtained specifically for these purposes unless image scrambling, voice distortion, or other identity-masking techniques can ensure adequate disguise (see also Standard 4.07, Use of Confidential Information for Didactic or Other Purposes).

The inclusion of the phrase "prior to recording their voices or images for data collection" allows investigators to record the consent procedure itself for documentation or other legitimate purposes as long as participant permission is obtained in advance and recording ceases if the individual refuses participation.

☑ A research team was conducting a study on HIV-related risk behaviors in community-dwelling adults with substance abuse disorders. Although there were gross measures of detecting consent incapacity (i.e., behavioral indicators of high levels of intoxication), the researchers realized there was little empirical evidence that could help evaluate whether the participants who might be suffering from comorbid disorders actually understood the informed consent information. Such comorbidity would only be formally evaluated once the individual consented to study participation. With approval from the IRB, the investigators decided to tape-record the informed consent procedures so that they could analyze in detail the participant's understanding of the information and develop ways of improving the process. At the beginning of the informed consent process, investigators told each prospective participant they were going to describe the study so the individual could decide if he or she wanted to participate. They also told prospective participants they would be asked questions to make sure they understood the consent information. They then asked for permission to tape-record responses to the questions. They pointed out that the participant's name would not be mentioned on the tape and that they could request that the tape be destroyed. Only the responses of individuals who gave permission were recorded.

Exceptions. Investigators may record the voices and images of persons without their consent if (a) observations occur in a public setting in which one would have no reasonable expectation of privacy, for example, a public park, a hotel lobby, a street corner; (b) procedures do not disturb or manipulate the natural surroundings; and (c) protections are in place to guard against personal identification and harm, especially when the behaviors observed place participants at legal or social risk, for example, street drug dealing. Investigators conducting deception research that meets the requirements of Standard 8.07, Deception in Research, can receive approval from their IRB to waive the requirement to obtain consent for recording prior to data collection, but they must seek permission to use recordings for data analysis from participants during debriefing. Recordings must be destroyed if the participant declines permission.

8.04 Client/Patient, Student, and Subordinate Research Participants

(a) When psychologists conduct research with clients/patients, students, or subordinates as participants, psychologists take steps to protect the prospective participants from adverse consequences of declining or withdrawing from participation. *[Modified for Clarity, 1992 Standard 6.11c, Informed Consent to Research]*

Clients/patients, students, employees, prisoners, or other institutionalized persons may not feel free to decline or withdraw participation in a study conducted by a psychologist serving as their treatment provider, professor, supervisor, employer, or member of the institutional staff. Standard 8.04a requires psychologists to take specific steps to ensure that (1) refusal to participate does not result in a reduction in the amount or quality of services, lowered grades, poor job performance evaluations, or loss of institutional privileges and (2) prospective participants are aware of these protections during recruitment and throughout the course of research (see 8.02, Informed Consent to Research). When power differentials inherent in an existing professional relationship are apparent (such as when the investigator is also the student's professor or a participant's service provider), psychologists should refrain from conducting the informed consent process and any research procedures involving direct contact with the individual (see also Standard 3.05, Multiple Relationships). In some settings, it may be desirable to appoint a participant advocate to (1) explain to prospective participants the purpose of the study, the role of the investigator, and protections against adverse consequences of nonparticipation; (2) determine if vulnerable persons wish to be approached by the research team to give informed consent; and (3) monitor the continued voluntariness of participation.

☑ A graduate student member of the APA received permission to collect data for her doctoral dissertation at her internship site. The methodology included individual

> interviews with patients at the veterans hospital where she interned. The graduate student restricted her recruitment to hospital patients who were not in the section in which she worked. In addition, she hired and trained a research assistant to recruit and obtain informed consent.

(b) When research participation is a course requirement or an opportunity for extra credit, the prospective participant is given the choice of equitable alternative activities. *[No Significant Change, 1992 Standard 6.11d, Informed Consent to Research]*

In many colleges and universities, psychology instructors require or give extra course credit for undergraduate student participation in research. The pedagogical rationale for research participation is to provide direct experience with the process of research. Yet the requirement can be coercive to students who do not want to be involved in experimental procedures. In addition, psychology faculty and graduate students conducting research at the university benefit from a yearly "subject pool" of prospective participants, creating the potential for student exploitation. Standard 8.04b addresses these concerns by requiring that psychologists offer students pedagogical alternatives equivalent in time and effort to research participation, such as watching a video on a research topic, summarizing an article on research techniques, or assisting with the conduct of an experiment.

> ☒ A psychology department instituted a 2-hour research participation requirement for all students enrolled in introductory psychology classes. Students who did not wish to participate in the research had to set up a meeting to explain their objection to the instructor and write a 15-page paper on a research topic approved by the professor. In anonymous course evaluations, many students said they had participated in the required research because they were afraid they would get a bad grade in the course if the professor knew they did not want to participate in the subject pool or they believed it would take more than 2 hours to complete a 15-page paper.

8.05 Dispensing With Informed Consent for Research

Psychologists may dispense with informed consent only (1) where research would not reasonably be assumed to create distress or harm and involves (a) the study of normal educational practices, curricula, or classroom management methods conducted in educational settings; (b) only anonymous questionnaires, naturalistic observations, or archival research for which disclosure of responses would not place participants at risk of criminal or civil liability or damage their financial standing, employability, or reputation, and confidentiality is protected; or (c) the study of factors related to job or organization effectiveness conducted in organizational settings for which there is no risk to participants' employability, and confidentiality is protected or (2) where otherwise permitted by law or federal or institutional regulations. *[Significant Change in Meaning, 1992 Standard 6.12, Dispensing With Informed Consent]*

This standard restricts dispensing with informed consent for research to three well-defined conditions—all of which are predicated on the condition that the research will not create distress or harm. Psychologists working in institutions receiving federal funds for research should remember that the determination of whether a study meets the criteria for dispensing with informed consent is the responsibility of the IRB and not the individual investigator. Therefore, when working in an institution with an IRB, investigators designing research that meets the criteria of Standard 8.05 must still obtain appropriate institutional approval for such waivers (Standard 8.01, Institutional Approval).

Research Conducted in Schools

Ethical justification for waiving the informed consent requirement for specific types of research conducted in educational settings is predicated on the right and responsibility of educational institutions to evaluate their own programs, practices, and policies to improve services as long as the research procedures themselves do not create distress or harm. Studies of normal educational practices that do not require informed consent include comparisons of different instructional methods and class-room management techniques, or evaluation of educational placements. In elementary and secondary school settings, dispensing with informed consent is a waiver of guardian permission for research involving persons who are legally incapable of consent. Irrespective of whether the type of research conducted meets the criteria for waiving parental permission under this standard, psychologists should consider state and federal laws and parental expectations regarding parental involvement in children's partici-pation in normal educational practices before deciding whether to dispense with parental permission or student assent. Psychologists conducting program evaluation in the schools should also be familiar with FERPA and other federal regulations that may require parental access to their child's school records irrespective of whether parental permission for the evaluation was required or obtained.

Permission to dispense with informed consent for research in educational settings does not apply to studies designed to describe or test hypotheses regarding the rela-tionship between student personality traits or mental health disorders and school performance (e.g., gender differences in math anxiety and its relationship to scores on a math achievement test). The assessment of such personal characteristics is not a part of normal educational practice and could constitute an invasion of privacy. In addition, some investigator-initiated school-based programs, such as drug prevention programs, may not be considered a normal educational practice or part of the school curricula and thus would not meet the Standard 8.05 criteria for waiver of parental permission or child/adolescent assent or consent. Investigators conducting such studies must either follow the consent requirements outlined in Standards 3.10, Informed Consent, and 8.02a, Informed Consent to Research, or obtain a waiver of parental permission from their IRB in compliance with Part 2 of this standard.

> ❌ A developmental psychologist received permission from a local school district to design and test a conflict resolution program for fifth and sixth graders. The school permitted her to offer the program during the regularly scheduled health classes. Half of the classes served as controls. The success of the program was evaluated by comparing baseline and postprogram responses of children to questions about their conflicts with peers, siblings, and parents. The psychologist told the school superintendent that according to the APA Ethics Code, parental permission would not be required for this type of research.

Anonymous, Naturalistic, or Archival Research

Informed consent is not required for investigations using anonymous questionnaires, naturalistic observations, or archival research when (1) confidentiality is protected; (2) disclosure of responses would not place participants at legal, financial, or social risk; and (3) the research methods would not reasonably be expected to cause distress or harm. The phrase "for which disclosure of responses would not place participants at risk" refers to both the certitude that participants could never be identified and the nature of data collected. Thus, unless anonymity can be assured, psychologists should avoid dispensing with informed consent when personal information collected would create participant distress or involve criminal activity, substance abuse, or other activities that if known would place the participant at risk. Psychologists using archival data that include PHI as defined by HIPAA should refer to the section below detailing the specific criteria for waiving the requirement for client/patient authorization for use and disclosure of data from their records.

What is anonymity? Anonymity is often confused with confidentiality. A questionnaire is not anonymous simply because it does not include a participant's name. Most investigations use only subject numbers on questionnaires to protect confidentiality. Anonymity occurs when neither the investigator nor the public can identify who participated in the study. Questionnaires are not anonymous when linked to other data or collected longitudinally. For questionnaires distributed through the Internet to be considered anonymous, investigators need to take steps to ensure that respondents cannot be identified through e-mail addresses or other electronic identifiers.

> ☑ An anonymous survey on attitudes toward caretaking of ill elderly household members included (1) a brief questionnaire asking for general demographic information such as

gender, age, and ethnicity of household members and (2) health-related information such as whether there was an ill elderly person living in the household, which family member did or would take care of an elder family member if he or she was ill, how the respondents rated the adequacy of their health insurance plan for elder care, and several questions tapping who the respondent thought should be most responsible for elder care, for example, spouses, adult children, private nursing homes, or government-run hospitals. The survey was mailed to 10,000 randomly selected households in a large metropolitan area where respondents could not reasonably be expected to be identified by their answers or zip code. No names were on the survey, and the mailed packet included a self-addressed stamped envelope.

Unique or small communities. Investigators should also consider whether the uniqueness of the population studied (e.g., individuals from small and geographically restricted ethnocultural communities; persons with rare genetic, medical, or psychological disorders) increases the probability that anonymous, naturalistic, or archival procedures may not be sufficient to safeguard identification of participants or their immediate community (Fisher et al., 2002).

❌ A health psychologist decided to conduct a naturalistic observation of the interactions among health care providers and patients in the emergency room of a small hospital in an isolated Appalachian town. He would sit in the back of the room on Saturday nights when the emergency room was most crowded. He dressed in such a way as to ensure that he would not be recognized from week to week. The psychologist took detailed notes on how specific doctors responded to the patients. He published an article highly critical of some of the interactions he had observed. Although the psychologist used pseudonyms for the hospital and the doctors, the unique location of the hospital, the medical events reported, and the detailed descriptions of the treatment staff made them readily identifiable. Following the publication, several members of the treatment staff were sued for malpractice.

Naturalistic observation on the Internet. Studies of individual responses in chat rooms and on listservs may be considered naturalistic observation if the users have no reasonable expectation of privacy and the investigator is not manipulating the discussion to test or elicit particular responses. Under Standard 8.05, psychologists may dispense with informed consent under these situations if protections are in place to guard against personal identification and harm.

Studies of Job or Organization Effectiveness

Subpart 1c is new and recognizes the right and responsibility of organizations to draw on the research expertise of psychologists to investigate factors related to job or organization effectiveness as long as (1) research participation does not pose a direct risk to an individual's current employment status, (2) confidentiality is adequately protected, and (3) the research procedures themselves would not be expected to create distress or harm. This standard is meant to apply to dispensing with informed consent to research directly linked to a specific organization's needs and not to studies designed to test general hypotheses regarding organizational effectiveness.

The phrase "not reasonably be assumed to create distress or harm" highlights the fact that in most circumstances it would be ethically inappropriate to dispense with informed consent for organizational effectiveness studies using measures of psychopathology or biological data because assessment of mental health or physiological responses without consent can violate an individual's right to privacy of information not directly related to job performance and be experienced as personally intrusive and distressful.

☑ An industrial-organizational psychologist collected criterion-related validation data on a test designed to select sales personnel by administering the test to all job incumbents. The incumbents were informed that their test performance would be kept confidential and would not affect employment status. To match the test data to measures of job performance (sales volume and supervisor performance ratings), the psychologist needed to collect identifying information on the test form. The psychologist maintained several levels of security on the test materials and associated database. As soon as the predictor test and performance criterion data were matched, all identifying information was stripped from both the hard copy test materials and electronic database. No information collected for purposes of the validation was released to anyone in the organization, and there were no consequences for those incumbents who performed poorly on the experimental test.

Where Otherwise Permitted by Law or Federal or Institutional Regulations

Part 2 of this standard permits psychologists to dispense with informed consent for reasons not included in part 1 where consent waiver is permitted by law or federal or institutional regulations. In such instances, researchers bear the burden of demonstrating that such conditions are met.

HIPAA requirements for use of PHI for research without client/patient authorization. Under HIPAA federal regulations, PHI may be used for research purposes without client/patient authorization if the covered entity who is being asked to disclose the PHI receives written documentation that waiver of patient authorization has been approved by an IRB in conformance with federal guidelines, and if

♦ The use or disclosure of PHI involves no more than minimal risk to the individuals.

♦ The alteration or waiver will not adversely affect the privacy rights and the welfare of the individuals.

♦ The research could not practicably be conducted without the alteration or waiver.

♦ The research could not practicably be conducted without access to and use of the PHI.

♦ The privacy risks to individuals whose PHI is to be used or disclosed are reasonable in relation to the anticipated benefits, if any, to the individuals, and the importance of the knowledge that may reasonably be expected to result from the research.

♦ There is an adequate plan to protect the identifiers from improper use and disclosure.

♦ There is an adequate plan to destroy the identifiers at the earliest opportunity consistent with conduct of the research, unless there is a health or research justification for retaining the identifiers or such retention is otherwise required by law.

♦ There are adequate written assurances that the PHI will not be reused or disclosed to any other person or entity, except as required by law, for authorized oversight of the research project, or for other research for which the use or disclosure of PHI would be permitted by the subpart (Rules for Research are under 45 CFR 164.501, 164.508[f], 164.512[i]).

Covered entities may also waive the requirement for client/patient authorization for the use and disclosure of their PHI for research under the following conditions (45 CFR 164.512[i]):

♦ Information is *de-identified* by the covered entity (de-identification has specific requirements under HIPAA; see 45 CFR 164.514). If de-identified information is later re-identified by the covered entity, a client/patient authorization is required.

♦ The researcher is reviewing the PHI for the sole purpose of preparing a research protocol or for similar purposes *preparatory to research,* the information is necessary for the research purposes, and the PHI is not removed from the covered entity's premises.

- Research is on *decedent's information* and the researcher provides the covered entity with representation that the use or disclosure sought is solely for research on the PHI of the decedents, the death is documented, and the PHI is necessary for the research.

- Disclosure is restricted to a *limited data set* (as specifically defined by HIPAA 45 CFR 164.513[e][2]) and the investigator enters into a "data use agreement" with the covered entity.

- The investigator signs a *business associate contract* with a covered entity to use PHI to conduct data analysis or quality assurance or other activities on behalf of the covered entity and to comply with all HIPAA regulations (45 CFR 160.103 and 164.504[e][1]).

8.06 Offering Inducements for Research Participation

(a) Psychologists make reasonable efforts to avoid offering excessive or inappropriate financial or other inducements for research participation when such inducements are likely to coerce participation. *[Modified for Clarity, 1992 Standard 6.14b, Offering Inducements for Research Participants]*

Selecting noncoercive compensation for research participation helps ensure that participation is voluntary and research burdens are not borne unequally by economically disadvantaged populations. Compensation for effort, time, and inconvenience of research is permitted if inducements do not encourage individuals to lie or conceal information that would disqualify them from the research or lure them into procedures they would otherwise choose to avoid. Some institutions adopt a standard compensation rate for all research participation. Others have defined noncoercive financial inducements as the amount of money a normal, healthy volunteer would lose in work and travel time or by fair market value for the work involved. Different economic and cultural circumstances may lead to varying perceptions of a cash inducement as fair or coercive. At the same time, fairness and justice entitle all persons to equal compensation for equal levels of participation in a particular research project (Principle D: Justice). Consulting with members of the population who will be recruited for research participation about different types of research compensation can help investigators and their IRBs determine the extent to which cash or nonmonetary compensation is fair or coercive.

(b) When offering professional services as an inducement for research participation, psychologists clarify the nature of the services, as well as the risks, obligations, and limitations. (See also Standard 6.05, Barter With Clients/Patients.) *[No Significant Change, 1992 Standard 6.14a, Offering Inducements for Research Participants]*

Providing psychological services as compensation for research participation is ethical when participants are fully aware of (a) the nature and risks of services (e.g., the type of treatment, the type of provider, risks to confidentiality), (b) the personal and financial obligations and time commitment involved in receiving the services, and (3) limitations of the type and in the length of services provided (see also Standards 6.04, Fees and Financial Arrangements; 6.05, Barter With Clients/Patients; and 10.01, Informed Consent to Therapy). Linking involvement in nontherapeutic research with treatment that immediately follows may benefit participants with mental health problems. However, psychologists should take special steps to ensure that offering such services does not compromise the voluntary nature of research participation of individuals who do not have access to adequate health care and social services.

8.07 Deception in Research

(a) Psychologists do not conduct a study involving deception unless they have determined that the use of deceptive techniques is justified by the study's significant prospective scientific, educational, or applied value and that effective nondeceptive alternative procedures are not feasible. *[No Significant Change, 1992 Standard 6.15a, Deception in Research]*

Deceptive techniques intentionally withhold information or misinform participants about the purpose of the study, the experimental procedures or equipment, or the roles of research team members (Sieber, 1982). By their very nature, deception studies compromise an individual's ability to make a fully informed decision about research participation. Deception research can have the advantage of keeping participants naïve about the purpose and procedures of a study, thereby increasing methodological realism and spontaneous response to experimental manipulation. However, these advantages may not be actualized if participants are predisposed to be suspicious of psychology experiments, or are actively engaged in hypotheses regarding an experiment's true purpose (Fisher & Fyrberg, 1994). Under Standard 8.07a, deception studies are ethically justified only if psychologists demonstrate that (1) prospective benefits to science or society significantly outweigh violating participants' right to determine whether they want to be involved in the type of experimental procedures for which they are recruited *and* (2) nondeceptive alternative procedures do not offer sufficient scientific controls to test the hypothesis under investigation. Some alternative methodologies that can be considered include naturalistic observation, field or game simulations, role-playing, or experimental methods. Failure to use scientifically valid nondeceptive alternative methods simply because of inconvenience or financial cost under some circumstances may be a violation of this standard.

(b) Psychologists do not deceive prospective participants about research that is reasonably expected to cause physical pain or severe emotional distress. *[Significant Change in Meaning, 1992 Standard 6.15b, Deception in Research]*

The 1992 version of this standard prohibited the use of deception techniques that expose persons to a wide range of mild to severe harms only if a psychologist could anticipate that these methods would affect the willingness of individuals to participate. The types of harm prohibited by the current Standard 8.08b are narrower and do not depend on speculation about whether knowledge of the procedures would influence participation decisions. Even if deceptive techniques have significant scientific, educational, or social value and thus meet the criteria of Standard 8.07a, 8.07b prohibits withholding or misleading prospective participants about procedures causing physical pain or severe emotional distress. The prohibitions in this standard are absolute and do not depend on the duration of physical pain or whether severe emotional harm can be alleviated during debriefing procedures.

> ☒ A psychologist at a university in New York City decided to study ways in which three types of warning systems would positively or negatively affect crowd behavior in response to a perceived terrorist attack a year following the September 11, 2001, attack on the United States. During one period of the day, the psychologist had confederates enter nine different classrooms and use of one of the three types of warning systems to instruct students in evacuation procedures for a "suspected bomb that might be planted in the building by a terrorist group." Many students started crying or screaming, some called their parents on cell phones to say goodbye, and two students fainted during the exercise.

(c) Psychologists explain any deception that is an integral feature of the design and conduct of an experiment to participants as early as is feasible, preferably at the conclusion of their participation, but no later than at the conclusion of the data collection, and permit participants to withdraw their data. (See also Standard 8.08, Debriefing.) *[Significant Change in Meaning, 1992 Standard 6.15c, Deception in Research]*

When deception is used, individuals must be informed about a study's deceptive aspects as soon as possible, preferably at the end of their participation. This procedure is often called dehoaxing. There may be situations in which explaining the deception can compromise the methodological validity of the research involving future participants, for example, if research is conducted in a small university where students are likely to speak with one another about their experiences. In such circumstances, dehoaxing may be delayed until data collection is completed. Psychologists must also take reasonable steps to alleviate psychological harm resulting from dehoaxing and may withhold information about deceptive procedures to protect the participant from harm (see Standard 8.08 b and c, Debriefing).

Data withdrawal. This standard includes a new requirement: Psychologists must permit participants to withdraw their data after learning about the deception. Although the standard stops short of requiring psychologists to ask participants if they want to withdraw their data, dehoaxing procedures should not preclude participants from making such a request. Giving individuals an opportunity to withdraw data should not be interpreted as implying their "deferred" consent to the deception—informed consent can only be prospectively obtained (OPRR, 1993).

8.08 Debriefing

(a) Psychologists provide a prompt opportunity for participants to obtain appropriate information about the nature, results, and conclusions of the research, and they take reasonable steps to correct any misconceptions that participants may have of which the psychologists are aware. *[Modified for Clarity, 1992 Standard 6.18a, Providing Participants With Information About the Study]*

To protect methodological validity, informed consent procedures often do not include the hypothesis or other information about the research that would not be expected to affect willingness to participate but might bias participant responding. Debriefing procedures provide participants the opportunity to be informed about such undisclosed information and to ask questions about the research. Standard 8.08a requires that psychologists take reasonable steps to correct any misconceptions about the research of which they are aware. The use of the terms "reasonable" and "aware" in this standard reflect the fact that despite the best efforts of a psychologist some participants may continue to hold misimpressions about the research or may not share these misperceptions with the investigator. As part of debriefing, psychologists should make a summary of the results of the research available to participants. Because data analysis and interpretation of results typically occur after data collection is completed, psychologists can make summaries available through mailings to participants, newsletters to the site at which the research occurred, Web site postings, or other mechanisms that do not incur unreasonable expense.

(b) If scientific or humane values justify delaying or withholding this information, psychologists take reasonable measures to reduce the risk of harm. *[No Significant Change, 1992 Standard 6.18b, Providing Participants With Information About the Study]*

There may be humane justification for withholding information about the nature, results, and conclusions of research. For example, individuals participating in deception research may experience loss of self-esteem or other negative psychological reactions if told they committed a social or moral breach of which they were not aware or which they did not know others had observed. In other situations, child participants may not have the recursive thinking skills to understand the rationale behind the research and feel confused upon debriefing or in the case of deception research may feel embarrassed or betrayed. In such circumstances, the study should be explained to the children's guardians.

☑ Investigators working with inpatient boys diagnosed with conduct disorder designed an analog task that could distinguish between the children's use of instrumental and hostile aggression. The task was a computer game in which the boys played against an unseen "boy" (in actuality formatted responses programmed by the investigators) in an adjacent room. According to the rules of the game, opponents could block each other's game (instrumental aggression) or send a noxious, but not harmful, noise through the computer headsets (hostile aggression). The investigators believed that these deceptive conditions were safer for the participants than alternative methodologies that manipulated or observed aggression in actual competitive situations. Parents thought the research was important but voiced concern that if the boys were told about the deception, they would lose trust in the staff at the facility. The investigators agreed. To minimize any distress that might emerge during the computer game, the boys could not see their scores during the game, and when the game was over, all boys were told they had won (adapted from Fisher, Hoagwood, & Jensen, 1996).

(c) When psychologists become aware that research procedures have harmed a participant, they take reasonable steps to minimize the harm. *[New]*

Psychologists must try to alleviate psychological distress or harm arising from research participation of which they are aware. In some cases, psychologists may not be able to anticipate participant stress reactions in response to debriefing. In such cases, psychologists might alleviate distress by explaining participant responses within the context of normative behavior if appropriate. In other situations, such as research involving genetic screening for predisposition to schizophrenia, psychologists may anticipate post-experimental stress if debriefing includes information concerning personal health vulnerabilities and should be prepared to provide referrals for appropriate counseling services.

☑ In a study to examine psychosocial factors contributing to the spread of the HIV/AIDS virus among intravenous drug users (IDUs), participants (a) answered questions about their drug use, needle sharing, sexual history, and sexual practices; (b) responded to standardized psychological assessments; and (c) had their blood tested for the HIV virus, hepatitis C, and other sexually transmitted diseases. The results of these blood tests were provided to participants during debriefing. The investigators developed two types of debriefing procedures. Aware that telling IDUs that they had tested negative for sexually transmitted diseases might lead them to falsely assume they were "AIDS safe," debriefing for these participants included counseling on continued risk of infection and risk reduction practices. Debriefing for participants who tested positive included counseling on availability of current treatments for these disorders, risk reduction practices, and referrals to appropriate health care providers.

8.09 Humane Care and Use of Animals in Research

The use of animals in research enables the control and manipulation of environmental, biological, and genetic factors leading to scientific discoveries producing tangible benefits for humans and animals not possible otherwise. The benefits of animal research never justify inhumane treatment. Psychologists conducting research involving animal subjects have a moral obligation to protect the animal subjects' welfare. Although protections for animal subjects articulated in the 1992 Ethics Code remain relatively unchanged in this revision, the intent of the 1992 Standard 6.20a has been incorporated into the revised general title to reflect the fact that Standards 8.09 a–g represent conditions that must be met to ensure care and use of animals in research is humane. [*Modified for Clarity, 1992 Standard 6.20a, Care and Use of Animals in Research*]

(a) *Psychologists acquire, care for, use, and dispose of animals in compliance with current federal, state, and local laws and regulations, and with professional standards.* [*No Significant Change, 1992 Standard 6.20b, Care and Use of Animals in Research*]

The federal government through the Health Research Extension Act of 1985 (Public Law 99-158) regulates the humane care and protection of animals used in research. The National Institutes of Health (NIH) through the Office of Laboratory Animal Welfare administers programs and provides guidance to institutions that must comply with the policy. Among the regulations is the requirement that all institutions covered by the act have an Institutional Animal Care and Use Committee (IACUC) to approve and monitor the ethical acquisition, care, use, and disposal of animals in research. The U.S. Department of Agriculture requires the planned and unscheduled inspections of animal research facilities twice a year to ensure that animal housing and research procedures are safe, sanitary, and appropriate for the particular environmental and nutritional needs of the species. In addition, animals not bred in the psychologist's laboratory must be acquired lawfully and with appropriate permits. States and local governments also have regulations regarding housing standards, veterinary care and inspection, research procedures, and disposal.

Animal research practices must also be in compliance with the Guidelines for Ethical Conduct in the Care and Use of Animals developed by the APA Committee on Animal Research and Ethics (CARE; 1996) (see http://www.apa.org/science/anguide.html). Other organizations such as the American Association for Laboratory Animal Science, the American Association for the Accreditation of Laboratory Animal Care, and the National Association for Biomedical Research have comprehensive rules for the conduct of animal research. Psychologists conducting research with animals must adhere to all relevant regulations and guidelines. The APA requires members working outside the United States to follow all applicable laws and regulations of the country in which the research is conducted.

(b) Psychologists trained in research methods and experienced in the care of laboratory animals supervise all procedures involving animals and are responsible for ensuring appropriate consideration of their comfort, health, and humane treatment. *[No Significant Change, 1992 Standard 6.20c, Care and Use of Animals in Research]*

This standard requires that psychologists conducting animal research have appropriate training and carefully supervise all personnel involved in the acquisition, care, research procedures, and disposal of animal subjects. Competencies include education, training, or experience with relevant animal research models; behavioral and surgical techniques; and knowledge of species-specific behavioral, social, and medical requirements. Psychologists conducting animal field research should have sufficient knowledge of the ecosystems they will observe to minimize harm to the natural behaviors and environment of the animal population under investigation and other plant and animal life.

(c) Psychologists ensure that all individuals under their supervision who are using animals have received instruction in research methods and in the care, maintenance, and handling of the species being used, to the extent appropriate to their role. (See also Standard 2.05, Delegation of Work to Others.) *[No Significant Change, 1992 Standard 6.20d, Care and Use of Animals in Research]*

Psychologists must ensure that all personnel involved in the housing, care, experimental methods, or disposal of animal research subjects are competent to fulfill these duties in a way that ensures animals are treated humanely and appropriately (see also Standard 2.05, Delegation of Work to Others). A wide range of animal species is used in research, and each species has its own unique housing, nutrition, medical, and psychological needs. Psychologists must make sure that individuals to whom animal care is delegated are sufficiently knowledgeable about the species and the duties they must perform through prior education, training by the psychologist, or close supervision.

❌ A psychologist who conducted research on aggressive behavior in male rats hired a research assistant to clean each animal's housing. Rather than provide direct supervision, the psychologist told the assistant to begin work and to feel free to ask the psychologists any questions that arose. To facilitate cleaning, the assistant decided to take three of the animals out of their separate housings and place them in a larger empty glass enclosure. The animals immediately began to fight with each other, incurring several injuries.

(d) Psychologists make reasonable efforts to minimize the discomfort, infection, illness, and pain of animal subjects. *[No Significant Change, 1992 Standard 6.20f, Care and Use of Animals in Research]*

Species-appropriate housing, sanitary conditions, feeding, regular veterinary check-ups, and development and monitoring of safety conditions during active experimentation should be implemented to protect the health and welfare of animal research subjects. Psychologists and their staff should be alert and competent to detect signs of illness or injury in animal subjects and be able to obtain the immediate and appropriate treatment. When alternative experimental procedures are available, psychologists should select the one that will produce the minimum amount of animal discomfort. The APA Guidelines for Ethical Conduct in the Care and Use of Animals also recommends that whenever possible psychologists should try to provide care and housing that can enrich the psychological well-being of the animal subject.

☑ A psychologist studying cognition in pigeons presented various landmarks and observed the pigeons' use of these cues. During initial testing, the psychologist unexpectedly found that some arrangements caused confusion resulting in minor injuries when several pigeons flew into the landmarks. The psychologist modified these arrangements to protect the animals' safety.

(e) Psychologists use a procedure subjecting animals to pain, stress, or privation only when an alternative procedure is unavailable and the goal is justified by its prospective scientific, educational, or applied value. *[No Significant Change, 1992 Standard 6.20g, Care and Use of Animals in Research]*

Exposing animals to experimentally induced pain or suffering is not ethically justified unless the psychologist can demonstrate that the knowledge produced from experimentation has the clear potential to substantially contribute to science, to teaching about animal behavior or research techniques, or to benefit other animals or humans. Animals should never be subjected to pain, physical or psychological stress, or food deprivation if alternative procedures have equal pedagogical value or can adequately test the research question. When aversive procedures cannot be avoided, psychologists must select the minimal level of pain, stress, or privation necessary to achieve the goals of the research.

☒ An introductory psychology laboratory instructor decided to demonstrate to the class how the phenomenon of learned helplessness is experimentally tested. The demonstration included placing laboratory rats in a cage with an electrified grid and preventing them from escaping when a painful shock was distributed through the grid.

(f) Psychologists perform surgical procedures under appropriate anesthesia and follow techniques to avoid infection and minimize pain during and after surgery. *[No Significant Change, 1992 Standard 6.20h, Care and Use of Animals in Research]*

Research requiring surgery must be conducted by appropriately trained psychologists or other competent personnel using methods that minimize risks of infection and pain. Unless there is a legitimate scientific or medical reason to do otherwise, animals must be anesthetized throughout the surgical procedure. Psychologists are responsible for monitoring postoperative care of research animals using appropriate medications to minimize discomfort and avoid infection. Exposing animals to multiple surgeries as a matter of convenience or to minimize cost is unethical.

☑ Researchers designed a study with rhesus monkeys to test the reinforcing effects of three commonly abused drugs. To enable the animals to reinforce their behavior with the drugs, a catheter was implanted in a jugular vein. The procedure was conducted under an effective anesthesia and aseptic conditions. Monkeys were treated postoperatively with antibiotics for 10 days and with an analgesic for 3 days. Testing was not begun until it was determined that the monkey was in good postoperative health. The investigators also determined that using a within-subjects design could minimize the number of monkeys needed to adequately test the reinforcing properties of the drugs. After the experiment, the catheters were removed under the same careful anesthesia and aseptic conditions and each monkey was given appropriate postoperative care.

(g) When it is appropriate that an animal's life be terminated, psychologists proceed rapidly, with an effort to minimize pain and in accordance with accepted procedures. *[No Significant Change, 1992 Standard 6.20i, Care and Use of Animals in Research]*

Humane or scientific considerations may necessitate terminating the life of animal research subjects when experimental procedures create chronic pain or discomfort that cannot be alleviated through medication or other remedies. Participation sometimes renders an animal unsuitable for future research, and returning it to the wild or giving it a home outside the laboratory is not safe or possible. Other times, autopsies are necessary to validate the efficacy of the surgical technique or to understand physiological processes and structures related to the psychological phenomenon under investigation. When termination is necessary, psychologists must use procedures that are humane, immediate, and appropriate for the species. According to the APA Guidelines for Ethical Conduct in the Care and Use of Animals, termination procedures should be in accordance with procedures of the latest version of the American Veterinary Medical Association Panel on Euthanasia, and disposal of euthanized animals should be consistent with law.

8.10 Reporting Research Results

(a) Psychologists do not fabricate data. (See also Standard 5.01a, Avoidance of False or Deceptive Statements.) *[Modified for Clarity, 1992 Standard 6.21a, Reporting of Results]*

Fraud in research is one of the most serious forms of scientific misconduct because it disrupts the scientific process and dilutes community confidence in the integrity of science. Psychologists do not falsify, make up, alter, or distort the responses of human participants or animal subjects or the results of data analysis. This standard is not limited to published reports and applies to the fabrication of data in journal entries or intentional manipulation of the data collection process itself that would lead to a false report. See Standard 5.01, Avoidance of False or Deceptive Statements, for additional prohibitions against publishing or presenting research findings psychologists know are false.

✗ After conducting planned statistical analyses of the data, a psychologist realized that if the data from just 4 of the 30 participants were eliminated, the statistical analyses would yield significance. The characteristics of these 4 participants met all the original inclusion criteria for the study and there was no deviation in the administration of testing procedures for these individuals. Reasoning that there must be some undetected characteristic responsible for these participants' outlier responses, the psychologist decided to eliminate their data from the analysis. Because there were no criteria other than their responses on which to exclude them, the psychologist decided not to report their elimination in a manuscript submitted for publication.

(b) If psychologists discover significant errors in their published data, they take reasonable steps to correct such errors in a correction, retraction, erratum, or other appropriate publication means. *[No Significant Change, 1992 Standard 6.21b, Reporting of Results]*

The research design, measurement tools, and analytic strategies selected by an investigator may lead to erroneous conclusions based on honest differences in interpretation, chance responding, or extraneous influences that are revealed only when new techniques are used to examine the hypothesis tested. Erroneous conclusions about natural phenomena based on methodologically sound research designs are themselves a natural part of the scientific process and are not unethical. A cornerstone of scientific progress is the process of self-correction in which the validity of results obtained in a single experiment can be confirmed or refuted following replication by others within the scientific community. Accurate reporting of research is essential to this process because it enables others to critique, replicate, dispute, and expand on the methods and interpretations reported.

The purpose of this standard is to safeguard the self-correction process by requiring that psychologists take steps to correct errors in published reports that compromise the readers' ability to replicate the research design or interpret the results because the methodology, data, or statistical analysis was incorrectly described. Informing the journal editor or publisher about the error and requesting a published correction can comply with this standard. The use of the phrase "reasonable steps" recognizes that investigators have limited control over editors or publishers who refuse to publish corrections.

> ☑ Following the publication of an article, a psychologist realized that the *F* values and probability levels in one of the tables had been wrongly transcribed. The psychologist wrote to the editor of the journal requesting that an addendum be published briefly describing the error and informing readers they can obtain the corrected table from the author. The psychologist also placed an addendum page onto all reprints distributed to other investigators.

8.11 Plagiarism

Psychologists do not present portions of another's work or data as their own, even if the other work or data source is cited occasionally. *[Modified for Clarity, 1992 Standard 6.22, Plagiarism]*

Plagiarism is the representation of another person's ideas or words without appropriate credit. A common misconception is that plagiarism is limited to word-for-word replication or paraphrasing of another's written work without appropriate citation. Whereas this form of plagiarism is clearly prohibited, violation of this standard also occurs when a psychologist knowingly presents throughout a publication or formal report another's ideas as his or her own citing the work from which it was drawn in a manner intended to obscure the original author's contribution. (See Standard 5.01, Avoidance of False or Deceptive Statements, for situations in which a psychologist may be in violation of the Ethics Code for appropriating the work of others outside the research or publication context.)

> ✗ In a manuscript submitted for publication, a psychologist used the organization, heading formats, and arguments presented by authors in an article published in an obscure journal. The psychologist cited the original article once in the opening paragraph of the manuscript. Two paragraphs duplicated word-for-word sentences in the original article—and many of the original article's paragraphs were paraphrased. The psychologist added five new references that appeared after the original article was published.

8.12 Publication Credit

(a) Psychologists take responsibility and credit, including authorship credit, only for work they have actually performed or to which they have substantially contributed. (See also Standard 8.12b, Publication Credit.) *[Modified for Clarity, 1992 Standard 6.23a, Publication Credit]*

This standard prohibits psychologists from taking credit for research they did not directly perform or for which they did not make a substantial intellectual contribution. Substantial intellectual contributions include formulating the hypothesis, developing the experimental design, selecting the analytic procedures, interpreting the data, writing the first draft of the article, or providing important intellectual revisions to the manuscript content (APA, 2001). According to this standard, any psychologist listed as an author must take responsibility for the content of the publication. This means that all coauthors must see drafts of the manuscript. In recent years, many scientific journals have required that all authors of a submitted manuscript sign a statement confirming that they contributed to the research and reviewed the written content of the paper.

☒ A junior faculty member asked a nationally recognized senior research psychologist to collaborate on an article based on data that the junior faculty member had collected. The junior member thought that including the accomplished researcher as an author would improve the chances of the manuscript being accepted for publication. The senior psychologist agreed to have his name included and told the junior faculty member that after hearing a description of the writing plan he would not have to read the manuscript before it was submitted for publication.

(b) Principal authorship and other publication credits accurately reflect the relative scientific or professional contributions of the individuals involved, regardless of their relative status. Mere possession of an institutional position, such as department chair, does not justify authorship credit. Minor contributions to the research or to the writing for publications are acknowledged appropriately, such as in footnotes or in an introductory statement. *[No Significant Change, 1992 Standard 6.23b, Publication Credit]*

Principal authorship must reflect the extent to which each individual contributed to the origination of the research problem, the research design, interpretation of results, and drafting of the manuscript. In addition to underscoring the importance of relative contribution as the determining factor for authorship credit, the wording of this standard is intended to protect students and junior faculty or research associates from exploitation by professors, supervisors, or senior administrators who might demand principal authorship based simply on the status of their position. The standard also requires that minor contributions not constituting authorship be acknowledged. Minor contributions include supportive functions such as designing or building the apparatus, suggesting or advising about the statistical analysis, collecting or entering the data, modifying or structuring a computer program, and recruiting participants or obtaining animals (APA, 2001).

☑ A psychologist was the director of a large research center where postdoctoral students were encouraged to apply for young investigator awards listing the director as mentor. The psychologist always commented on drafts of manuscripts that the highly competent postdoctoral students submitted for publication, but had a policy of being included as an author only if she directly contributed to the design, implementation, analysis, data interpretation, or writing.

(c) Except under exceptional circumstances, a student is listed as principal author on any multiple-authored article that is substantially based on the student's doctoral dissertation. Faculty advisors discuss publication credit with students as early as feasible and throughout the research and publication process as appropriate. (See also Standard 8.12b, Publication Credit.) *[Significant Change in Meaning, 1992 Standard 6.23c, Publication Credit]*

This standard recognizes that doctoral work is expected to represent an independent and original contribution devised and conducted largely by the student. Consequently, doctoral students should receive principal authorship on publications substantially based on their dissertation. The rare exception to this standard might occur when a student's doctoral dissertation is published in monograph form as part of a collection of studies by other researchers that cumulatively substantiates a phenomenon or supports or refutes a hypothesis.

Following the publication of the 1992 Ethics Code, there was significant discussion within the academic community regarding the inclusion of "thesis" as a requirement for student principal authorship. In contrast to general agreement regarding the student's primary contribution to his or her dissertation, students conducting master's and undergraduate honors research theses often work within an apprenticeship model distinctly different from the independent work model of the dissertation (Fine & Kurdek, 1993; Fisher & Younggren, 1997). The current standard has eliminated "thesis" from this requirement, recognizing that the apprenticeship model can provide undergraduate- and master's-level students who are just beginning to acquire the theoretical, methodological, statistical, and writing skills necessary to make a primary scientific contribution the opportunity to learn these skills through collaboration on faculty-originated projects.

When honors or master's-level students make the primary contributions to a project, their right to be listed as first author is protected by Standard 8.12b. Standard 8.12c affords additional student protections by requiring that faculty advisors discuss publication credit with students as early as is feasible to provide students an opportunity to evaluate their skills and select the best mentoring experience (apprenticeship vs. independent scholar model) to meet their training needs and expectations for publication credit. Recognizing that research collaboration is a dynamic process in which relative contribution can change over time, research mentors should discuss with students any such changes they observe or anticipate that would affect publication credit at the point at which they emerge. For all student-faculty research collaborations, assignment of principal authorship must follow the rule of relative scientific contribution established in Standard 8.12b.

8.13 Duplicate Publication of Data

Psychologists do not publish, as original data, data that have been previously published. This does not preclude republishing data when they are accompanied by proper acknowledgment. *[No Significant Change, 1992 Standard 6.24, Duplicate Publication of Data]*

Scientific knowledge is based on cumulative evidence of the reliability of observations and relationships among variables tested over time and in different experimental contexts. When psychologists present the same data in different publications without proper acknowledgment, they jeopardize the evolution of scientific knowledge by giving the erroneous impression that replication of results has occurred. Publishing original data in more than one source without proper attribution misrepresents the amount of experimental work the author has actually conducted and in some instances may result in violation of copyright law. This standard does not prohibit psychologists from publishing the same data in different journals or on Web sites for the purpose of reaching different audiences as long as proper citations of the original publication source are provided. Publishing multiple or piecemeal reports of different aspects of a single research project may be unethical without a reasonable theoretical, methodological, or practical justification for doing so. In such cases, investigators should inform the editor of the publication to which the manuscript is submitted about their plans for publishing different parts of the study.

8.14 Sharing Research Data for Verification

(a) After research results are published, psychologists do not withhold the data on which their conclusions are based from other competent professionals who seek to verify the substantive claims through reanalysis and who intend to use such data only for that purpose, provided that the confidentiality of the participants can be protected and unless legal rights concerning proprietary data preclude their release. This does not preclude psychologists from requiring that such individuals or groups be responsible for costs associated with the provision of such information. *[Modified for Clarity, 1992 Standard 6.25, Sharing Data]*

The self-correcting nature of science requires investigators to share research data for the purpose of replication and reanalysis. Such openness protects the integrity of science through independent validation of data coding, analysis, and interpretation. Psychologists should follow appropriate guidelines for retention of data (see also Standard 6.01, Documentation of Professional and Scientific Work and Maintenance of Records). For example, authors of articles published in APA journals are required to have their raw data available for at least 5 years after the date of publication (APA, 2001).

The term "competent professionals" as used in this standard limits the obligation to provide data to individuals competent in the research methods and data analytic techniques necessary to substantiate claims through reanalysis. Psychologists are not required to share data with individuals for purposes of developing and testing new theories or other goals beyond reanalysis and verification of data. The standard recognizes there may be legitimate ethical, legal, and financial barriers to data sharing. In some instances, it may be impossible to de-identify data to adequately protect the confidentiality rights of those who participated in the research. In other instances, a third party who is not a psychologist may own the proprietary rights to the data. To avoid subjecting investigators to financial hardship or harassment, the standard permits psychologists to require that costs of the exchange be borne by the requesting party.

(b) Psychologists who request data from other psychologists to verify the substantive claims through reanalysis may use shared data only for the declared purpose. Requesting psychologists obtain prior written agreement for all other uses of the data. *[New]*

This standard protects the intellectual property rights of the owner of the data by prohibiting the requesting psychologist from piggybacking on the work of another by using the data for any purpose other than reanalysis or to verify substantive claims. The data cannot be used to test related or peripheral hypotheses or to develop new research or analytic techniques unless the psychologist obtains prior written agreement.

> ❎ On the basis of a written request, a psychologist received data from another psychologist to verify through inspection of the data and reanalysis the interpretation of findings stated in a recent publication. After receiving the data, the psychologist realized that there were several additional hypotheses that could be tested with the data set. The psychologist quickly developed an analytic plan and got together a team of graduate students to implement the plan in time to submit the analysis of new hypotheses for presentation at an upcoming professional meeting.

8.15 Reviewers

Psychologists who review material submitted for presentation, publication, grant, or research proposal review respect the confidentiality of and the proprietary rights in such information of those who submitted it. *[Expanded, 1992 Standard 6.26, Professional Reviewers]*

Psychologists are prohibited from using privileged and proprietary information obtained through confidential review of research materials including the review of grant applications and papers submitted for publication or presentation at professional meetings. This standard protects the intellectual property rights of individuals who describe their theories, research designs, and data in unpublished materials from use by others who obtain this information during the peer review process.

☑ A research psychologist on an NIH special emphasis panel was primary reviewer on an R01 grant application addressing a conceptual problem the psychologist had been tackling in her own lab. The psychologist wrote a critical review of the proposal and argued strongly for a score in the unfundable range. Several months later, the principal investigator of the R01 application was distressed to learn that the psychologist had begun a series of studies almost identical to those in the rejected proposal.

CHAPTER 12

Standards on Assessment

9. ASSESSMENT

9.01 Bases for Assessments

(a) Psychologists base the opinions contained in their recommendations, reports, and diagnostic or evaluative statements, including forensic testimony, on information and techniques sufficient to substantiate their findings. (See also Standard 2.04, Bases for Scientific and Professional Judgments.) *[Modified for Clarity/ Behavioral Specificity, 1992 Standard 2.01b, Evaluation, Diagnosis, and Interventions in Professional Context]*

Psychological assessment serves the public good by providing information to guide decisions affecting the well-being of individuals, families, groups, organizations, and institutions. Psychologists who draw their conclusions on information and techniques based in the scientific and professional knowledge of the discipline are uniquely qualified to interpret the results of psychological assessments in ways that merit the public trust. However, the public and the profession are harmed when psychologists provide opinions unsubstantiated by information obtained or drawn from data gathered through improper assessment techniques. Standard 9.01a of the American Psychological Association (APA) Ethics Code (2002) prohibits psychologists from providing written or oral opinions that cannot be sufficiently substantiated by the information obtained or the techniques employed.

The standard is broadly worded to apply to all written and oral professional opinions irrespective of information recipient, setting, or type of assessment.

Information recipient. The standard prohibits unfounded professional opinions offered to, among others, (1) individual clients/patients or their representatives; (2) other professionals; (3) third-party payors; (4) administrative and professional staff at schools, hospitals, and other institutions; (5) businesses, agencies, and other organizations; (6) the courts; (7) the military or other governing legal authorities; and (8) callers to talk-radio programs or those interacting with psychologists through other media.

Setting. Standard 9.01a applies to (1) diagnostic opinions offered orally in the office of a private practitioner; (2) written reports provided to clients/patients, other practitioners, or third-party payors through the mail, the Internet, or other forms of electronic transmission; (3) testimony provided in the courts; and (4) opinions about an individual's mental health offered over the Internet, radio, television, or other electronic media.

Types of assessment. The standard pertains to all unfounded opinions claiming to be based on any form of evaluation including but not limited to (1) standardized psychological, educational, or neuropsychological tests; (2) diagnostic information gained through clinical interviews; (3) collateral data obtained through discussions with family members, teachers, employee supervisors, or other informants; (4) observational techniques; or (5) brief discussion or correspondence with an individual via radio, television, telephone, or the Internet.

Violations of this standard are often related to failure to comply with other standards including Standards 2.04, Bases for Scientific and Professional Judgments; 9.01b, Bases for Assessments; and 9.02b, Use of Assessments. Below are examples of opinions based on insufficient information or techniques that would be considered violations under this standard:

☒ Testifying on the validity of a child abuse allegation based on the results of an idiosyncratic, improperly constructed parent checklist of child behaviors

☒ Diagnosing an adult with impaired decisional capacity as mentally retarded without taking a developmental history

☒ Providing preemployment recommendations on the basis of a personality test with no proven relationship to job performance

☒ Submitting a diagnosis of neurological impairment to a health insurance company based solely on information derived during therapy sessions

☒ Informing parents that their preschooler is autistic on the basis of a single observational session

☒ Recommending a child for special education placement solely on the basis of scores on a standardized intelligence test

☒ Offering a diagnosis of post-traumatic stress disorder based on a 5-minute discussion with a listener to a radio program hosted by the psychologist

---

(b) Except as noted in 9.01c, psychologists provide opinions of the psychological characteristics of individuals only after they have conducted an examination of the individuals adequate to support their statements or conclusions. When, despite reasonable efforts, such an examination is not practical, psychologists document the efforts they made and the result of those efforts, clarify the probable impact of their limited information on the reliability and validity of their opinions, and appropriately limit the nature and extent of their conclusions or recommendations. (See also Standards 2.01, Boundaries of Competence, and 9.06, Interpreting Assessment Results.) *[Expanded, 1992 Standard 7.02b 7.02c, Forensic Assessments]*

Standard 9.01b specifically addresses the importance of in-person evaluations of individuals about whom psychologists will offer a professional opinion. Under this standard, with few exceptions psychologists must conduct individual examinations sufficient to obtain personal verification of information on which to base their professional opinions and refrain from providing opinions about the psychological characteristics of an individual if they themselves have not conducted an examination of the individual adequate to support their statements or conclusions.

> ☒ A psychologist testified about a parent's psychological fitness for visitation rights drawing his opinion solely from comments made by the child and divorced spouse in the absence of an individual examination of the parent.
>
> ☒ A psychologist contracted by an insurance company to evaluate an individual's mental health as part of a current disability claim provided an opinion based solely on job performance evaluations written by the insured's immediate supervisors and diagnostic information collected by another psychologist prior to the incident cited in the claim.
>
> ☒ A psychologist working in a correctional facility who was asked to recommend whether a prison guard's mental status was a risk to prisoner protections did not personally exam the guard but instead gave an opinion based on reports by facility administrators, staff, and prisoners.

Standard 9.01b also recognizes that in some cases a personal examination may not be possible. For example, an individual involved in a child custody suit, a disability claim, or performance evaluation may refuse or because of relocation or other reasons be unavailable for a personal examination. The standard requires that psychologists make "reasonable efforts" to conduct a personal examination. Efforts that would not be considered reasonable in the prevailing professional judgment of psychologists engaged in similar activities would be considered a violation of this standard. Consider the following two examples of potential violations:

> ☒ A psychologist was contracted by a prison to evaluate the job potential of guards hired for a probationary period. Without conducting an individual interview, the psychologist

wrote a report concluding that one job candidate's emotional instability made him ineligible for full-time employment. The psychologist justified the lack of a personal examination on the fact that several coworkers claimed the guard was too dangerous to interview.

☒ A psychologist hired by the attorney of a husband engaged in a custody suit provided court testimony on the wife's parenting inadequacies without having interviewed her personally. The psychologist claimed the wife did not respond to the psychologist's letter requesting the interview. On cross-examination, it was revealed that the letter written by the psychologist included the following language seemingly designed to discourage agreement to be examined: "I have reason to believe from interviews with your spouse and an examination of your children that you are responsible for the children's current mental health problems and would like to conduct an examination to confirm or dispute these assumptions."

When, despite reasonable efforts, a personal interview is not feasible, under Standard 9.01b psychologists in their written or oral opinions must document and explain the results of their efforts, clarify the probable impact failure to personally examine an individual may have on the reliability and validity of their opinions, and appropriately limit their conclusions or recommendations to information they can personally verify. For example:

☑ A court-appointed psychologist attempted to contact the biological parent of a child currently in foster care to make recommendations regarding parental visitation. The parent was no longer at the last known residence and had not left a forwarding address. In testimony, the psychologist described the current mental health status of the child, the child's statements regarding the biological parent, and the observed relationship between the child and foster parents. In referring to the biological parent, the psychologist informed the court of efforts to contact the parent, described how failure to interview the parent limited any conclusions that could be drawn regarding the parent's psychological characteristics and parenting competence, and clarified that recommendations regarding visitation were based on the child's attitudes, mental health, and foster care arrangements.

(c) When psychologists conduct a record review or provide consultation or supervision and an individual examination is not warranted or necessary for the opinion, psychologists explain this and the sources of information on which they based their conclusions and recommendations. *[New]*

This standard applies to those assessment-related activities for which an individual examination is not warranted or necessary for the psychological opinion. Such activities include record or file reviews where psychologists are called on to review preexisting records and reports to assist or evaluate decisions made by schools, courts, health insurance companies, organizations, or other psychologists they supervise or with whom they consult. Record reviews can be performed to (1) determine whether a previously conducted assessment was appropriate or sufficient; (2) evaluate the appropriateness of treatment, placement, employment, or the continuation of benefits based on the previously gathered information and reports; (3) adjudicate a disability or professional liability claim based on existing records; or (4) resolve conflicts over the applicability of records to interpretations of federal and state laws in administrative law or due process hearings (Hadjistavropoulos & Bieling, 2001; Krivacska & Margolis, 1995).

According to Standard 9.01c, psychologists who provide such services must clarify to the appropriate parties the source of the information on which the opinion is based and why an individual interview conducted by the psychologist is not necessary for the opinion.

Simply complying with this standard may not be sufficient for psychologists who are in supervisory roles that carry legal responsibility for the conduct of assessments by unlicensed supervisees or employees. In many of those instances, psychologists may be directly responsible for ensuring that individuals are qualified to conduct the assessments and do so competently (see Standard 2.05, Delegation of Work to Others).

9.02 Use of Assessments

(a) Psychologists administer, adapt, score, interpret, or use assessment techniques, interviews, tests, or instruments in a manner and for purposes that are appropriate in light of the research on or evidence of the usefulness and proper application of the techniques. *[Expanded, 1992 Standard 2.02a, Competence and Appropriate Use of Assessments and Interventions]*

The appropriate use of psychological assessments can benefit individuals, families, organizations, and society by providing information on which educational placements, mental health treatments, health insurance coverage, employee selection, job placement, workers' compensation, program development, legal decisions, and government policies can be based. The inappropriate use of assessments can lead to harmful diagnostic, educational, institutional, legal, and social policy decisions based on inaccurate and misleading information.

Standard 9.02a is concerned with the proper selection, interpretation, scoring, and administration of assessments. It refers to the full range of assessment techniques used by psychologists including interviews and standardized tests administered in person, through the Internet, or other media. According to this standard, ethical justification for the use of assessments is determined by research on or evidence supporting the purpose for which the test is administered, the method of administration, and

interpretation of scores. To comply with the standard, psychologists should be familiar with the data and other information provided in test manuals detailing (1) theoretical and empirical support for test use for specific purposes and populations, (2) administration procedures, and (3) how test scores are to be calculated and interpreted. Psychologists should also keep apprised of ongoing research or evidence of a test's usefulness or obsolescence over time (see also Standards 2.03, Maintaining Competence; 2.04, Basis for Scientific and Professional Judgments; and 9.08b, Obsolete Tests and Outdated Test Results).

Violations of this standard occur when psychologists use assessments in a manner or for a purpose that is not supported by evidence in the field.

❌ A psychologist contracted to conduct employment testing for an organization administered a series of personality inventories with little or no validity evidence supporting the link between scores on the inventories and actual job performance.

❌ A counseling psychologist working with an isolated rural community administered a series of tests over the Internet without previously establishing whether the Internet-mediated scores measure the same construct as scores from the paper-and-pencil version (Buchanan, 2002).

❌ A school psychologist working under pressure to meet the school system's quotas for weekly testing gave the same battery of tests to all students irrespective of their grade level or presenting problem.

❌ A neuropsychologist conducted a forensic examination of a prisoner in a room occupied by other prisoners thereby compromising the validity of score interpretation based on norms established under standardized distraction-free testing environments.

❌ A psychologist who had just obtained prescription privileges prescribed for an elderly client a medication for depression based solely on the administration of a self-report depression inventory.

Test administration for individuals with disabilities may require modifications and adaptations in testing administration to minimize the effect of test-taker characteristics incidental to the purpose of the assessment. Standard 9.02a permits departure from a standard administration protocol if the method of test adaptation can be justified by research or other evidence. For example, converting a written test to Braille for a blind individual, physically assisting a client with cerebral palsy to circle items on a written test, or providing breaks for an individual with a disability associated with

prior to selecting, administering, or interpreting tests, psychologists must consider both the language preference and language competence of the testee.

Whereas the inappropriateness of English-only-based psychological testing is obvious when testees speak little or no English, the hazards of English-only testing for bilingual persons or oral-language-only assessment of persons with hearing disabilities who can read lips and communicate in sign language are often overlooked. The linguistic competencies of individuals who are bilingual often vary with the mode of communication (e.g., oral vs. written language), language function (e.g., social, educational, or job related), and topical domain (e.g., science, mathematics, interpersonal relationships, self-evaluations). In addition, individuals' language preferences do not always reflect their language competence. Individuals may be embarrassed to reveal that their English or oral language is poor, believe non-English or nonhearing testing will negatively affect their evaluations, or misjudge their language proficiency.

The Standards for Educational and Psychological Testing (AERA, APA, and NCME, 1999) recommend a number of steps that can help psychologists comply with Standard 9.02c:

☑ Psychologists can use language tests that assess multiple language domains to determine language dominance and proficiency relevant to different modes of assessment (e.g., written, oral) and topics (e.g., academic, interpersonal).

☑ Whenever possible, psychologists should use test translations that have been developed according to accepted methods of test construction (see Standard 9.05, Test Construction). For example, the Standards for Educational and Psychological Testing recommend the use of an iterative process more akin to test construction and validation rather than sole reliance on back translation (translating the translation of the test back into the original language).

☑ Additional testing or observation may be necessary to determine whether what appears to be eccentric behavior (e.g., short phrases or reticence in response to test questions) reflects differences in cultural communication styles or an individual characteristic.

☑ To the extent feasible, psychologists must ensure the language competence of the test administrator (see also Standards 2.05, Delegation of Work to Others, and 9.03c, Informed Consent in Assessments).

☑ When interpreting assessment results, test norms for native speakers of English should not be used for individuals for whom English is a second language or should be interpreted in part as reflecting level of English proficiency.

There are instances where proficiency in English or another language is essential to the goal of the assessment. For example, the ability to communicate with English-speaking employees may be a necessary qualification for a successful applicant for a personnel position. Evaluating a student's English proficiency may be necessary to determine appropriate educational placement. The ability to read and speak English may be important to certain service positions responsible for protecting public health, safety, and welfare (AERA, APA, and NCME, 1999). Inclusion of the phrase "unless the use of an alternative language is relevant to the assessment issues" indicates that Standard 9.02c permits psychologists to use tests in a language in which the testee may not be proficient, if effective job performance, school placement, or other goals of assessment require the ability to communicate in that language.

9.03 Informed Consent in Assessments

(a) Psychologists obtain informed consent for assessments, evaluations, or diagnostic services, as described in Standard 3.10, Informed Consent, except when (1) testing is mandated by law or governmental regulations; (2) informed consent is implied because testing is conducted as a routine educational, institutional, or organizational activity (e.g., when participants voluntarily agree to assessment when applying for a job); or (3) one purpose of the testing is to evaluate decisional capacity. Informed consent includes an explanation of the nature and purpose of the assessment, fees, involvement of third parties, and limits of confidentiality and sufficient opportunity for the client/patient to ask questions and receive answers. *[New]*

To comply with this standard, with few exceptions psychologists must obtain and document written or oral consent in the manner set forth in Standard 3.10, Informed Consent. Psychologists must provide individuals who will be assessed, and when appropriate their legal guardians, a clear explanation of the nature and purpose of the assessment, fees, involvement of third parties, and the limits of confidentiality.

Core Elements of Informed Consent in Assessments

Nature of the assessment. The *nature* of an assessment refers to (1) the general category of the assessment (e.g., personality, psychopathology, competency, parenting skills, neuropsychological abilities and deficits, employment skills, developmental disabilities), (2) procedures and testing format (e.g., oral interviews, written self-report checklists, behavioral observation, skills assessment), and (3) duration of the assessment (e.g., hours or multiple assessments).

Purpose of the assessment. The *purpose* of the assessment refers to its potential use, for example, in employment decisions, school placement, custody decisions, disability benefits, treatment decisions, and plans for or evaluation of rehabilitation of criminal offenders.

Fees. Discussion of *fees* must include the cost of the assessment and payment schedule and should be consistent with requirements of Standard 6.04, Fees and Financial Arrangements. When applicable and to the extent feasible, psychologists must also discuss with relevant parties the extent to which their services will be covered by the individual's health plan, school district, employer, or others (see Standards 6.04a and d, Fees and Financial Arrangements).

Third parties. Involvement of *third parties* refers to other individuals (e.g., legal guardians), health maintenance organizations (HMOs), employers, organizations, or legal or other governing authorities that have requested the assessment and to whom the results of the assessments will be provided. Psychologists should be familiar with ethical standards, state law, and federal regulations relevant to the appropriate role of third parties and the release and documentation of release of such information to others (see Standard 4.05, Disclosures). Psychologists asked to evaluate a child by one parent should clarify custody issues to determine if another parent must give permission.

Confidentiality. Informed consent to assessments must provide a clear explanation of the extent and limits of *confidentiality,* including (1) when the psychologist must comply with reporting requirements such as mandated child abuse reporting or duty-to-warn laws and (2) in the case of assessments involving minors, guardian access to records (see discussion of parental access involving HIPAA, FERPA, and other regulations in Standards 4.01, Maintaining Confidentiality; 4.02; Discussing the Limits of Confidentiality; and 3.10, Informed Consent). Psychologists who administer assessments over the Internet must inform clients/patients, research participants, or others about the procedures that will be used to protect confidentiality and the threats to confidentiality unique to this form of electronic transmission of information (see also Standard 4.02c, Discussing the Limits of Confidentiality).

Implications of HIPAA for Confidentiality-Relevant Information

To effectively provide information relevant to confidentiality during informed consent as required in Standard 9.03a, psychologists who will be electronically recording, storing, or disseminating to third parties protected health information (PHI) gathered during an assessment need to be familiar with the Health Insurance Portability and Accountability Act of 1996 (HIPAA; http://www.hhs.gov/ocr/hipaa/finalreg.html). PHI is defined as any information transmitted or maintained in any form or medium relating to the past, present, or future physical or mental health condition, provision of care, or payment for provision of care for an individual that either identifies or can be used to identify the individual (45 CFR 160.102). Not all psychologists who are administering or using assessments are covered entities under HIPAA. A covered entity is a (a) health plan, (b) health care clearinghouse, or (c) health care provider who transmits any health information in electronic form in connection with a financial or administrative transaction. HIPAA regulations apply to a psychologist's practice and not to individual clients/patients. Therefore, psychologists who are covered entities as that relates to a single client/patient must comply with HIPAA regulations for all their clients/patients.

The HIPAA regulation most relevant to informed consent in assessments is the Notice of Privacy Practices. At the beginning of the professional relationship, covered entities must provide clients/patients a written document detailing routine uses and disclosures of PHI and the individual's rights and the covered entities' legal duties with respect to PHI (45 CFR 164.520). Psychologists conducting assessments should also be familiar with HIPAA-compliant authorization forms for use and release of PHI and HIPAA requirements for Accounting of Disclosures. These regulations are described in greater detail in the section "A Word About HIPAA" in the Preface of this book and in discussions of Standard 3.10, Informed Consent, in Chapter 6; Standards 4.01, Maintaining Confidentiality, and 4.05, Disclosures, in Chapter 7; Standard 6.01, Documentation of Professional and Scientific Work and Maintenance of Records, in Chapter 9; and Standard 9.04, Release of Test Data, in this chapter. Psychologists conducting assessments may wish to use the HIPAA-compliant model forms developed by the APA Insurance Trust (APAIT) and the APA Practice Directorate (www.apa.org/apait).

Dispensing With Informed Consent

Under Standard 9.03a, informed consent may be waived when consent is implied because testing is conducted as (1) a routine educational activity, such as end-of-term reading or math achievement testing in elementary and high schools; (2) regular institutional activities, such as student and teaching evaluations in academic institutions or consumer satisfaction questionnaires in hospitals or social service agencies; or (3) organizational activity, such as when individuals voluntarily agree to preemployment testing when applying for a job.

Standard 9.03a permits psychologists to dispense with informed consent in assessment when testing is mandated by law or other governing legal authority or when one purpose of testing is to determine the capacity of the individual to give consent. Ethical steps that must be taken in these contexts are discussed next under Standard 9.03b.

(b) Psychologists inform persons with questionable capacity to consent or for whom testing is mandated by law or governmental regulations about the nature and purpose of the proposed assessment services, using language that is reasonably understandable to the person being assessed. *[New]*

Under Standards 3.10b, Informed Consent, and 9.03a, Informed Consent in Assessments, informed consent in assessment is not required when an individual has been determined to be legally incapable of giving informed consent, when testing is mandated by law or other governing legal authority, or when one purpose of testing is to determine consent capacity. These waivers reflect the fact that the term "consent" refers to a person's legal status to make autonomous decisions based on age, mental capacity, or the legal decision under consideration. Consistent with the moral value of respect for the dignity and worth of all persons articulated in Principle E: Respect for People's Rights and Dignity, under Standard 9.03c psychologists must provide all individuals irrespective of their legal status appropriate explanations of the nature and purpose of the proposed assessment.

Standard 9.03a often applies in situations where assessment is requested by parents of children under 18 years or family members of adults with suspected cognitive impairments. In these situations, the psychologist must provide assent information in a language and at a language level that is reasonably understandable to the child or adult being assessed. When both guardian consent and child assent are sought, psychologists working with populations for whom English is not a first language should be alert to situations in which prospective clients/patients and their legal guardians may have different language preferences and proficiencies.

Psychologists conducting forensic, military, or other assessments that have been legally mandated should explain to the person being tested the nature and purpose of the testing, who has requested the testing, and who will receive copies of the report. APAIT provides a useful sample of a Forensic Informed Consent Contract developed by Jeffrey Younggren, Eric Harris, and Bruce Bennett (www.apa.org/apait).

(c) Psychologists using the services of an interpreter obtain informed consent from the client/patient to use that interpreter, ensure that confidentiality of test results and test security are maintained, and include in their recommendations, reports, and diagnostic or evaluative statements, including forensic testimony, discussion of any limitations on the data obtained. (See also Standards 2.05, Delegation of Work to Others; 4.01, Maintaining Confidentiality; 9.01, Bases for Assessments; 9.06, Interpreting Assessment Results; and 9.07, Assessment by Unqualified Persons.) *[New]*

Compliance with the consent requirements outlined in Standard 3.10 obligates psychologists to provide information in a language and at a language level that are reasonably understandable to the client/patient and where applicable his or her legally authorized representative. Psychologists may use the services of an interpreter when they do not possess the skills to obtain consent in the language in which the client/patient is proficient.

When delegating informed consent responsibilities to an interpreter, psychologists must ensure not only that the interpreter is competent in the consent relevant language (see Standard 2.05, Delegation of Work to Others) but that the interpreter understands and complies with procedures necessary to protect the confidentiality of test results and test security. An interpreter who revealed the identity of a client/patient or the nature of specific test items used during the assessment would place the psychologist who hired the interpreter in potential violation of this standard.

Because test validity and reliability may be vulnerable to errors in interpretation, Standard 9.03c also requires that the involvement of the interpreter and any related limitations on the data obtained be clearly indicated and discussed in any assessment-based report, recommendation, diagnostic or evaluative statement, or forensic testimony.

9.04 Release of Test Data

(a) The term *test data* refers to raw and scaled scores, client/patient responses to test questions or stimuli, and psychologists' notes and recordings concerning client/patient statements and behavior during an examination. Those portions of test materials that include client/patient responses are included in the definition of *test data*. Pursuant to a client/patient release, psychologists provide test data to the client/patient or other persons identified in the release. Psychologists may refrain from releasing test data to protect a client/patient or others from substantial harm or misuse or misrepresentation of the data or the test, recognizing that in many instances release of confidential information under these circumstances is regulated by law. (See also Standard 9.11, Maintaining Test Security.) *[Significant Change in Meaning, 1992 Standard 2.02b, Competence and Appropriate Use of Assessments and Interventions]*

This standard reflects perhaps the most significant shift in ethical requirements from the 1992 Ethics Code to the current version. The 1992 code included reference to the release of "raw test data" within a standard broadly prohibiting the misuse of assessment techniques, results, or interpretations by psychologists and others not qualified to use such information (Standard 2.02b, Competence and Appropriate Use of Assessments and Interventions; APA, 1992). The older standard required psychologists to refrain "from releasing raw test results or raw data to persons, other than to patients and clients as appropriate, who are not qualified to use such information." This standard produced numerous member requests to the APA Ethics Office and the APA Committee on Legal Issues (COLI) for guidance regarding (a) the nature of test responses and materials defined as "raw test results" or "raw data"; (b) appropriate conditions for the release of such data to clients/patients; (c) how to determine whether another professional was qualified to use such information; and (d) how to respond to attorney requests, subpoenas, and court orders. Standard 9.04a of the 2002 Ethics Code was crafted to provide increased clarity of terms, reflect the evolving relationship between psychology and law, and take into account new state and federal laws governing individual rights to health records.

Definition of Test Data

In Standard 9.04a, the term "test data" refers to the client's/patient's actual responses to test items, the raw or scaled scores such responses receive, and a psychologist's written notes or recordings of the client's/patient's specific responses or behaviors during the testing. The term "notes" in this standard is limited to the assessment context and does not include psychotherapy notes documenting or analyzing the contents of conversation during a private counseling session.

Test data and test materials. Recognizing that availability of test questions and scoring criteria may compromise the validity of a test for future use with a client/patient or other individuals exposed to the information, Standard 9.04a distinguishes "test data," which under most circumstances must be provided upon a client/patient release, from "test materials," which under most circumstances should not (see Standard 9.11, Maintaining Test Security). The definition of "test data" does *not* include test manuals, protocols for administering or scoring responses, or test items *unless* these materials include the client's/patient's responses or scores or the psychologist's contemporaneous notes on the client's/patient's testing responses or behaviors. If testing protocols allow, it is good practice for psychologists to record client/patient responses on a form separated from the test items themselves to ensure that upon client/patient request only the test data and not the test material itself need be released.

The Affirmative Duty to Provide Test Data to Clients/Patients and Others Identified in a Client's/Patient's Release

Release to clients/patients. Under Standard 9.04a, psychologists have an affirmative duty to provide test data as defined above to the client/patient or other persons identified in a client/patient release. The obligation set forth by Standard 9.04a to respect clients'/patients' right to their test data is consistent with legal trends toward greater patient autonomy and the self-determination rights of clients/patients as set forth in Principle E: Respect for People's Rights and Dignity. Although not explicitly stated in the standard, it is always good practice for psychologists to have a signed release or authorization from the client/patient even if the data are to be given directly to the client/patient. This standard does not preclude psychologists from discussing with a client/patient the potential for misuse of the information by individuals unqualified to interpret it.

Release to others. The requirement to provide test data to any person identified in a client/patient release is also in sharp contrast to the 1992 Ethics Code's prohibition against release to persons unqualified to use such information. The rationale for eliminating this prohibition was influenced by several factors. First, whether a person is qualified to use test data is determined by the context of the proposed use. For example, restricting release of test data to individuals with advanced degrees or licensure in professional psychology would preclude other qualified health care professionals from using the information. Broadening the definition of "qualified" person to health professionals might jeopardize appropriate judicial scrutiny of psychological tests and a client's/patient's right to the discovery process to challenge their use in court. Second, even if a consensus of "qualified" person could be achieved, requiring a psychologist to confirm the education, training, degrees, or certifications of other professionals would pose burdens that might not be possible or feasible to meet.

Third, as described below, HIPAA regulations require that covered entities provide clients/patients and their personal representatives access to PHI.

Withholding Test Data

Standard 9.04a permits psychologists to withhold test data to protect the client/patient or another individual from substantial harm. The standard also permits withholding test data to protect misuse or misrepresentation of the data or the test. Before refusing to release test data under this clause, psychologists should carefully consider the proviso that such decisions may be regulated by law.

Organizations, courts, and government agencies. The use of the term "client/patient" in this standard refers to the individual testee and not to an organizational client. This standard does not require industrial-organizational or consulting psychologists to release test data to either an organizational client or an employee when testing is conducted to evaluate job candidacy or employee or organization effectiveness and does not assess factors directly related to medical or mental health conditions or services. Psychologists working in these contexts would not be required to provide the test data to the employees themselves under this standard, because the organization, not the employee, is the client (see also Standard 3.07, Third-Party Requests for Services; 3.11, Psychological Services Delivered To or Through Organizations; and 9.03, Informed Consent in Assessments). Similarly, forensic psychologists, military psychologists, and others working under governing legal authority are permitted by the Ethics Code to withhold release of test data from a testee when the client is an attorney, the court, or other governing legal authority. Finally, all psychologists are permitted by the Ethics Code to withhold release of test data when required by law (Standard 1.02, Conflicts Between Ethics and Law, Regulations, or Other Governing Legal Authority).

Implications of HIPAA. Requiring psychologists to release test data to the client/patient or others pursuant to a client/patient release reflects a sea change in the legal landscape from paternalistic to autonomy-based rules governing access to health records. In particular, HIPAA establishes the right of access of individuals to inspect and receive copies of medical and billing records maintained and used by the provider for decisions about the client/patient (45 CFR 524). This requirement does not include psychotherapy notes or information compiled in reasonable anticipation of or use in civil, criminal, or administrative actions or proceedings. In addition, psychologists who are covered entities under HIPAA must also provide such access to a client's/patient's personal representative (45 CFR 164.502[g][1]).

HIPAA severely limits the ability of covered entities to use professional judgment to determine the appropriateness of release of test data to clients/patients and their personal representatives. For example, the right of clients/patients to obtain their own test data under HIPAA regulations means in practice that they can pass it on to other individuals of their choice. Thus, requiring psychologists to deny a request from a client/patient to release information to other persons in essence becomes an ineffective and burdensome obligation.

HIPAA and withholding test data. Standard 9.04a permits psychologists to withhold test data to protect the client/patient or another individual from substantial harm or to protect misuse or misrepresentation of the data or the test, with the proviso that in many instances these decisions may be constrained by law. Under HIPAA, psychologists who are covered entities can deny client/patient access to test data only if it is reasonably likely to endanger the life or physical safety of the individual or another person or in some cases likely to cause equally substantial harm. In addition, psychologists must allow clients/patients the right to have the denial reviewed by a designated licensed health care professional. HIPAA regulations thus severely limit psychologists' ability to exercise their professional judgment as to what constitutes substantial harm to clients/patients.

In addition, HIPAA does not recognize the protection of test materials (e.g., test security) as a legitimate reason to withhold test data that meets the HIPAA definition of PHI and is appropriately requested by a client/patient. There are instances, however, where HIPAA constraints are not at issue. For example, HIPAA does not require release of PHI to clients in situations in which information is compiled in reasonable anticipation of, or for use in, civil, criminal, or administrative actions or proceedings. In other instances, such as certain educational evaluations, test data may not come under the PHI classification and thus the HIPAA Privacy Rule would not apply (see Standard 4.01, Maintaining Confidentiality).

(b) In the absence of a client/patient release, psychologists provide test data only as required by law or court order. *[New]*

Standard 9.04b recognizes the clients'/patients' right to expect that in the absence of their release or authorization, psychologists will protect the confidentiality of test data. The standard does permit psychologists to disclose test data without the consent of the client/patient in response to a court order (including subpoenas that are court ordered) or in other situations required by law (e.g., an order from an administrative tribunal). In such instances, psychologists are wise to seek legal counsel to determine their legal responsibility to respond to the request (see also Standard 4.05b, Disclosures). Psychologists may also ask the court or other legal authority for a protective order to prevent the inappropriate disclosure of confidential information or suggest that the information be submitted to another psychologist for qualified review.

Implications of HIPAA. Standard 9.04b provides stricter protection of confidential test data than HIPAA. Under the HIPAA Privacy Rule, PHI may be disclosed in response to a subpoena, discovery request, or other lawful process that is not accompanied by an order of a court or administrative tribunal, if the covered entity receives satisfactory assurance from the party seeking the information either that reasonable efforts have been made to ensure that the client/patient has been notified of the request or reasonable efforts have been made to secure a qualified protective order (45 CFR 164.512[e][1]). Psychologists who disclosed information in such an instance would be in violation of 9.04b. The greater protection provided by 9.04b is consistent with most states' more stringent psychotherapist-patient privilege communication statutes.

9.05 Test Construction

Psychologists who develop tests and other assessment techniques use appropriate psychometric procedures and current scientific or professional knowledge for test design, standardization, validation, reduction or elimination of bias, and recommendations for use. *[Modified for Clarity, 1992 Standard 2.03, Test Construction]*

Test development is the foundation of good psychological assessment. Psychologists who construct assessment techniques must be familiar with and apply psychometric methods for establishing the validity and reliability of tests, developing standardized administration instructions, selecting items that reduce or eliminate bias, and drawing on current scientific or professional knowledge for recommendations about the use of test results (see also Standard 2.01, Boundaries of Competence).

Standard 9.05 applies to all test development activities, not just those implemented in professional testing services or research settings. Psychologists who develop tests or other assessment techniques to serve private practice clients/patients, organizational clients, or the courts can violate this standard if they fail to use proper psychometric methods for test construction.

Psychometric Procedures

To be in compliance with Standard 9.05, psychologists must be familiar with and competent to implement appropriate psychometric procedures to establish the usefulness of the test (Standard 2.01, Boundaries of Competence). A good resource for complying with this standard in the Ethics Code is the Standards for Educational and Psychological Testing (AERA, APA, and NCME, 1999). Below are brief definitions of psychometric procedures presented in greater detail by AERA, APA, and NCME.

Validity, reliability, and standardization. Validity is the degree to which theory and empirical evidence support specific interpretations of test scores. Methods for establishing test validity include content, concurrent, construct, and predictive validity as well as evidence-based response processes, internal structure of a test, and consequences of testing. *Reliability* is the degree to which test scores for a group of test takers are consistent over repeated administrations of a test or for items within a test.

Methods for establishing test reliability include internal consistency coefficients, analysis of the standard error of measure, test-retest, split-half, or alternative form comparisons. *Standardization* refers to the establishment of scoring norms based on the test performance of a representative sample of individuals from populations for which the test is intended.

Validity and reliability must be appropriately assessed for each total score, subscore, or combination of scores that will be interpreted. Where relevant, descriptions of the test to users, school personnel, organizational clients, and the courts should include a description of the psychometric procedures used during test development.

> ❎ Over the years, a school psychologist had observed that students who had been removed from their homes because of child abuse or neglect frequently gave a set of common and unique narrative responses to items on the Wechsler Intelligence Scale for Children (WISC; Wechsler, 1991) Comprehension subtest. Cognizant of school psychologists' legal duty to report suspected child abuse, she constructed a test composed of 10 narrative statements she believed were typical of abused and neglected children. She developed a scoring system where 0-1 indicated that the child was probably not abused or neglected, 2-3 suggested that the child should be further observed, and 4-10 supported a suspicion of child abuse or neglect that should be reported to child protective services. She began to use the scale to decide whether to make a report of child abuse. When she became district supervisor of psychological and social services, she required all school psychologists and social workers to administer the scale to children with whom they worked despite the lack of evidence of its validity.

Reduction or elimination of test bias. *Test bias* may refer to systematic errors in test scoring. The term is more frequently associated with test fairness and refers to assessment norms applied to persons from different populations that fail to establish measurement equivalence: the degree to which reliability and validity coefficients associated with a measure are similar across populations. Depending on the purpose and nature of testing, failure to determine item, functional, scalar, or predictive measurement equivalence when developing a test can lead to over- or underdiagnosis, faulty personnel recommendations, inappropriate educational placements, and misinformation to the courts (AERA, APA, and NCME, 1999; Knight & Hill, 1998).

> ❎ An industrial-organizational psychologist developed a prescreening employment test for a large personnel department. After demonstrating high levels of interitem and test-retest reliability, the scale was touted as a culture-free measure of employment preparedness. However, the psychologist did not examine whether the factor structure,

> predictive validity of the test for job performance, or other psychometric factors were equivalent across the major ethnic/cultural groups in the city who applied for positions in the company.

Recommendations for Use

In their recommendations for use, test developers must provide adequate guidance to allow users to administer tests in a standardized fashion and score and interpret responses according to established criteria. Psychologists who develop tests or assessment techniques must provide explanations of the meaning and intended interpretation of reported scores to users, school personnel, organizational clients, the courts, and others as appropriate. For example, score interpretation can be facilitated through norm-referenced and criterion-referenced scoring, scaling, or cut scores.

> **☒** A psychologist working for a test company was responsible for developing a test for premorbid speech and language predictors of childhood-onset schizophrenia. Child inpatients who had already been diagnosed with schizophrenia were the only population available for test development. The test yielded good test-retest reliability and was validated on correlations with practitioner diagnoses of childhood schizophrenia. In writing the test manual, the psychologist described the test as useful for identifying children at risk for the disorder. The manual did not indicate that test norms were applicable only to inpatients who had already manifested the disorder.

Test Revisions

Once tests have been developed, test developers are responsible for monitoring conditions that might warrant test revision, modifications in recommendations for test interpretation, or limitations or withdrawal of test use. According to the Standards for Educational and Psychological Testing, tests "should be amended or revised when new research data, significant changes in the domain represented, or newly recommended conditions of test use may lower the validity of test score interpretations" (AERA, APA, and NCME, 1999, Standard 3.25, p. 48). The scope of test revision will depend on the conditions warranting change and may include revisions in test stimuli, administration procedures, scales or units of measure, norms or psychometric features, or applications (Butcher, 2000).

> **☒** A test company sold a popular test to help determine cognitive decline in newly admitted nursing home patients. The test had been used for more than 15 years. During the

past 5 years, the psychologist directing the geropsychological test department of the company had been getting complaints that patients were being underdiagnosed. The psychologist reasoned that the test norms established 15 years ago might not be applicable to a better-educated cohort of elderly persons. However, the company's current 5-year plan focused on the development of new depression inventories and had no budget for revisions of current tests. The psychologists decided not to rock the boat and to wait for the next 5-year plan to recommend a revision of the test.

9.06 Interpreting Assessment Results

When interpreting assessment results, including automated interpretations, psychologists take into account the purpose of the assessment as well as the various test factors, test-taking abilities, and other characteristics of the person being assessed, such as situational, personal, linguistic, and cultural differences, that might affect psychologists' judgments or reduce the accuracy of their interpretations. They indicate any significant limitations of their interpretations. (See also Standards 2.01b and c, Boundaries of Competence, and 3.01, Unfair Discrimination.) *[Expanded, 1992 Standard 2.05, Interpreting Assessment Results]*

Accurate interpretations of assessment results are critical to ensure that appropriate decisions are made regarding an individual's diagnosis, treatment plan, legal status, educational placement, or employment and promotion opportunities. It is ethically imperative that when providing interpretations, psychologists take into account the purpose of the test and testee characteristics and indicate any significant limitations of their interpretations.

The Purpose of the Test

As required by Standard 9.06, the *purpose* of the assessment must be carefully considered in the interpretation of test scores. At the same time, psychologists must also resist allowing test interpretations to be biased by pressures from school personnel, parents, employers, attorneys, managed care companies, or others with an invested interest in a particular interpretation (AERA, APA, and NCME, 1999).

When offering recommendations, drawing conclusions, or making predictions from test scores, psychologists should refer to test manuals prepared by the test developer as well as the relevant body of research to understand the extent to which the tests in isolation or within the context of other tests are directly related to the purpose of testing.

☒ A neuropsychologist was hired by an insurance claims company to evaluate whether an individual insured by the company had sustained neurological damage following a car accident or whether the individual was feigning symptoms. Following administration of a battery of tests, the psychologist determined that the individual's test scores were at the lower boundaries of normal functioning. Although the psychologist made no effort to obtain information regarding the patient's neurological functioning before the accident, he concluded in his report that there was no evidence to support an injury claim.

Test factors and examinee characteristics. With the exception of perhaps some employment-related screenings, interpretations should never be based solely on test scores. Standard 9.06 requires psychologists to consider factors associated with the testing context, the examinee's test-taking abilities, and other characteristics that may affect or inappropriately bias interpretations. When relevant, psychologists should take into account observations of test-taking styles, fatigue, perceptual and motor impairments, illness, limited fluency in the language of the test, or lack of cultural familiarity with test items that would introduce construct-irrelevant variability into a test score (AERA, APA, and NCME, 1999).

In addition to familiarity with the test itself, psychologists should have the specialized knowledge necessary to formulate professional judgments about the meaning of test scores as they relate to the individual examinee (see Standards 2.01b and c, Boundaries of Competence).

Test takers' scores should not be interpreted in isolation of other information about the characteristics of the person being assessed. Such information may be gained from interviews, additional testing, or collateral information from teachers, employers, supervisors, parents, or school or employment records. Such information may lead to alternative explanations for examinees' test performance.

☒ An inpatient at a psychiatric hospital had a Monday appointment with a psychologist to help determine whether he was well enough to go home for the weekend. When he arrived for the appointment, he was obviously distressed and told the psychologist that the patient he shared his room with had threatened to kill him. The psychologist confirmed this story with one of the orderlies. Rather than reschedule the appointment, the psychologist decided to conduct the required standardized assessment and clinical interview. In his report, the psychologist noted that the patient had high MMPI scores on the Minnesota Multiphasic Personality Inventory (MMPI) (Butcher, Dahlstrom, Graham, Tellegen, & Kaemmer, 2002) indicating paranoid tendencies and high levels of stress that might be interpreted as a lack of readiness to go home. The psychologist's report did not address how the events surrounding the roommate's threats might have influenced MMPI scores and responses to interview questions.

Limitations. Under Standard 9.06, psychologists must indicate any significant limitations of their interpretations. In general, interpretive remarks that are not supported by validity and reliability information should be presented as hypotheses. When test batteries are used, interpretations of patterns of relationships among different test scores should be based on identifiable evidence. If none are available, this must be stated in the report. Interpretations of test results often include recommendations for placement, treatment, employment, or legal status based on validity evidence and professional experience. Psychologists should refrain from implying that empirical relationships exist between test results and recommendations when they do not, and distinguish between recommendations based on empirical evidence and those based on professional judgment.

Automated interpretations. Computer-generated interpretations are based on accumulated empirical data and expert judgment but cannot take into account the special characteristics of the examinee (AERA, APA, and NCME, 1999). Psychologists should use interpretations provided by automated and other types of services with caution and indicate their relevant limitations.

9.07 Assessment by Unqualified Persons

Psychologists do not promote the use of psychological assessment techniques by unqualified persons, except when such use is conducted for training purposes with appropriate supervision. (See also Standard 2.05, Delegation of Work to Others.) *[Modified for Clarity, 1992 Standard 2.06, Unqualified Persons]*

Psychologists' professional and scientific responsibilities to society and those with whom they work include helping to ensure that the administration, scoring, interpretation, and use of psychological tests are conducted only by those who are competent to do so by virtue of their education, training, or experience. Standard 9.07 prohibits psychologists from promoting the use of psychological assessment techniques by unqualified persons. For example, psychologists should not employ persons who have not received formal graduate-level training in psychological assessments to administer, score, or interpret psychological tests that will be used to determine an individual's educational placement, psychological characteristics for employment or promotion, competence to stand trial, parenting skills relevant to child custody, mental health status or diagnosis, or treatment plan.

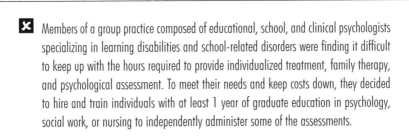

Members of a group practice composed of educational, school, and clinical psychologists specializing in learning disabilities and school-related disorders were finding it difficult to keep up with the hours required to provide individualized treatment, family therapy, and psychological assessment. To meet their needs and keep costs down, they decided to hire and train individuals with at least 1 year of graduate education in psychology, social work, or nursing to independently administer some of the assessments.

Psychological
Assessments Conducted by Trainees

Standard 9.07 does not prohibit psychologists from supervising trainees in the administration, scoring, and interpretation of tests. However, (a) the trainees must be qualified on the basis of their enrollment in a graduate or postdoctoral psychology program or externship or internship, and (b) supervision must be appropriate to their level of training. For example, psychologists teaching a first-year graduate-level personality assessment course that requires students to submit scored protocols of individuals they have independently assessed must ensure that (a) the course adequately prepares students for initial testing situations and (b) students inform persons tested or their legal guardians that the testing is for training purposes only and not for individual assessment. Faculty who have students registered in advanced practica, externships, or internships must provide a level of supervision themselves or ensure on-site supervision that is appropriate to the trainees' previous education and experience and see that trainees administer, score, and interpret tests competently (see also Standard 2.05, Delegation of Work to Others).

9.08 Obsolete Tests and Outdated Test Results

(a) Psychologists do not base their assessment or intervention decisions or recommendations on data or test results that are outdated for the current purpose. *[No Significant Change, 1992 Standard 2.07a, Obsolete Tests and Outdated Test Results]*

Standard 9.08a prohibits psychologists from making evaluative, intervention, or treatment decisions or recommendations based on outdated data or test results, unless such information is specifically relevant to the diagnostic or placement decision. The standard applies to psychologists who administer, score, and interpret the test as well as to psychologists who use test results for intervention decisions or recommendations. Whether test data or results are outdated for the current purpose may be determined by whether the test from which scores were derived is itself obsolete (see Standard 9.08b below).

Standard 9.08a is addressed to the use of test scores that may have been derived from currently used tests but are obsolete for the purposes of the evaluation. Previous scores derived from an up-to-date version of a test may be obsolete if individuals might be expected to score differently or require a different test based on (1) the amount of time between the previous administration and the current need for assessment, (2) maturational and other developmental changes, (3) educational advancement, (4) job training or employment experiences, (5) change in health status, (6) new symptomatology, (7) change in work or family status, or (8) an accident or traumatic experience.

❎ A psychologist was asked to provide an assessment of learning disabilities in support of an 18-year-old high school senior's request to be admitted to special learning support programs at the colleges to which he was applying. The psychologist had conducted such an assessment with the student 6 years earlier when he was applying for special educational support in junior high school. The psychologist wrote the report for colleges based on the test data from the earlier test administration.

In some instances, it may be appropriate to use outdated test scores as a basis of comparison with new test results to evaluate the long-term effectiveness of an educational program or intervention or to help identify cognitive decline or a sudden change in mental health or adaptive functioning relevant to treatment, placement in an appropriate educational or health care environment, disability claims, competency hearings, or custody suits. When outdated data or results are used, psychologists' reports and recommendations should include explanations for their use and their limitations (see Standard 9.06, Interpreting Assessment Results).

☑ A neuropsychologist was asked to evaluate cognitive and personality factors that might be responsible for a sudden change in adaptive functioning of an 80-year-old nursing home resident. The resident had been given a battery of intelligence and personality tests 5 years previously upon admission to the nursing home. Advances in geropsychology in the past 5 years had resulted in more developmentally appropriate and sensitive assessment instruments for this age group. The psychologist conducted a new evaluation using the more valid instruments. In her summary, she compared the results of the assessment to the results of the earlier evaluation accompanied by a discussion of the limitations of comparing current performance to the older test results.

Psychologists should resist pressures to use obsolete test results from schools, health care delivery systems, or other agencies or organizations that seek to cut expenses by using outdated test results for placement or services (see Standard 1.03, Conflicts Between Ethics and Organizational Demands).

(b) Psychologists do not base such decisions or recommendations on tests and measures that are obsolete and not useful for the current purpose. *[No Significant Change, 1992 Standard 2.07b, Obsolete Tests and Outdated Test Results]*

Test developers often construct new versions of a test to reflect significant (1) advances in the theoretical constructs underlying the psychological characteristic assessed; (2) transformations in cultural, educational, linguistic, or societal influences

that challenge the extent to which current test items validly reflect content domains; or (3) changes in the demographic characteristics of the population to be tested affecting interpretations that can be drawn from standardized scores. Standard 9.08b prohibits psychologists from using outdated versions of tests for assessment or intervention decisions when interpretations drawn from the test are of questionable validity or otherwise not useful for the purpose of testing.

The expense of purchasing the most up-to-date version of a test is not an ethical justification for using obsolete tests when the validity of interpretations drawn from such tests is compromised. Psychologists working with schools, businesses, government agencies, courts, HMOs, and health care delivery systems that resist purchasing updated tests because of costs or ease of record keeping should clarify the nature of the problem, urge organizational reconsideration, and if such recommendations are not heeded strive to the extent feasible to limit harms that will arise from misapplication of the test results (see Standards 1.02, Conflicts Between Ethics and Law, Regulations, or Other Governing Legal Authority, and 1.03, Conflicts Between Ethics and Organizational Demands).

The standard does permit psychologists to use obsolete versions of a test when there is a valid purpose for doing so. In most cases, the purpose will be to compare past and current test performance. When use of an obsolete test is appropriate to the purpose of assessment, psychologists should clarify to schools, courts, or others that will use the test results which version of the test was used, why that version was selected, and the test norms used to interpret the results.

☑ A psychologist asked to evaluate an employee's claim that an industrial accident was responsible for a current disabling psychological disorder learned that the employee had been administered a battery of cognitive and personality tests several years before during preemployment screening. The psychologist decided it would be useful and appropriate to compare the complainant's current performance to his performance on test scores obtained prior to the accident. One of the previous scores was derived from an older version of a test that had recently been updated and revised. The psychologist decided to administer the older version of the test to better determine whether functioning had been affected by the accident. The psychologist's report included a rationale for the use of the older version of the test.

9.09 Test Scoring and Interpretation Services

(a) Psychologists who offer assessment or scoring services to other professionals accurately describe the purpose, norms, validity, reliability, and applications of the procedures and any special qualifications applicable to their use. *[No Significant Change, 1992 Standard 2.08a, Test Scoring and Interpretation Services]*

Standard 9.09 applies to psychologists who develop or sell computerized, automated, Web-linked, or other test scoring and interpretation services to other professionals. Psychologists offering these services must provide in manuals, instructions, brochures, and advertisements accurate statements about the purpose, basis and method of scoring, validity and reliability of scores derived from the service, the professional contexts in which the scores can be applied, and any special user qualifications necessary to competently use the service.

When test interpretations in addition to scores will be provided to users of the services, psychologists providing the services must document the sources, theoretical rationale, and psychometric evidence for the validity and reliability of the particular interpretation method employed. The Standards for Educational and Psychological Testing recommend that scoring services provide a summary of the evidence supporting the interpretations that includes the nature, rationale, and formulas for cut-off scores or configural scoring rules (rules for scoring test items or subtests that depend on a pattern of responses) (AERA, APA, and NCME, 1999). If algorithms or other rules for scoring jeopardize proprietary interests, copyrights, or other intellectual property rights issues, owners of the intellectual property are nevertheless responsible for documenting in some way evidence in support of the validity of score interpretations (AERA, APA, and NCME, 1999; Bersoff & Hofer, 1991).

Descriptions of the application of test scoring and interpretation procedures must include a discussion of their limitations. For example, computer-generated or automated systems may not be able to take into account specific features of the examinee that are relevant to test interpretation such as medical history, gender, age, ethnicity, employment history, education, or competence in the language of the test, motor problems that might interfere with test taking, current life stressors, or special conditions of the testing environment.

(b) Psychologists select scoring and interpretation services (including automated services) on the basis of evidence of the validity of the program and procedures as well as on other appropriate considerations. (See also Standard 2.01b and c, Boundaries of Competence.) *[No Significant Change, 1992 Standard 2.08b, Testing Scoring and Interpretation Services]*

Standard 9.09b applies to psychologists who use computerized, automated, Web-linked, or other test scoring and interpretation services developed by other professionals or test vendors. Psychologists should select only test scoring and interpretation services that provide evidence of the validity of the program and procedures for the types of evaluation or treatment decisions that are to be informed by the assessment and that are appropriate for the individual case under consideration. Psychologists should not use scoring and interpretation services if the psychometric information provided by the test scoring or interpretation services is inadequate or fails to support the applicability of the scoring and interpretation methods to the goals of the particular assessment.

Implications of HIPAA. When the test data to be scored and interpreted by the service comes under the HIPAA definition of PHI, psychologists must include this information in the notice of privacy practices or obtain a valid authorization from the client/patient to transmit the information to the service (see more detailed discussion on core requirements for valid HIPAA authorizations under Standard 4.05a, Disclosures). Psychologists must ensure that the service receives, stores, transmits, and discloses client/patient information in a manner that is HIPAA compliant. In most instances, psychologists will enter into a business associate agreement with the testing service (45 CFR 160.103 and 164.504[e]). Under HIPAA, a "business associate" is a person who acts on behalf of a covered entity but not as an employee of the covered entity. As part of the business associate contract, the service must provide assurances to the psychologist that information will be appropriately safeguarded. If a psychologist discovers the service has violated HIPAA regulations in some way, the psychologist must correct the error or terminate the business associate contract.

(c) Psychologists retain responsibility for the appropriate application, interpretation, and use of assessment instruments, whether they score and interpret such tests themselves or use automated or other services. *[No Significant Change, 1992 Standard 2.08c, Test Scoring and Interpretation Services]*

Irrespective of whether psychologists use a service or score and interpret test data themselves, the psychologist is ultimately responsible for the appropriate selection, administration, scoring, interpretation, and use of the test. Under Standard 9.09c, psychologists must acknowledge this responsibility and take appropriate steps to ensure that tests were properly scored and interpreted.

To be in compliance with Standard 9.09c, psychologists must

♦ Have sufficient familiarity with scoring and interpretation techniques to adequately perform these tasks themselves, detect errors in test scores provided by a service, and critically evaluate canned interpretations.

♦ Be able to identify the limitations of test service interpretations and know when collateral test scores and other relevant information are necessary to adequately interpret and apply test results. Such information might include an examinee's health status, culture, gender, age, employment history, educational experiences, language competencies, physical disabilities, symptoms of or empirical evidence to assume comorbid disorders, current life stressors, and special conditions of the testing environment.

♦ Avoid simplified interpretations of test scores that can lead to misdiagnosis, inadequate or iatrogenic treatment plans, or unfair or invalid personnel decisions or that can mislead the trier of fact in judicial and government hearings (AERA, APA, and NCME, 1999).

9.10 Explaining Assessment Results

Regardless of whether the scoring and interpretation are done by psychologists, by employees or assistants, or by automated or other outside services, psychologists take reasonable steps to ensure that explanations of results are given to the individual or designated representative unless the nature of the relationship precludes provision of an explanation of results (such as in some organizational consulting, preemployment or security screenings, and forensic evaluations), and this fact has been clearly explained to the person being assessed in advance. *[Modified for Clarity, 1992 Standard 2.09, Explaining Assessment Results]*

Psychologists who administer, supervise, or otherwise are responsible for test administration are also responsible for ensuring that the individuals tested, their guardians, or personal representative receives an explanation of the assessment results. The purpose of an explanation is to enable a client/patient to understand the meaning of a test score or test score interpretation as it relates to its purpose, implications, and potential consequences. According to the Standards for Educational and Psychological Testing, an appropriate explanation "should describe in simple language what the test covers, what scores mean, the precision of the scores, common misinterpretations of the test scores, and how scores will be used" (AERA, APA, and NCME, 1999, Standard 5.10, p. 65). Whenever possible and clinically appropriate, psychologists assessing children and adolescents should provide feedback to the child as well as his or her guardian; the feedback should be appropriate to the child's developmental level.

Employees and Trainees

According to Standard 9.10, the responsibility for appropriate test explanation lies with the psychologist whether or not he or she personally scored or interpreted the test, assigned the scoring or interpretation to an employee or assistant, or used an outside service. The standard does not require that psychologists provide the explanation but that they take reasonable steps to ensure that one is given. The term "reasonable steps" is used to acknowledge situations in which the examinee may not wish to or is unable to meet for an explanation of results or an employee has misinformed the psychologist about an explanation taking place. If, however, a psychologist is aware that appropriate staff is unavailable or unable to provide the explanation, the psychologist must do so personally.

> ☒ A psychologist supervised several interns at an outpatient unit of a veterans hospital. The interns were responsible for administering a battery of psychological tests to new patients. Weekly supervision meetings with the interns included discussion of test selection, administration, scoring, and interpretation. The psychologist paid only cursory attention to instructing the supervisees on how to explain test results to patients. The clinic director received several complaints that interns' explanations of test results were confusing and distressing to patients.

Use of Automated Scoring Services

A psychologist who asks a scoring service to send a computerized interpretation to a client/patient should take reasonable steps to ensure that the computerized interpretation provides an explanation adequate for conveying test performance information to examinees. As discussed under Standard 9.09b, psychologists who are covered entities under HIPAA who use scoring services must include this information in the notice of privacy practices or obtain a specific client/patient authorization to use such services and ensure that the service transmits information and protects client/patient privacy in a HIPAA-compliant manner.

☑ A psychologist decided to use a popular scoring service for some frequently administered tests, after examination of the company's materials indicated the scoring system was reliable and valid. An added benefit of the service was that it would send test interpretations directly to the client. For the first set of test data the psychologist sent to the service, she asked the service to send her the test interpretation that is usually mailed directly to the client. The psychologist reviewed the interpretive materials and believed the information was too sparse to adequately inform clients and might create confusion. She therefore decided to continue using the service for scoring but did not permit the service to send explanations directly to the client.

Exceptions

Standard 9.10 permits exceptions to this requirement when an explanation of the results is precluded by the psychologist-examinee relationship, such as instances where an organization or the court is the psychologist's client/patient rather than the test taker. For example, it is usually inappropriate for psychologists to provide an explanation of test results directly to the examinee when testing is court ordered, when it involves employment testing, or when it involves eligibility for security clearances for government work. In such situations, prior to administering assessments, psychologists are required to inform examinees that the psychologist will not be providing them with an explanation of the test results. If legally permissible, the psychologist should provide the reason why an explanation will not be given (see Standards 3.10c, Informed Consent; 3.11, Psychological Services Delivered To or Through Organizations; and 9.03, Informed Consent in Assessment).

9.11 Maintaining Test Security

The term *test materials* refers to manuals, instruments, protocols, and test questions or stimuli and does not include *test data* as defined in Standard 9.04, Release of Test Data. Psychologists make reasonable efforts to maintain the integrity and security of test materials and other assessment techniques consistent with law and contractual obligations, and in a manner that permits adherence to this Ethics Code. *[Significant Change in Meaning, 1992 Standard 2.10, Maintaining Test Security]*

An assumption of test validity is that individuals take the test under prescribed standardized conditions. For many tests, a critical aspect of standardization is that testees are equally unfamiliar with the test items. When some testees have access to test items prior to the administration of the test, the test norms and thus interpretations based on scaled scores may not be psychometrically defensible. Duplicating test materials or making video or audio recordings of an assessment session that subsequently enters the public domain also threatens the ongoing validity of tests. Individuals who have had uncontrolled access to test content can manipulate or coach others to manipulate test results that harm the public by enabling individuals to malinger or to obtain positions for which they are unqualified. Many tests consist of a static number of items that are costly to develop, take years to construct, and are not easily replaced. Thus, release of test materials can compromise the validity and usefulness of a test and harm the intellectual property rights of test authors and publishers.

Definition of Test Materials and Test Security

Under Standard 9.11, "test materials" are manuals, instruments, protocols, and test questions or stimuli that do not come under the definition of "test data" as defined in Standard 9.04a, Release of Test Data. Under Standard 9.11, psychologists have a duty to make reasonable efforts to protect the integrity and security of test materials and other assessment techniques. With few exceptions, test materials that do not include client/patient responses should never be released to clients/patients or others unqualified to use the instruments. Unless specifically recommended by the test developer, self-administered tests should not be given to clients/patients to take home. Additional security precautions need to be taken for tests administered through the Internet. Psychologists should consult test developers and if necessary seek legal consultation before distributing copyrighted tests over the Internet.

This standard does not prohibit psychologists from discussing individual test items with clients/patients if it assists in explaining test results (Standard 9.10, Explaining Assessment Results). Psychologists may also send test materials to other qualified health professionals bound by their ethical guidelines to protect the security of the instruments, taking appropriate steps not to violate copyright laws.

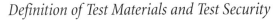

> ❌ A patient of a psychologist in independent practice was discussing her anxiety about an upcoming psychological evaluation for a job promotion that required security clearance. To reduce the patient's anxiety, the psychologist took out from his files several of the standardized tests that are usually administered for such purposes and went over them with the patient.

Laws Governing Release of Records

Implications of HIPAA. As a matter of practice, psychologists should keep test materials separated from a client's/patient's mental health records so the materials do not come under the HIPAA-defined "designated record set," which may under federal law not be withheld pursuant to client/patient release. Test materials do not have to be included in the patient's record if "test data," as defined by Standard 9.04, Release of Test Data, are not recorded on the test material itself. "Separated" does not necessarily mean that the test data and test material must be kept in a separate file cabinet, but it does require that they are separated by a folder or binding unit so they are not confused or commingled with the test data records. Psychologists should seek legal advice before making such a determination and be mindful that removing clients'/patients' responses from the test protocol after it has been recorded on the material can constitute unlawful alteration of the patient's record.

Implications of FERPA. School psychologists may also find that laws governing the release of school records supersede the requirements of Standard 9.11. The Family Education Rights and Privacy Act (FERPA) establishes the right of parents to obtain copies of their children's school records where failure to provide the copies would effectively prevent a parent or eligible student from exercising his or her right to inspect and review the education records (20 U.S.C. § 1232G[a][1][A]; 34 CFR § 99.11b; http://www.ed.gov/offices/OM/fpco/ferpa/index.html). Schools are not required to provide copies of the records unless because of distance or other considerations it is impossible for the parent or student to review the records. Psychologists working in schools may also release test materials to attorneys or other nonprofessionals in response to a court order. In these situations, psychologists can request that the court issue a protective order requiring that test items not be duplicated or made available to the public as part of the court record and returned to the psychologist at the end of the proceedings.

Additional legal caveats. Release of "test data" that includes client/patient responses recorded on the test protocol itself can raise issues of copyright protection and fair use by test development companies. If testing protocols allow, psychologists may wish to record client/patient responses on a form separated from the test items themselves to protect the test materials from HIPAA regulations. The extent to which HIPAA, state privacy rules, and Standard 9.04 of the Ethics Code will conflict with test copyright and fair use laws will be determined over time. Psychologists are reminded that Standard 1.02 of the new Ethics Code permits psychologists to adhere to the requirements of the law when such conflicts cannot be resolved. The release of client/patient records is becoming a highly regulated area of health care practice. In this new and evolving legal arena, psychologists are wise to consult with attorneys and to seek guidance from continually updated materials provided by the APA Practice Directorate and APA Insurance Trust.

CHAPTER 13

Standards on Therapy

10. THERAPY

10.01 Informed Consent to Therapy

(a) When obtaining informed consent to therapy as required in Standard 3.10, Informed Consent, psychologists inform clients/patients as early as is feasible in the therapeutic relationship about the nature and anticipated course of therapy, fees, involvement of third parties, and limits of confidentiality and provide sufficient opportunity for the client/patient to ask questions and receive answers. (See also Standards 4.02, Discussing the Limits of Confidentiality, and 6.04, Fees and Financial Arrangements.) *[Expanded, 1992 Standard 4.01, Structuring the Relationship]*

To comply with this standard of the American Psychological Association (APA) Ethics Code (2002), psychologists must obtain and document written or oral consent in the manner set forth in Standard 3.10, Informed Consent. Psychologists must also provide prospective therapy clients/patients, and when appropriate their legal guardians, a clear explanation of the nature and anticipated course of therapy, fees, involvement of third parties, and the limits of confidentiality. This information must be presented in a language reasonably understandable to the client/patient, and the consent process must provide sufficient opportunity for questions and answers.

Standard 10.01 explicitly uses the phrase "as early as is feasible" to indicate that in some cases obtaining informed consent during the first therapy session may not be possible or clinically appropriate. Psychologists may need to wait for feedback from a client's/patient's health maintenance organization (HMO) before consent discussions regarding fees can be completed. Informed consent during the first session may be clinically contraindicated if a new client/patient is suicidal or experiencing some other crisis needing immediate therapeutic attention. In such situations, consent is obtained as soon as all information is available or the crisis has subsided. In many instances, informed consent to therapy will be an ongoing process determined, for example, by the extent to which the nature of a client's/patient's treatment needs are immediately diagnosed or gradually identified over a series of sessions, cognitive and social maturation in child clients/patients, or functional declines in clients/patients with progressive disorders.

> ☑ At the beginning of a first session, it became apparent that a new client was having difficulty communicating in a coherent fashion. With probing the psychologist learned that the client had a history of schizophrenia and had recently gone off his medications because of the intolerable side effects. The psychologist postponed discussion relevant to informed consent and spent the rest of the session working with the client to determine the best course of action to deal with the immediate situation.

Nature of the therapy. The *nature* of the therapy refers to information about the therapeutic process that would reasonably be expected to affect clients'/patients' decisions to enter into therapy with the psychologist. Informed consent should include discussion of the duration of each session (e.g., 50 minutes), appointment schedule (e.g., weekly), and the general objectives of treatment (e.g., crisis management, symptom reduction). Depending on the treatment modality, the consent process might inform clients/patients that therapy entails participating in biofeedback sessions, relaxation exercises, behavioral contracts, homework assignments, discussion of dreams and developmental history, collateral treatments, or other aspects of the therapeutic process relevant to an informed consent decision. Psychologists should not assume that all clients/patients are familiar with the nature of psychotherapy.

> ☑ A new patient who had recently immigrated to the United States from West Africa told a psychologist that his general practitioner had recommended that he see the psychologist because of headaches that had not responded to traditional medications. The psychologist explained her cognitive therapy approach to working with such problems, standard confidentiality procedures, and issues relevant to the patient's health plan and then turned to discussion of issues relevant to the patient's presenting problem. Toward the end of the session, the psychologist asked the patient if he had any additional questions. The patient asked the psychologist if she was ready to give him the prescription for the new medication that will cure his headaches. The psychologist then carefully explained in greater detail the nature of cognitive therapy and the difference between such therapy and psychopharmacological approaches.

Anticipated course of the therapy. The *anticipated course* of the therapy refers to the number of sessions expected given the psychologist's current knowledge of the client's/patient's presenting problem and when applicable the company, institutional, or health plan policies that may affect the number of sessions. Depending on the treatment modality, consent discussions would also include expectable modifications such as the evolving nature of systematic desensitization or exposure therapy; the uncovering of as yet unidentified treatment issues; or if the practitioner is a prescribing psychologist, adjustments in dosage levels of psychopharmacological medications.

> ☒ A psychologist saw a new client whose presenting problems appeared to be related to a debilitating social phobia. The client was to pay privately for treatment because her health plan did not cover psychotherapy. The client asked the psychologist how long she might have to be in therapy before she saw some relief from her symptoms. The psychologist responded, "We'll just see how it goes."
>
> ☑ A psychologist saw a new patient who appeared to be suffering from a mild form of agoraphobia. The psychologist explained his behavioral approach to this type of problem and the average number of sessions after which patients often feel some relief from their symptoms. The psychologist stressed that each individual responds differently and that together they would reassess the patient's progress after a specific number of sessions.

Fees. Discussion of *fees* must include the cost of the therapy; the types of reimbursement accepted (e.g., checks, credit card payments, direct payment from insurance companies), the payment schedule (e.g., weekly, monthly), when fees are reevaluated (e.g., annual raise in rates), and policies regarding late payments and missed appointments. When appropriate and as soon as such information can be verified, psychologists must also discuss with clients/patients the percentage of therapy costs reimbursed under the client's/patient's health plan and limitations on the number of sessions that can be anticipated because of limitations in insurance or other sources of client/patient financing (see also Standard 6.04, Fees and Financial Arrangements). Psychologists directly contracted with HMOs may have capitated or other types of business agreements that provide financial incentives to limit the number of treatment sessions. When permitted by law and contractual agreement, psychologists should inform clients/patients about such arrangements (Acuff et al., 1999; see also Standard 3.06, Conflict of Interest).

> ☒ On the initial visit, a psychologist told a client her fee for each session. At the end of the first month in treatment when the client asked the psychologist to fill out an insurance form for treatment, he was shocked to learn that the psychologist did not accept third-party reimbursement for services.

Involvement of third parties. The term "third parties" as used in this standard refers to legal guardians, health insurance companies, employers, organizations, or legal or other governing authorities that may be involved in the therapy. Psychologists should inform clients/patients if such parties have requested or ordered mental health treatment, are paying for the therapy, are entitled to receive diagnostic information or details of the therapy based on law or contractual agreement, and to whom information may be provided, contingent on the client's/patient's appropriate written release or authorization (see section below on implications of the Health Insurance Portability and Accountability Act [HIPAA]). Psychologists asked to evaluate a child by one parent should when appropriate clarify custody issues to determine if the other parent must also give permission.

☑ A psychologist was assigned to see a couple for court-ordered therapy following the removal of their children from their home based on a finding of child abuse and neglect. The psychologist informed the couple that the treatment was mandatory, that it was paid for by a court-affiliated child protective services agency, and that the psychologist would be providing to the court a summary of the couple's compliance with and progress in therapy.

Confidentiality. Informed consent to therapy must provide a clear explanation of the extent and limits of *confidentiality,* including (1) when the psychologist must comply with reporting requirements such as mandated child abuse reporting or duty-to-warn laws and (2) in the case of therapy involving minors or individuals with impaired consent capacities, guardian access to records. Psychologists who provide therapy over the Internet must inform clients/patients about the procedures that will be used to protect confidentiality and the threats to confidentiality unique to this form of electronic transmission of information (see also Standard 4.02c, Discussing the Limits of Confidentiality). Clients/patients enrolled in health plans must be informed about the extent to which treatment plans, diagnosis, or other sensitive information must be disclosed to case managers for precertification or continuing authorization for treatment (Acuff et al., 1999).

☑ A psychologist had an initial appointment with an adolescent and his parents to discuss the 14-year-old's entry into individual psychotherapy for depression. The psychologist discussed with both the prospective patient and his parents what information concerning the adolescent's treatment would and would not be shared with the parents, including her confidentiality and disclosure policies regarding adolescent risk behaviors such as sexual activity and use of illegal drugs. She also informed them about her legal obligations to report suspected child abuse or neglect and her own policy regarding disclosure of information pertaining to patient imminent self-harm or harm to others. In addition, she described the parents' right to access of the adolescent's health records under HIPAA (see below).

> ❌ A psychologist began therapy with a client over the Internet. The psychologist failed to inform the client of the need to password protect the home computer from which the client would be interacting with the psychologist. The client's spouse opened the files in which therapeutic communications had been saved and printed them out to use against the client in petitioning for divorce.

Implications of HIPAA

Psychologists who are covered entities under HIPAA (see "A Word About HIPAA" in the Preface of this book) must inform clients/patients about their rights regarding the use and disclosures of their health information. A covered entity is defined as a health care provider who transmits any health information in electronic form in connection with a transaction related to financial or administrative activities related to health care (45 CFR 160.102[a][3] and 160.103). The designation of "covered entity" is not specific to an individual client/patient but to the psychologist's practice. Thus, even if a psychologist is not electronically transmitting health information about a particular client/patient, HIPAA is triggered if the psychologist has conducted any such transactions for other clients/patients.

Notice of Privacy Practices. Clients/patients have certain rights regarding their protected health information (PHI) characterized as individually identifiable health information created or received by a health care provider relating to the past, present, or future health; provision of health care; or payment for health care (45 CFR 160.103 and 160.501). These rights include access to their PHI (excluding psychotherapy notes), the right to amend their PHI, the right to request restriction of uses and disclosures, and the right to an accounting of disclosures made by the provider to others during the past 6 years (45 CFR 164.522, 164.524, 164.526, 164.528; see also discussions under Standard 3.10, Informed Consent, in Chapter 6; Standards 4.01, Maintaining Confidentiality, and 4.05, Disclosures, in Chapter 7; and Standard 6.01, Documentation of Professional and Scientific Work and Maintenance of Records). HIPAA requires that if under applicable law a person has authority to act on behalf of a client/patient in decisions related to health care, a covered entity must provide such a person (called a personal representative) with all information that would be given to the client/patient, except if there is reason to believe the client/patient has been abused or is endangered by the personal representative or that treating the individual as a personal representative would not be in the best interests of the client/patient (45 CFR 164.502[g]).

At the beginning of treatment, covered entities are required to provide clients/patients with a Notice of Privacy Practices that explains the uses and disclosures of PHI that may be made by the covered entity, and the individual's rights and covered entity's legal duties with respect to PHI (45 CFR 164.520). The notice should be provided to the client/patient in written form and separate from other informed consent procedures or documents.

Authorization. HIPAA requires that covered entities obtain written valid authorization from the individual or his or her personal representative prior to releasing PHI (45 CFR 164.508) to others. The authorization must include the following:

- A specific description of information to be disclosed

- Specific identification of the person or class of persons who can make the authorization

- The specific persons or class of persons to whom information may be disclosed

- A description of each purpose of the use or disclosure

- A statement explaining the client's/patient's rights including the right to revoke the authorization in writing

- Exceptions to the right to revoke

- An expiration date

- Client/patient signature

The client/patient must also receive a copy of the authorization. In addition, when appropriate release and authorizations are obtained, the HIPAA Privacy Rule requires that psychologists share only the minimum amount of information necessary for billing agencies and non-health provider internal staff to perform their roles (45 CFR 164.502[b]). Psychologists may wish to use the HIPAA-compliant Notice of Privacy Practices and authorization model forms that have been developed by the APA Insurance Trust and the APA Practice Directorate to be compatible with the laws governing practice in each state (see http://apait.org/hipaa and http://apa.org/practice).

Authorization is not required to use or disclose PHI for cover entities to carry out their own treatment, payment, or health care operations as long as appropriate consent has been obtained and Notice of Privacy Practices provided at the beginning of the professional relationship (164.506[b]).

Psychotherapy notes. HIPAA is highly protective of psychotherapy notes, defined as notes recorded by a health care provider who is a mental health professional documenting or analyzing the contents of conversation during a private counseling session or a group, joint, or family counseling session and that are separated from the rest of the individual's medical record. Psychotherapy notes as defined by HIPAA do *not* include medication prescription and monitoring, counseling session start and stop times, the modalities and frequencies of treatment furnished, results of clinical tests, and any summary of the following items: diagnosis, functional status, the treatment plan, symptoms, prognosis, and progress to date (45 CFR 164.501).

Patients do *not* have a right of access to psychotherapy notes, and a separate authorization is required for the release of psychotherapy notes when a covered entity agrees to their release. In addition, HMOs are prohibited from requiring patient authorization to disclose psychotherapy notes as a condition for evaluating eligibility. For additional discussion of HIPAA regulations in other chapters, see the standards listed under HIPAA in the topical table of contents.

(b) When obtaining informed consent for treatment for which generally recognized techniques and procedures have not been established, psychologists inform their clients/patients of the developing nature of the treatment, the potential risks involved, alternative treatments that may be available, and the voluntary nature of their participation. (See also Standards 2.01e, Boundaries of Competence, and 3.10, Informed Consent.) *[New]*

Most techniques that are now accepted practice in the profession of psychology emerged from treatment needs unmet by existing therapies. Standard 10.01b recognizes that innovation in mental health services is critical if a profession is to continue to adequately serve a diverse and dynamic public. The standard also recognizes that during the development and refinement of new therapeutic techniques the risks and benefits to clients/patients are unknown. Consequently, respect for a client's/patient's right to informed, rational, and voluntary consent requires that when the treatment needs of a client/patient call for innovative techniques, during informed consent psychologists have the obligation to explain the relatively new and untried nature of the therapy, clearly describe alternative established treatments that may be available, and clarify the client's/patient's right to dissent in favor of more established treatments whether they are offered by the psychologist obtaining the consent or other mental health professionals.

At the time that the 2002 Ethics Code was adopted, consensus on techniques and procedures to provide therapy over the Internet (e.g., e-mail, chat rooms, video conferencing) were just emerging, and the mental health benefits and risks of different forms of telehealth for different patients/clients were being actively explored and debated in the literature. Many psychologists using such techniques are pioneers in the field. During the period in which the 2002 Ethics Code will be effective, different forms of behavioral telehealth will most likely become standard practices. Below is an example of how a psychologist using such a technique in the earliest days of its development could comply with Standard 10.01b.

 A psychologist working in a large, underserved rural community found that a number of his clients could not afford to make the 100-mile trip to his office on a weekly basis.

After attending an intensive workshop on e-mail therapy and developing a network of colleagues to consult with on behavioral telehealth techniques, the psychologist decided to use this form of therapy. He adopted the procedure of having an initial in-person meeting with each client who might be appropriate for e-mail therapy. During the informed consent provided at this session, he explained the following: (1) E-mail therapy is a new and still developing form of therapy; (2) although there was reason to believe this form of therapy would serve the client's mental health needs, the extent of such benefits was still largely unknown; (3) current risks associated with e-mail therapy include confidentiality concerns and lack of immediacy; (4) there are traditional treatments available for the client's presenting problem; and (5) that if the client preferred to receive a more traditional therapy the psychologist would try to work out a schedule that could accommodate the client's travel difficulties.

Informed consent should be conceptualized as a continuing process in which the clinically determined need to shift to treatment strategies distinctly different from those that were originally agreed on during informed consent are discussed with the client/patient at appropriate points during the course of psychotherapy. If, after several sessions, a client's/patient's treatment needs call for a shift to innovative techniques that have not been widely used or accepted by practitioners in the field, the psychologist should follow the requirements of Standard 10.01b. The case below illustrates a potential violation of this standard.

❌ A psychologist had just returned from a professional meeting where she heard several other practitioners discuss a new technique for anxiety disorders that involved viewing video clips of people reacting to natural or humanmade catastrophes. She decided to try this untested technique with one of her patients who had not been responding to traditional psychodynamic approaches to anxiety. At the next session, she told the patient that as part of his ongoing treatment they would look at a video together. The patient experienced an anxiety attack following exposure to the video and apologized to the therapist for failing to improve after so many sessions.

(c) When the therapist is a trainee and the legal responsibility for the treatment provided resides with the supervisor, the client/patient, as part of the informed consent procedure, is informed that the therapist is in training and is being supervised and is given the name of the supervisor. *[Modified for Clarity, 1992 Standard 4.01b, Structuring the Relationship]*

Standard 10.01c applies to therapy conducted and supervised as part of practica, internships, or other training experiences in which the legal responsibility for treatment resides with the supervisor. In these contexts, clients/patients must be informed that the therapist is a trainee and that the therapy is supervised and is given the name and contact information of the supervisor. Both the trainee and the supervisor would be in potential violation of this standard if the supervisee failed to include this information during informed consent. This standard does not apply to therapy conducted by licensed psychologists obtaining postdoctoral training and supervision, because in such contexts the legal responsibility most often resides with the psychologist.

> ☒ A student interning at a veterans hospital was concerned that her ability to help the patients would be compromised if she told them that she was a trainee. When she discussed this with her supervisor, the supervisor told her the decision was up to her.

10.02 Therapy Involving Couples or Families

(a) When psychologists agree to provide services to several persons who have a relationship (such as spouses, significant others, or parents and children), they take reasonable steps to clarify at the outset (1) which of the individuals are clients/patients and (2) the relationship the psychologist will have with each person. This clarification includes the psychologist's role and the probable uses of the services provided or the information obtained. (See also Standard 4.02, Discussing the Limits of Confidentiality.) *[Modified for Clarity, 1992 Standard 4.03a, Couples and Family Relationships]*

Steps required to inform prospective clients/patients in couples or family therapy about the nature of treatment go beyond those described in Standard 10.01, Informed Consent to Therapy. In addition to the features of informed consent described in Standard 10.01, under Standard 10.02, psychologists must identify and explain which members of the couple or family is the primary client/patient. In some treatment modalities, the client/patient is the multiperson unit and the primary obligation of the psychologist is to the parties as a whole. In other modalities, the primary client/patient is a single individual with other persons involved only to provide collateral support for the client's/patient's treatment.

> ☑ A divorced couple with joint custody of their children began family therapy to help their 10-year-old son, who had been having problems in school and in adjusting to living in two different homes. The father indicated that he was just attending sessions to support his son's therapy. The psychologist explained to the father, mother, and child that she offered family therapy in which all members are clients and their feelings and behaviors equally explored during the treatment sessions. She also told them that if there was some indication that the son needed individual therapy, she would recommend an appropriate practitioner specializing in childhood disorders.

Clarifying the psychologist's role and goals of therapy. In addition to identifying who is the client/patient, discussions at the outset of couple or family therapy must clarify (1) the psychologist's responsibilities in balancing the interests of different individuals, (2) whether the psychologist will conduct individual or conjoint sessions, and (3) how often the psychologist will meet with each party. The modifier "reasonable" indicates that a violation of this standard is limited to instances when psychologists do not take steps to clarify information in a manner that would be considered appropriate in the prevailing judgment of other similarly engaged psychologists. Clients'/patients' failure to understand the full implications of this information is not in itself sufficient evidence of violation.

☑ An elderly couple entered therapy to help them address feelings and conflicts arising from the husband's terminal illness. Upon initial assessment of their situation, the psychologist determined that the wife's and husband's emotional reactions to the illness should be explored in individual sessions before it would be helpful for the couple to meet with the therapist together. The therapist outlined a treatment plan that included scheduling of individual and joint sessions.

In many instances, the goals of treatment may be different for the individuals involved. For example, one member of a couple may see therapy as a means of strengthening the relationship, whereas the other sees it as a means of ending the relationship. Psychologists must take reasonable steps to correct such misimpressions.

☑ An interfaith couple began premarital counseling to help resolve conflicts regarding issues such as which clergy should perform their wedding ceremony and the religious upbringing of their children. In the first 10 minutes of the initial session, it became clear that one member of the couple believed the purpose of counseling was to convince his fiancée to agree to conduct the wedding ceremony and to raise the children in his faith, whereas the fiancée was participating in the counseling to ease the way for her breaking the engagement. During the process of informed consent and in subsequent sessions, the psychologist continued to clarify that involvement in premarital counseling could not promise the direction the couple's relationship would take.

Confidentiality. Psychologists working with couples and families must take reasonable steps to clarify how confidential information will be handled. Will the psychologist keep information received from one party secret from the other? Or will all information be shared? (see Margolin, 1982). Psychologists must also clearly articulate their legal obligations and policies regarding confidentiality and disclosure of information about child abuse, domestic abuse, HIV notification, high-risk behaviors of adolescent clients/patients, and other instances of potential harm.

> ✖ A gay couple had been in couples counseling for several sessions. One member of the couple called the psychologist and revealed that without the knowledge of his significant other, he had begun seeing his former wife in what was progressing toward a renewal of their sexual relationship. The client asked the psychologist to keep the information secret. Although the psychologist had communicated a general confidentiality policy to the couple at the outset of therapy, she had not specifically discussed with them her policy regarding information sharing among her and each member of the couple. She now felt in a terrible bind. If she refused to keep the information secret, she would violate the presumption of confidentiality held by the client who had called. If she respected the request for secrecy, she might be violating the other client's trust and expectation of openness.

(b) If it becomes apparent that psychologists may be called on to perform potentially conflicting roles (such as family therapist and then witness for one party in divorce proceedings), psychologists take reasonable steps to clarify and modify, or withdraw from, roles appropriately. (See also Standard 3.05c, Multiple Relationships.) *[Modified for Clarity, 1992 Standard 4.03b, Couple and Family Relationships]*

It is not unusual for individuals who have sought couples or family therapy to become involved in litigation involving divorce, child custody, child abuse allegations, petitions for child or family services, or mental competency hearings. In such situations, psychologists may be asked by one party to testify on his or her behalf or receive a court order to serve as a fact witness for the legal matter at issue. When such situations arise, under Standard 10.02b, psychologists must first take steps to clarify to clients/patients the nature of the two roles and the potential effect on each party involved in the therapy. To comply with this standard, psychologists will need to be aware of and communicate to their patients/clients the extent to which state law defines as public or private the information revealed in couples or family therapy and whether one or all parties must agree to disclosure of information in court.

As with other forms of multiple relationships, sometimes the request to serve in a dual capacity risks impairing performance of one or both professional roles. In such cases, psychologists are required to take reasonable steps to modify or withdraw from one of the roles to ensure that services continue to be objective and effective and to avoid exploitation or harm to parties involved.

> ☑ A psychologist providing therapy for a family with a terminally ill child received a court order to serve as a fact witness for a case against the couple alleging child neglect. The

> psychologist informed the parents of the court's request and took steps to clarify the nature of this role to them. The psychologist was concerned that testifying in court would harm the therapeutic relationship achieved with this family and informed the judge in writing of these concerns. The judge refused to comply with the psychologist's request not to testify. The psychologist discussed the situation further with the family, and they mutually agreed to a referral to another therapist.

10.03 Group Therapy

When psychologists provide services to several persons in a group setting, they describe at the outset the roles and responsibilities of all parties and the limits of confidentiality. *[New]*

In addition to responsibilities described in Standard 10.01, Informed Consent to Therapy, psychologists conducting group therapy must describe at the outset of treatment the unique roles and responsibilities of both therapist and clients/patients in multiperson therapies. Such information may include discussion of (a) differences between the exclusivity of the therapist's attention in individual therapy compared to attention to group dynamics in multiperson treatments; (b) group member responsibilities including turn taking and prohibitions against group members socializing outside of sessions; and (c) policies regarding such client/patient responsibilities as acceptance of diverse opinions, abusive language, coercive or aggressive behaviors, or member scapegoating.

Confidentiality. A frequently misunderstood aspect of group therapy concerns the limits of confidentiality. Although psychologists are professionally obligated to maintain the confidentiality of most statements made during group therapy sessions, decisions by members of a therapy group to disclose confidential information are neither bound by professional codes nor subject to legal liability. At the outset of group therapy, and each time a new member enters an ongoing group, psychologists must take reasonable steps to clarify that they can request, but not guarantee, that all group members maintain the confidentiality of statements made during sessions. Psychologists should also be familiar with and inform group members about state laws protecting or denying client/patient privilege (the right to limit the psychologist's disclosures to courts) for information shared during group therapy. When group therapy is conducted in response to court-ordered counseling, psychologists must also clarify to group members the parties in the justice system that will receive information learned during group therapy and how such information may be used.

Clients/Patients in Concurrent Single and Group Therapy

Psychologists who see clients/patients concurrently in individual and group therapy must take special precautions to ensure that they do not inadvertently reveal during a group session confidential information gained about a client/patient during an individual session. Psychologists must also clarify in advance to such clients differences between the goals, processes, and therapist-client relationships in single versus group therapy. When recommending that a client/patient seen in individual therapy also participate in group therapy conducted by the psychologist, steps should be taken to ensure that clients/patients understand that such a decision is voluntary and that reluctance to participate in the group will not compromise the current therapeutic relationship. This does not prohibit psychologists from having a policy of only accepting individuals as clients/patients if they participate in group therapy if (1) such multimodal treatment is clinically indicated and (2) clients/patients are informed of this requirement prior to or at the outset of therapy.

10.04 Providing Therapy to Those Served by Others

In deciding whether to offer or provide services to those already receiving mental health services elsewhere, psychologists carefully consider the treatment issues and the potential client's/patient's welfare. Psychologists discuss these issues with the client/patient or another legally authorized person on behalf of the client/patient in order to minimize the risk of confusion and conflict, consult with the other service providers when appropriate, and proceed with caution and sensitivity to the therapeutic issues. *[No Significant Change, 1992 Standard 4.04, Providing Mental Health Services to Those Served by Others]*

There may be instances in which psychologists professionally encounter an individual already receiving mental health services from another professional who might benefit from or is requesting additional therapy with the psychologist. Standard 10.04 recognizes the rights of clients/patients to seek additional services and the potential benefits of collateral therapy, as well as the potential harm that can result from client/patient involvement in concurrent therapies.

Under this standard, careful consideration of the client's/patient's welfare and treatment needs determines the ethical appropriateness of providing therapy to those served by others. In some instances, clients/patients may benefit from consultation with a psychologist when they are uncertain about the effectiveness of their current therapy or uncomfortable with what they perceive as their current provider's boundary violations. In other instances, the expertise of the psychologist may provide needed collateral treatment, for example, when a client/patient who is under the care of a psychiatrist for psychopharmacological treatment of depression would also benefit from psychosocial or behavioral treatment. On the other hand, provision of concurrent services may be harmful if clients/patients consciously or unconsciously seek to use a second therapist as a means of triangulating issues arising in their current therapy, if they begin to receive conflicting therapeutic messages from two different service providers, or if the psychologist's choice to see the patient is governed by the psychologist's own financial interests rather than client/patient welfare (see also Standards 3.08, Exploitative Relationships, and 5.06, In-Person Solicitation).

> ☑ A psychologist had an initial consultation with an individual who was currently in treatment with another provider. During the consultation, the patient frequently asked questions about the appropriateness of certain therapeutic styles. The psychologist asked the patient why he sought the consultation. He stated that he liked his current therapist but thought he would benefit from two different perspectives on his problems. During further discussions, there was no evidence that the patient's current treatment was inadequate or that the psychologist could provide collateral therapy that would be helpful. The psychologist explained this to the patient and told him that under such circumstances it would not be appropriate for her to see him as a regular patient.

In addition to careful consideration of the treatment issues and client/patient harm, under Standard 10.04, psychologists should take steps to minimize the risk that providing therapy to an individual already receiving mental health services will lead to confusion and conflicts that could jeopardize client/patient welfare. Such steps include discussing with the client/patient or his or her legally authorized representative the potential consequences of entering into a second therapeutic relationship and obtaining authorization from the client/patient to consult with the other service provider about the appropriateness and effectiveness of conjoint services (see discussion of Standard 10.01a for additional information regarding HIPAA).

> ☑ An individual met with a psychologist to discuss joining one of the psychologist's therapy groups. The client was currently in individual psychotherapy with another practitioner and informed the psychologist that her current therapist suggested that concurrent participation in group therapy might be helpful in addressing some of the social anxiety issues they had been discussing in treatment. The psychologist explained the differences in goals and modalities of group and single therapy and received written authorization from the client to discuss the treatment recommendation with her current therapist. After a conversation with the current therapist, the psychologist agreed that the client could be further helped through participation in group therapy.

Because conflicts and issues associated with providing therapy to those served by others may continue to emerge over the course of treatment, Standard 10.04 also requires that psychologists who decide to offer such services continue to monitor and proceed cautiously and sensitively in response to therapeutic issues that may arise.

10.05 Sexual Intimacies With Current Therapy Clients/Patients

Psychologists do not engage in sexual intimacies with current therapy clients/patients. *[No Significant Change, 1992 Standard 4.05, Sexual Intimacies With Current Patients or Clients]*

Sexual intimacies of any kind with a current therapy client/patient are harmful and prohibited by Standard 10.05. Sexual intimacies are broadly interpreted and include fondling, intercourse, kissing, masturbation in front of a client, telephone sex, touching of genitals, erotic hugging, verbal invitations to engage in sexual relationships, or communications (in person or via electronic transmission) intended to erotically arouse the patient. The ethical obligation to avoid sexual intimacies with clients/patients lies solely with the therapist, not with the client/patient. Any sexual intimacy between psychologists and clients/patients represents a violation of this standard regardless of whether clients/patients initiated sexual contact or voluntarily or involuntarily responded to therapists' overtures.

Sexual intimacies with current clients/patients exploit the explicit power differential and influence that psychologists have over those they treat in therapy and the vulnerabilities that led clients/patients to treatment in the first place. Sexual intimacies further harm clients/patients by impairing the provider's ability to objectively evaluate treatment issues and the client's/patient's ability to trust and respond to the psychologist in his or her professional role. In many cases, therapist-client sex exacerbates client's/patient's symptoms or leads to more serious mental disorders (Sonne & Pope, 1991).

Nonsexual physical contact with clients/patients such as handshakes or nonerotic hugging is not a violation of Standard 10.05. However, the nonerotic intentions of a therapist are often misperceived as sexualized by clients/patients. In addition, research indicates that for some psychologists such seemingly minor blurring of boundaries as hugs, self-disclosures, or meetings outside the therapist's office are often precursors of sexual misconduct (Lamb & Catanzaro, 1998).

10.06 Sexual Intimacies With Relatives or Significant Others of Current Therapy Clients/Patients

Psychologists do not engage in sexual intimacies with individuals they know to be close relatives, guardians, or significant others of current clients/patients. Psychologists do not terminate therapy to circumvent this standard. *[New]*

Engaging in sexual intimacies with another person who is related to or in a significant relationship with a current client/patient is prohibited. Sexual intimacies with such persons harm the client/patient by impairing the psychologist's treatment objectivity, blurring the therapist-client roles and relationships, and risking exploitation of the client/patient to attain or maintain a sexual relationship with a third party. This standard applies to a client's/patient's parents, siblings, children, legal guardians, and significant others. It may also apply to other relatives if they are emotionally or otherwise close to the client/patient. The phrase "they know to be" applies to the rare instance when psychologists are unaware that someone they are seeing romantically is a close relative, guardian, or significant other of a current client/patient. Standard 10.06 also prohibits psychologists from terminating therapy to circumvent the prohibition.

> ☒ A psychologist began dating the mother of a child who was currently in therapy with the psychologist.
>
> ☒ A psychologist terminated marriage therapy with a couple with the intent to begin a sexual relationship with one of the spouses.

10.07 Therapy With Former Sexual Partners

Psychologists do not accept as therapy clients/patients persons with whom they have engaged in sexual intimacies. *[No Significant Change, 1992 Standard 4.06, Therapy With Former Sexual Partners]*

Under 10.07, psychologists are prohibited from providing therapy to former sexual partners. Conducting therapy with individuals with whom psychologists have had a previous sexual relationship risks compromising the effectiveness of professional services. The knowledge gained about the individual from former sexual relationships and romantic and sexualized feelings that may reemerge during therapy can impair the psychologist's ability to objectively evaluate the client's/patient's treatment needs and response to treatment. In addition, intimate and personal knowledge about the psychologist that the client/patient gained during the former relationship can create role confusion and interfere with the client's/patient's ability to benefit from the psychologist's professional communications.

> ☒ A psychologist received a call from a man with whom she had a sexual relationship during college. The man asked if he could see her professionally to discuss some serious problems that had recently arisen in his life. The psychologist told him that she did not think it was a good idea for her to see him professionally because they had been in a previous personal relationship. The man started crying and told the psychologist that he had just moved to the town in which the psychologist practices and she was the only person he could trust with his problems. The psychologist agreed to see him for just one session.

10.08 Sexual Intimacies With Former Therapy Clients/Patients

(a) Psychologists do not engage in sexual intimacies with former clients/patients for at least two years after cessation or termination of therapy. *[No Significant Change, 1992 Standard 4.07a, Sexual Intimacies With Former Therapy Patients]*

Standard 10.08a prohibits psychologists from engaging in sexual intimacies for at least 2 years after the therapy has ended. Posttherapy sexual relationships can be harmful to clients/patients in many ways including (1) depriving former clients/patients of

future services with a practitioner who is familiar with their mental history and with whom they had a good therapeutic rapport, (2) threatening client/patient privilege when the blurring of personal and professional boundaries allows the court to require a psychologist to testify about the former client/patient in his or her personal role, (3) compromising the credibility of previous professional reports written by the psychologist about the client/patient and jeopardizing the credibility of court testimony that may be needed regarding the client's/patient's past mental status, and (4) client/patient exploitation and psychological deterioration.

Two-year moratorium. Under Standard 10.08a, any sexual intimacies with a former client/patient within 2 years following the last professional contact are an ethical violation. The standard has a 2-year moratorium period rather than a permanent prohibition against sex with former clients/patients because most complaints involving sexual intimacies with former clients/patients received by the APA Ethics Committee and licensing boards pertain to relationships that began during the first year following the cessation of therapy and complaints about relationships that began 2 years posttherapy are infrequent. However, as discussed below under Standard 10.08b, such behavior is not unconditionally acceptable after 2 years.

❌ A year after therapy ended, a traumatic event in a former patient's life created a need for additional treatment. The patient had begun a sexual relationship with his psychologist a few months following termination of treatment and thus could not reenter therapy with the psychologist. The former patient, fearful that another psychologist would be critical of his relationship with his former therapist, chose not to seek needed treatment.

❌ Several months after therapy terminated, a client entered into a sexual relationship with her former therapist and continued to discuss her mental health problems in this nonprofessional relationship. During this period, she became involved in a sexual harassment suit and wanted to exert her privilege to keep her mental status and thus her involvement in therapy confidential. Due to the blurring of personal and professional boundaries, the court agreed to call the psychologist as a witness.

❌ A psychologist began a sexual relationship with a former patient soon after therapy was terminated. Several months later, the former patient was injured on the job and his attorney advised him to pursue a disability insurance claim for mental distress created by the accident. The patient needed the psychologist to testify regarding his mental status prior to the injury. However, the psychologist-client sexual relationship compromised the psychologist's ability to provide or appear to provide objective information to the court.

> ❌ A client with a history of child sexual abuse had transferred to the psychologist the feelings of both powerlessness and eroticism that she felt for her childhood abuser. The psychologist took advantage of these feelings and told the client that she could overcome the mental health consequences of this early trauma by terminating therapy and becoming his lover. The patient agreed to end therapy. A few weeks into the post-therapy sexual relationship with the psychologist, her depression escalated and she attempted suicide.

(b) Psychologists do not engage in sexual intimacies with former clients/patients even after a two-year interval except in the most unusual circumstances. Psychologists who engage in such activity after the two years following cessation or termination of therapy and of having no sexual contact with the former client/patient bear the burden of demonstrating that there has been no exploitation, in light of all relevant factors, including (1) the amount of time that has passed since therapy terminated; (2) the nature, duration, and intensity of the therapy; (3) the circumstances of termination; (4) the client's/patient's personal history; (5) the client's/patient's current mental status; (6) the likelihood of adverse impact on the client/patient; and (7) any statements or actions made by the therapist during the course of therapy suggesting or inviting the possibility of a posttermination sexual or romantic relationship with the client/patient. (See also Standard 3.05, Multiple Relationships.) *[Modified for Clarity, 1992 Standard 4.07b, Sexual Intimacies With Former Patients]*

Standard 10.08a prohibits psychologists from engaging in a sexual relationship with a former client/patient for at least 2 years following the termination of therapy. However, sexual intimacies with former clients/patients even 2 years following the cessation of therapy can result in exploitation and harm. If an ethics complaint is made against the psychologist regarding a 2-year posttermination sexual relationship, Standard 10.08b places the ethical burden on the psychologist to demonstrate that the sexual relationship is not exploitative. The standard describes seven relevant factors that could be applied to determine such exploitation. Below these factors are listed along with examples of how they might be applied to a finding of violation of this standard.

1. *The amount of time that has passed since therapy terminated.* A sexual relationship was initiated immediately following the 24-month period.

2. *The nature, duration, and intensity of the therapy.* The client/patient was seen by the psychologist three times a week for several years in intensive psychodynamic psychotherapy.

3. *The circumstances of termination.* The client/patient abruptly stopped coming to therapy after expressing strong erotic fantasies for the psychologist.

4. *The client's/patient's personal history.* The client-patient had been sexually abused as a child and was diagnosed with borderline personality disorder and severe attachment needs.

5. *The client's/patient's current mental status.* When the posttermination sexual relationship with the psychologist began, the patient was being treated by another psychologist for major depression.

6. *The likelihood of adverse impact on the client/patient.* Based on a sexual abuse history, borderline diagnosis, and current major depression, it was reasonable to assume that a client/patient would be extremely vulnerable to reexperiencing some of the early trauma if engaged in a sexual relationship with his former therapist whom he perceived as a powerful parent figure.

7. *Any statements or actions made by the therapist during the course of therapy suggesting or inviting the possibility of a posttermination sexual or romantic relationship with the client/patient.* The psychologist had a habit of hugging the client/patient at the end of each therapy session.

10.09 Interruption of Therapy

When entering into employment or contractual relationships, psychologists make reasonable efforts to provide for orderly and appropriate resolution of responsibility for client/patient care in the event that the employment or contractual relationship ends, with paramount consideration given to the welfare of the client/patient. (See also Standard 3.12, Interruption of Psychological Services.) *[Modified for Clarity, 1992 Standard 4.08b, Interruption of Services]*

This standard applies to ethical obligations of psychologists at the time they enter into employment or contractual agreements with other providers, group practices, managed care providers, institutions, or agencies. Employment or contractual agreements can end when psychologists have a time-limited contract or employment period, when they elect to leave for professional or personal reasons, or when the employer or company terminates their position or contract. Under Standard 10.09, psychologists must make reasonable efforts to ensure at the outset that the employment agreement or contract provides for orderly and appropriate resolution of responsibility in the event that the employment or contractual arrangement ends.

Psychologists can comply with Standard 10.09 by determining through preemployment discussions whether the organization, group practice, or other entity in which a work arrangement is being considered has policies designed to ensure continuity of care when a practitioner can no longer provide services. If no such policies exist, psychologists can help to develop such policies or include in their employment or contractual agreements permission to appropriately resolve treatment responsibility in the event their employment or contract ends. Steps the psychologist can recommend be taken to protect client/patient welfare when treatment can no longer be provided by the psychologist include providing pretermination counseling and referrals, supervising appropriate transfer and storage of client/patient records, assisting in the transition of the client/patient to a new treatment provider if clinically indicated, or continuing treatment with the client/patient in a different venue. The phrase "make reasonable efforts" recognizes that in some situations employers, organizations, group practices, or other providers will refuse to promise or follow through on promises to protect client/patient welfare through an orderly and appropriate resolution of care when there is a change in staff.

☑ A school psychologist was hired on a 9-month (October through June) contract to provide counseling services for grade-school students who had lost parents in the September 11, 2001, attack on the World Trade Center. It was reasonable to assume that some children might need continued care during the summer. The school psychologist raised this issue when asked to take the position. The school superintendent responded that such services were not available through the schools during the summer. The psychologist worked with the superintendent to develop an agreement with a social services agency to provide treatment for students who needed continued care over the summer. The superintendent also agreed to set up a system that facilitated the appropriate transfer of student records to the social service agency. The psychologist also laid out a plan for identifying children who would need summer services and for informing their guardians about the availability of such services.

Standard 10.09 does not prohibit psychologists from signing a non-compete clause barring the psychologist from continuing to see specific clients/patients after the employment or contractual agreement has ended as long as other provisions for protecting client/patient welfare are in place.

10.10 Terminating Therapy

(a) Psychologists terminate therapy when it becomes reasonably clear that the client/patient no longer needs the service, is not likely to benefit, or is being harmed by continued service. *[No Significant Change, 1992 Standard 4.09b, Terminating the Professional Relationship]*

Psychologists are committed to improving the condition of individuals with whom they work and to do no harm (Preamble; Principle A: Beneficence and Nonmaleficence). In some instances, continued therapy with a client/patient may be nonbeneficial or harmful. Standard 10.10a requires psychologists to terminate therapy under three conditions that either fail to benefit clients/patients or could be harmful if therapy is continued. Although the need to continue or terminate a therapeutic relationship requires professional judgment based on knowledge of the specific treatment context, the phrase "reasonably clear" in this standard indicates that it is ethically inappropriate for a psychologist to continue therapy under conditions in which most psychologists engaged in similar activities in similar circumstances would judge it unnecessary, nonbeneficial, or harmful.

Services are no longer needed. Psychologists who continue to see clients/patients professionally after they no longer need mental health services are in violation of this standard. The need for continued services depends on the nature of the client's/patient's disorder and the goals of treatment as identified during the initial informed consent and throughout the therapeutic process. Psychologists who continue to treat clients/patients when the problems associated with entering treatment have been adequately addressed violate this standard. The standard does not prohibit psychologists and clients/patients from reevaluating treatment needs and continuing in a therapeutic relationship to address additional mental health needs. However, failure to reevaluate the need for continued therapy after treatment goals are met would violate the standard. Psychologists who continue to see clients/patients solely to fulfill the psychologists' own training requirements or for financial gain violate this standard and also risk violating Standard 3.08, Exploitative Relationships. Psychologists who continue to bill a third-party payor for mental health services when the services are no longer required place themselves at risk for accusations of insurance fraud and are in potential violation of Standards 6.04b, Fees and Financial Arrangements, and 6.06, Accuracy in Reports to Payors and Funding Sources.

☒ A licensed psychologist in independent practice had sought additional training at a prestigious postgraduate psychotherapy institute. The institute required a certain number of hours of supervision with clients with specific disorders to obtain a certificate of completion. The psychologist had 8 more hours of supervision for treatment of anxiety disorders to complete before he could qualify for the certificate. The client who met the diagnostic criteria for supervision had been doing very well in treatment. She had resolved most of the problems at work and at home that had brought her to therapy and viewed terminating treatment with eagerness and a sense of pride. She asked the therapist whether they could have one final session to complete the therapy. The psychologist told her that although she had been doing well there were a few unresolved issues that would take about eight more sessions to adequately address. The client reluctantly agreed.

The client/patient is not likely to benefit. Psychologists must also terminate therapy when the client/patient is not likely to benefit from the treatment. This criterion applies when during the course of therapy it becomes reasonably clear that the client/patient is not responding to treatment, a newly uncovered aspect of the client's/patient's disorder is not amenable to the type of treatment modality in which the psychologist has been trained (see also Standard 2.01a, Boundaries of Competence), or a client/patient is unwilling or unable to comply with treatment (e.g., when a client/patient continuously refuses to follow the terms of a behavioral contract).

☑ A counseling psychologist had been seeing a client for career counseling who was recently fired from a management position that he had held for 10 years. The client was angry and believed that the termination was undeserved. After three sessions, the psychologist determined that there was a clinically paranoid feature to the client's distress and that more intensive psychotherapy was needed before career counseling could be beneficial. The psychologist discussed her concerns with the client and referred him to another practitioner who worked with more seriously disturbed clients. The psychologist also informed the client that her services would be available to him when he was ready to resume career counseling.

The client/patient is being harmed by continued service. Psychologists are prohibited from continuing therapy if it is reasonably clear that the client/patient is being harmed by the treatment. For example, in some instances clients/patients may unexpectedly respond to therapy with major depression, a psychotic episode, or addictive behaviors that do not respond to continued efforts by the psychologist. The phrase "reasonably clear" indicates that the criteria for determining whether a client/patient is being harmed by continued services are determined by what would be the prevailing judgment of psychologists engaged in similar activities in similar circumstances, given the knowledge the psychologist had or should have had at the time. Psychologists who find that a client's/patient's mental health is deteriorating may find it helpful therefore to consult with colleagues regarding whether services should be continued. When it is appropriate to terminate, patients should be referred to alternative treatments that may be more effective.

☑ A psychologist was providing psychoanalytic therapy to a patient with narcissistic personality disorder. The treatment appeared to be going well until the patient began to discuss in detail a traumatic rape experience that occurred when she was a young adult. In the weeks that followed, the patient kept putting herself in dangerous situations that appeared to be reenactments of the earlier event. She was engaging in sexual relationships with men she barely knew, engaging in unprotected sex, and frequenting dangerous areas of the city. In therapy during the next 6 weeks, the psychologist continued to explore with the patient her feelings and behaviors associated with the initial trauma. Instead of abating the risky behavior, each session appeared to lead to more extreme behaviors. The psychologist was concerned that the patient might again be raped, assaulted, or contract HIV/AIDS and consulted with several colleagues regarding continuation of services. Based on these consultations, he concluded that continuing the therapy would be harmful to this patient and that she might benefit from a different therapeutic approach. He discussed this with the patient over several sessions and referred her to a group practice specializing in treatments for rape trauma.

(b) Psychologists may terminate therapy when threatened or otherwise endangered by the client/patient or another person with whom the client/patient has a relationship. *[New]*

Standard 10.10b permits psychologists to abruptly terminate therapy if they are threatened or endangered by a client/patient or another person with whom the client/patient has a relationship such as a family member, significant other, friend, employer, or employee. Such situations can include verbal or physical threats or any other evidence that the psychologist is endangered. In such situations, neither advance notification of termination nor pretermination counseling as described in Standard 10.10c is required. Psychologists may also request a protective order against clients/patients or others whom they suspect will threaten or harm them. Prohibitions against revealing confidential information do not apply when psychologists must call on authorities or others to protect them from threats or harm (see Standard 4.05b, Disclosures).

(c) Except where precluded by the actions of clients/patients or third-party payors, prior to termination psychologists provide pretermination counseling and suggest alternative service providers as appropriate. *[Expanded, 1992 Standard 4.09c, Terminating the Professional Relationship]*

A noteworthy change in the 2002 Ethics Code is the elimination of the 1992 code's broadly worded prohibition against abandoning the client (Standard 4.09a, Terminating the Professional Relationship). Termination based on reasonable professional judgment and proper pretermination counseling is ethically appropriate. In addition to the situations described in Standards 10.10a and 10.10b, above, ethically permissible and professionally appropriate reasons to end a therapeutic relationship include the following: (1) an organized system of health or managed care company rejects a psychologist's recommendations for additional therapy sessions; (2) an unforeseen potentially harmful multiple relationship arises (Standards 3.05b, Multiple Relationships; 10.02b, Therapy Involving Couples or Families); (3) a client/patient repeatedly refuses to pay for services (Standard 6.04e, Fees and Financial Arrangements); (4) a psychologist becomes ill or finds therapy with a particular client/patient stressful in a manner that risks compromising professional services (Standard 2.06b, Personal Problems and Conflicts); (5) during the course of therapy, unexpected treatment needs arise that are outside the psychologist's area of expertise (Standard 2.01, Boundaries of Competence); or (6) the psychologist is relocating or retiring.

Under Standard 10.10c, psychologists must provide pretermination counseling prior to ending a therapeutic relationship. Pretermination counseling includes (1) providing clients/patients sufficient advance notice of termination (when possible), (2) discussing with the client/patient the reasons for the termination, (3) encouraging the client/patient to ask questions regarding termination, and (4) providing referrals to alternate service providers when appropriate. Psychologists are not in violation of this standard if pretermination counseling is precluded by client/patient or third-party payor actions. For example, parents may abruptly end their child's therapy making further contact with the child inappropriate or unfeasible; health plans may prohibit or place restrictions on provider referrals.

☑ A psychotherapy patient changed to a health plan that she later realized would not reimburse her current psychologist's services. She told the psychologist that she would not be able to come to any more sessions because she could not afford to pay for therapy out of pocket and thus would be continuing services with a provider covered by her new health plan. The psychologist discussed the patient's concerns about leaving therapy. The patient appeared ready to terminate the relationship. The psychologist told her that he was not familiar with any of her new health plan's approved providers, but, with her authorization, would be willing to speak with her new therapist if the need arose.

☑ A psychologist in independent practice accepted a job offer from a treatment center in another state. The psychologist agreed to start the new position in 4 weeks. At their next sessions, the psychologist told each of her clients that she would be relocating at the end of the month and that they would have time to discuss over the next few weeks their feelings about terminating therapy and their plans for the future. At each of the remaining sessions, she encouraged clients to discuss any concerns they might have about the termination. The psychologist provided appropriate referrals to those who wished to continue in therapy with another professional. She told the other clients how to contact her if they wished a referral in the future. One client had serious difficulty adjusting to the termination. The psychologist offered to have phone sessions with this client until a suitable referral could be found.

☑ A patient who recently lost his job had not paid his last two monthly bills for psychotherapy. The psychologist had discussed the issue of nonpayment with the patient several times during the past month. Neither a reduced fee nor payment plan was economically feasible for the patient. The psychologist told the patient that she would not be able to continue to see him pro bono indefinitely and that they would have two more sessions to discuss any questions he might have and his plans for the future. She also provided the patient with a list of several free clinics in the area that offered therapy.

Part III

Ethics in Action

CHAPTER 14

The APA Ethics Code and Ethical Decision Making

The American Psychological Association's (APA) Ethics Code provides a set of aspirational principles and behavioral rules written broadly to apply to psychologists' varied roles and the diverse contexts in which the science and practice of psychology are conducted. Previous chapters of this book have provided rationales, explanations, and examples of the application of each Ethical Standard to psychologists' work. In their everyday activities, psychologists will find many instances in which familiarity with and adherence to specific Ethical Standards provide adequate foundation for ethical actions. There will also be many instances in which (1) the means by which to comply with a standard are not readily apparent, (2) two seemingly competing standards appear equally appropriate, (3) application of a single standard or set of standards appears consistent with one aspirational principle but inconsistent with another, or (4) a judgment is required to determine if exemption criteria for a particular standard are met.

The Ethics Code is not a formula for solving these ethical challenges. The Ethics Code provides psychologists with a set of aspirations and broad general rules of conduct that must be interpreted and applied as a function of the unique scientific and professional roles and relationships in which they are embedded. Psychologists are not moral technocrats simply working their way through a maze of ethical rules. Successful application of the principles and standards of the Ethics Code involves a conception of psychologists as active moral agents committed to the good and just practice and science of psychology. Ethical decision making thus involves a commitment to applying the Ethics Code to construct rather than simply discover solutions to ethical quandaries.

This chapter steps back from discussion of specific standards to reflect on ethical attitudes and decision-making strategies that can help psychologists prepare for, identify, and resolve ethical challenges as they continuously emerge and evolve in the dynamic discipline of psychology.

Ethical Commitment

The development of a dynamic set of ethical standards for psychologists' work-related conduct requires a personal commitment and lifelong effort to act ethically; to encourage ethical behavior by students, supervisees, employees, and colleagues; and to consult with others concerning ethical problems.

—*APA (2002, Preamble)*

Ethical commitment refers to a strong desire to do what is right because it is right (Josephson Institute of Ethics, 1999). In psychology, this commitment reflects a moral disposition and emotional responsiveness that move psychologists to creatively apply the APA's Ethics Code principles and standards to the unique ethical demands of the scientific or professional context.

The desire to do the right thing has often been associated with moral virtues or moral character defined as a disposition to act and feel in accordance with moral principles, obligations, and ideals—a disposition that is neither principle bound nor situation specific (Beauchamp & Childress, 2001; MacIntyre, 1984). Virtues are dispositional habits acquired through social nurturance and professional education that provide psychologists with the motivation and skills necessary to apply the ideals and standards of the profession (see, e.g., Hauerwas, 1981; Jordan & Meara, 1990; May, 1984).

Focal Virtues for Psychology

Many moral dispositions have been proposed for the virtuous professional (Beauchamp & Childress, 2001; Keenan, 1995; MacIntyre, 1984; May, 1984). For disciplines such as psychology, in which codes of conduct dictate the general parameters but not the context-specific nature of ethical conduct, conscientiousness, discernment, and prudence are requisite virtues.

- A *conscientious* psychologist is motivated to do what is right because it is right, diligently tries to determine what is right, and makes reasonable attempts to do the right thing.

- A *discerning* psychologist brings contextually and relationally sensitive insight, good judgment, and appropriately detached understanding to determine what is right.

- A *prudent* psychologist applies practical wisdom to ethical challenges leading to right solutions that can be realized given the nature of the problem and the individuals involved.

Some moral dispositions can be understood as derivative of their corresponding principles (Beauchamp & Childress, 2001). Drawing on the five APA General Principles, Table 14.1 lists corresponding virtues.

The virtues considered most salient by members of a profession will vary with differences in role responsibilities. Benevolence, care, and compassion are often associated

Table 14.1   APA Ethics Code General Principles and Corresponding Virtues

APA General Principle	Corresponding Virtues
Principle A: Beneficence and Nonmaleficence	Compassionate, nonmalevolent, and prudent
Principle B: Fidelity and Responsibility	Faithful, dependable, and conscientious
Principle C: Integrity	Honest, reliable, and genuine
Principle D: Justice	Judicious and fair
Principle E: Respect for People's Rights and Dignity	Respectful and considerate

with the provision of mental health services. Prudence, discretion, and trustworthiness have been considered salient in scientific decision making. Fidelity, integrity, and wisdom are moral characteristics frequently associated with teaching and consultation.

Can virtues be taught? Some have argued that psychology professors cannot change graduate students' moral character through classroom teaching and therefore ethics education should focus on understanding the ethics code rather than instilling moral dispositions to right action. Without question, however, senior members of the discipline through teaching and through their own examples can enhance the ability of students and young professionals to understand the centrality of ethical commitment to ethical practice.

Ethical Awareness

In the process of making decisions regarding their professional behavior, psychologists must consider this Ethics Code, in addition to applicable laws and psychology board regulations.

—*APA (2002, Introduction)*

Lack of awareness or misunderstanding of an ethical standard is not itself a defense to a charge of unethical conduct.

—*APA (2002, Introduction)*

Ethical commitment is just the first step in effective ethical decision making. Good intentions are insufficient if psychologists fail to identify the ethical situations to which they should be applied. Psychologists found in violation of Ethical Standards or licensure regulations have too often harmed others or damaged their own careers or the careers of others because of ethical ignorance. Conscientious psychologists understand that identification of situations requiring ethical attention is dependent on familiarity and understanding of the APA Ethics Code, relevant scientific and professional guidelines, and laws and regulations applicable to their specific work-related activities.

Table 14.2 APA Ethics Code General Principles and the Ethical Awareness Necessary to Apply the Principles

APA General Principle	Corresponding Ethical Awareness
Principle A: Beneficence and Nonmaleficence	Psychologists should be able to identify what is in the best interests of those with whom they work, when a situation threatens the welfare of individuals, and the competencies required to achieve the greatest good and avoid or minimize harm.
Principle B: Fidelity and Responsibility	Psychologists should be aware of their obligations to the individuals and communities affected by their work, including their responsibilities to the profession and obligations under the law.
Principle C: Integrity	Psychologist should know what is possible before making professional commitments and be able to identify when it is necessary to correct misconceptions or mistrust.
Principle D: Justice	Psychologists should be able to identify individual or group vulnerabilities that can lead to exploitation and recognize when a course of action would or has resulted in unfair or unjust practices.
Principle E: Respect for People's Rights and Dignity	Psychologists must be aware of special safeguards necessary to protect the autonomy, privacy, and dignity of members from the diverse populations with whom psychologists work.

Moral Values and Ethical Awareness

To identify a situation as warranting ethical consideration, psychologists must be aware of the moral values of the discipline. Although the Ethics Code's General Principles are not exhaustive, they do identify the major moral ideals of psychology as a field. Familiarity with the General Principles, however, is not sufficient for good ethical decision making. Psychologists need to be aware when situations call for consideration of these principles. Table 14.2 identifies types of ethical awareness corresponding to each General Principle.

Ethical Awareness and Ethical Planning

Too often psychologists approach ethics as an afterthought to assessment or treatment plans, research designs, course preparation, or groundwork for forensic or consulting activities. Ethical planning based on familiarity with ethical standards, professional guidelines, state and federal laws, and organizational and institutional policies should be seen as integral rather than tangential to psychologists' work.

Ethical Standards. Familiarity with the rules of conduct set forth in the Ethical Standards enables psychologists to take preventive measures to avoid the harms, injustices, and violations of individual rights that often lead to ethical complaints. For example, psychologists familiar with the standards on confidentiality and disclosure discussed in Chapter 7 will take steps in advance to (1) develop appropriate procedures to protect the confidentiality of information obtained during their work-related activities; (2) appropriately inform research participants, clients/patients, organizational clients, and others in advance about the extent and limitations of confidentiality; and (3) develop specific plans and lists of appropriate professionals, agencies, and institutions to be used if disclosure of confidential information becomes necessary.

Guidelines. Good ethical planning also involves familiarity with guidelines for responsible practice and science. The APA and other professional and scientific organizations publish guidelines for responsible practice appropriate to particular psychological activities. Guidelines, unlike ethical standards, are essentially aspirational and unenforceable. As a result, compared with the enforceable Ethics Code standards, guidelines can include recommendations for and examples of responsible conduct with greater specificity to role, activity, and context. Guidelines shed light on specific steps that other psychologists in similar situations have taken to successfully resolve ethical quandaries. The crafters of guidelines developed by APA constituencies usually attempt to ensure that their recommendations are consistent with the most current APA Ethics Code—readers should refer back to Chapter 3 of this book to help identify where changes in the 2002 Ethics Code may render some guideline recommendations obsolete.

Laws, regulations, and policies. Another important element of information gathering is identifying and understanding applicable laws, government regulations, and institutional and organizational policies that may dictate or limit specific courses of actions necessary to resolve an ethical problem. There are state and federal laws and organizational policies governing patient privacy, mandated reporting, research with humans and animals, conduct among military enlistees and officers, employment discrimination, conflicts of interest, billing, and treatment. As discussed in previous chapters, only a handful of Ethical Standards require psychologists to adhere to laws or institutional rules. However, choosing an ethical path that violates law, institutional rules, or company policy can have serious consequences for psychologists and others. Laws and policies should not dictate ethics, but familiarity with legal and organizational rules is essential for informed ethical decision making.

Ethical Decision Making

Ethical commitment and well-informed ethical planning will reduce but not eliminate ethical challenges that emerge during the course of psychologists' work. Ethical problems often arise when two or more principles or standards appear to be in conflict, from unforeseen reactions of those with whom a psychologist works, or unexpected events. There is no ethical menu from which the right ethical actions can simply be selected.

Many ethical challenges are unique in time, place, and persons involved. The very process of generating and evaluating alternative courses of action helps place in vivid relief the moral principles underlying such conflicts and stimulates creative strategies that may resolve or eliminate them.

Evaluating Alternatives and Consequences

Ethical decisions are neither singular nor static. They involve a series of steps, each of which will be determined by the consequences of previous steps. Evaluation of alternative ethical solutions should take a narrative approach that sequentially considers the potential risks and benefits of each action. Understanding of relevant laws and regulations as well as the nature of institutions, companies, or organizations in which the activities will take place is similarly essential for adequate evaluation of the reactions and restraints imposed by the specific ethical context.

Stakeholders. Ethical decision making requires sensitivity to and compassion for the views of individuals affected by actions taken. Discussions with stakeholders can clarify the multifaceted nature of an ethical problem, illuminate ethical principles that are in jeopardy of being violated or ignored, and alert psychologists to potential unintended consequences of specific action choices. By taking steps to understand the concerns, values, and perceptions of clients/patients, research participants, family members, organizational clients, students, corporate compliance or institutional review boards, and others with whom they work, psychologists can avoid ethical decisions that would be ineffective or harmful (Fisher, 1999, 2000).

Moral theories. In evaluating each alternative, psychologists should reflect on the rights and obligations of all involved and aspirational principles that can or cannot be achieved at each step. Awareness of the moral framework guiding one's concerns can also help clarify the values underlying a choice of alternative strategies (Beauchamp & Childress, 2001; Fisher, 1999; Kitchener, 1984). Consider the following ethical dilemma and the ways in which the moral theories listed below might lead to different ethical choices.

> ☑ A psychotherapy client who was an executive at a large company was in treatment for his addiction to heroin. A month ago, the client had learned that he tested positive for the HIV virus and had reacted with bouts of depression and rage since then. During a session, the client told the psychologist that he had been saving the needles he used to inject himself with heroin so that he could infect others with the HIV virus. He further revealed that he invited a group of colleagues who he knew to be drug users to a party that evening to carry out his plan. As the session was ending, it became obvious that the psychologist's attempts to convince the client not to carry out

this plan were unsuccessful. The state in which the psychologist worked did not have laws either compelling or prohibiting professionals from disclosing such information. The psychologist could decide to keep the information confidential. Such a decision would be compatible with Standard 4.01, Maintaining Confidentiality, which stresses psychologists' primary obligation to protect confidential information. The psychologist could also decide to alert authorities or others about the party. Such a decision would be compatible with Standard 4.05b, Disclosures, which permits psychologists to disclose confidential information without the consent of the individual to protect others from harm.

Deontology. Deontological theory prioritizes absolute obligations over consequences (Kant, 1785/1959). In this moral framework, ethical decision making is the rational act of applying universal principals to all situations irrespective of specific relationships, contexts, or consequences. For Kant, respect for the worth of all persons was a categorical imperative. A course of action that results in a person being used simply as a means for others' gains would be ethically unacceptable. In the above case, a psychologist following deontological theory might decide to maintain client confidentiality under the premise that respect for a person's autonomy and privacy rights is a universal principle that should always be followed irrespective of consequences in particular situations.

Utilitarianism. Utilitarian theory prioritizes the consequences (or utility) of an act over the application of universal principles (Mill, 1861/1957). From this perspective, an ethical decision is situation specific and must be governed by a risk-benefit calculus that determines which act will produce the greatest possible balance of good over bad consequences. An "act utilitarian" makes an ethical decision by evaluating the consequences of an act for a given situation. A "rule utilitarian" makes an ethical decision by evaluating whether following a general rule in all similar situations would create the greater good. Like deontology, utilitarianism is impersonal. Psychologists' obligations to those with whom they work can be superseded by an action that would produce a greater good for others. A psychologist adhering to act utilitarianism might decide in the above case to disclose information about the client's intentions because to do so could produce benefits for many others, whereas maintaining confidentiality might benefit only the client. A rule utilitarian might decide to maintain confidentiality because if other clients with drug addictions began to suspect that psychologists would disclose personal information, the value of therapy to many others would be jeopardized.

Communitarianism. Communitarian theory assumes right actions derive from community values, goals, traditions, and cooperative virtues. Accordingly, different populations with whom a psychologist works may require different conceptualizations of what is ethically appropriate (MacIntyre, 1989; Walzer, 1983). Psychologists who have extensive experience working with individuals with drug addictions often obtain a perspective on how the majority of such individuals view needle sharing by heroin addicts who know that they are HIV positive. In the above case, psychologists holding a communitarian perspective might base their decision to maintain confidentiality or disclose the client's intentions based on their understanding of attitudes within the drug-addicted community.

Feminist ethics. Feminist ethics, or an ethics of care, sees emotional commitment to act on behalf of persons with whom one has a significant relationship as central to ethical decision making. This moral theory rejects the primacy of universal and individual rights in favor of relationally specific obligations (Baier, 1985; Brabeck, 2000; Gilligan, 1982). Feminist psychologists in the above case might decide that the professional relationship with the client, the obligation to help him overcome his addiction, and the importance of maintaining his trust in the therapeutic relationship supersede the responsibility to protect individuals with whom a psychologist has no relationship.

Steps in Ethical Decision Making

A number of psychologists have proposed excellent ethical decision-making models to guide the responsible conduct of psychological science and practice (e.g., Canter, Bennett, Jones, & Nagy, 1994; Kitchener, 1984; Koocher & Keith-Spiegel, 1998; Newman, Gray, & Fuqua, 1996; Rest, 1983; Staal & King, 2000). Drawing on these models and the importance of ethical commitment, awareness, and competence, an 8-step model is proposed:

Step 1: Develop and sustain a professional commitment to doing what is right.

Step 2: Acquire sufficient familiarity with the APA Ethics Code General Principles and Ethical Standards to be able to anticipate situations that require ethical planning and to identify unanticipated situations that require ethical decision making.

Step 3: Gather additional facts relevant to the specific ethical situation from professional guidelines, state and federal laws, and organizational policies.

Step 4: Make efforts to understand the perspective of different stakeholders who will be affected by the decision and consult with colleagues.

Step 5: Apply Steps 1-4 to generate ethical alternatives and evaluate each alternative in terms of moral theories, General Principles and Ethical Standards.

Step 6: Select and implement an ethical course of action.

Step 7: Monitor and evaluate the effectiveness of the course of action.

Step 8: Modify and continue to evaluate the ethical plan if necessary.

Doing Good Well

Ethical decision making in psychology requires flexibility and sensitivity to the context, role responsibilities, and stakeholder expectations unique to each work endeavor. At their best, ethical choices reflect the reciprocal interplay between psychological activities and ethical standards in which each is continuously informed and transformed by the other. The specific manner in which the APA Ethics Code General Principles and Ethical Standards are applied should reflect a "goodness of fit" between ethical alternatives and the psychologist's professional role, work setting, and stakeholder needs (Fisher, 2002a, 2003). Envisioning the responsible conduct of psychology as a process that draws on psychologists' human responsiveness to those with whom they work and their awareness of their own boundaries, competencies, and obligations will sustain a profession that is both effective and ethical.

Ethics requires self-reflection and the courage to analyze and challenge one's values and actions. Ethical practice is ensured only to the extent that there is a personal commitment accompanied by ethical awareness and active engagement in the ongoing construction, evaluation, and modification of ethical actions. In their commitment to the ongoing identification of key ethical crossroads and the construction of contextually sensitive ethical courses of action, psychologists reflect the highest ideals of the profession and merit the trust of those with whom they work.

Appendix

Ethical Principles of Psychologists and Code of Conduct, American Psychological Association (2002)

Ethical Principles of Psychologists and Code Of Conduct
2002

History and Effective Date Footnote

CONTENTS

INTRODUCTION AND APPLICABILITY

The American Psychological Association's (APA's) Ethical Principles of Psychologists and Code of Conduct (hereinafter referred to as the Ethics Code) consists of an Introduction, a Preamble, five General Principles (A – E), and specific Ethical Standards. The Introduction discusses the intent, organization, procedural considerations, and scope of application of the Ethics Code. The Preamble and General Principles are aspirational goals to guide psychologists toward the highest ideals of psychology. Although the Preamble and General Principles are not themselves enforceable rules, they should be considered by psychologists in arriving at an ethical course of action. The Ethical Standards set forth enforceable rules for conduct as psychologists. Most of the Ethical Standards are written broadly, in order to apply to psychologists in varied roles, although the application of an Ethical Standard may vary depending on the context. The Ethical Standards are not exhaustive. The fact that a given conduct is not specifically addressed by an Ethical Standard does not mean that it is necessarily either ethical or unethical.

This Ethics Code applies only to psychologists' activities that are part of their scientific, educational, or professional roles as psychologists. Areas covered include but are not limited to the clinical, counseling, and school practice of psychology; research; teaching; supervision of trainees; public service; policy development; social intervention; development of assessment instruments; conducting assessments; educational counseling; organizational consulting; forensic activities; program design and evaluation; and administration. This Ethics Code applies to these activities across a variety of contexts, such as in person, postal, telephone, internet, and other electronic transmissions. These activities shall be distinguished from the purely private conduct of psychologists, which is not within the purview of the Ethics Code.

Membership in the APA commits members and student affiliates to comply with the standards of the APA Ethics Code and to the rules and procedures used to enforce them. Lack of awareness or misunderstanding of an Ethical Standard is not itself a defense to a charge of unethical conduct.

The procedures for filing, investigating, and resolving complaints of unethical conduct are described in the current Rules and Procedures of the APA Ethics Committee. APA may impose sanctions on its members for violations of the standards of the Ethics Code, including termination of APA membership, and may notify other bodies and individuals of its actions. Actions that violate the standards of the Ethics Code may also lead to the imposition of sanctions on psychologists or students whether or not they are APA members by bodies other than APA, including state psychological associations, other professional groups, psychology boards, other state or federal agencies, and payors for health services. In addition, APA may take action against a member after his or her conviction of a felony, expulsion or suspension from an affiliated state psychological association, or suspension or loss of licensure. When the sanction to be imposed by APA is less than expulsion, the 2001 Rules and Procedures do not guarantee an opportunity for an in-person hearing, but generally provide that complaints will be resolved only on the basis of a submitted record.

The Ethics Code is intended to provide guidance for psychologists and standards of professional conduct that can be applied by the APA and by other bodies that choose to adopt them. The Ethics Code is not intended to be a basis of civil liability. Whether a psychologist has violated the Ethics Code standards does not by itself determine whether the psychologist is legally liable in a court action, whether a contract is enforceable, or whether other legal consequences occur.

The modifiers used in some of the standards of this Ethics Code (e.g., *reasonably, appropriate, potentially*) are included in the standards when they would (1) allow professional judgment on the part of psychologists, (2) eliminate injustice or inequality that would occur without the modifier, (3) ensure applicability across the broad range of activities conducted by psychologists, or (4) guard against a set of rigid rules that might be quickly outdated. As used in this Ethics Code, the term *reasonable* means the prevailing professional judgment of psychologists engaged in similar activities in similar circumstances, given the knowledge the psychologist had or should have had at the time.

In the process of making decisions regarding their professional behavior, psychologists must consider this Ethics Code in addition to applicable laws and psychology board regulations. In applying the Ethics Code to their professional work, psychologists may consider other materials and guidelines that have been adopted or endorsed by scientific and professional psychological organizations and the dictates of their own conscience, as well as consult with others within the field. If this Ethics Code establishes a higher standard of conduct than is required by law, psychologists must meet the higher ethical standard. If psychologists' ethical responsibilities conflict with law, regulations, or other governing legal authority, psychologists make known their commitment to this Ethics Code and take steps to resolve the conflict in a responsible manner. If the conflict is unresolvable via such means, psychologists may adhere to the requirements of the law, regulations, or other governing authority in keeping with basic principles of human rights.

PREAMBLE

Psychologists are committed to increasing scientific and professional knowledge of behavior and people's understanding of themselves and others and to the use of such knowledge to improve the condition of individuals, organizations, and society. Psychologists respect and protect civil and human rights and the central importance of freedom of inquiry and expression in research, teaching, and publication. They strive to help the public in developing informed judgments and choices concerning human behavior. In doing so, they perform many roles, such as researcher, educator, diagnostician, therapist, supervisor, consultant, administrator, social interventionist, and expert witness. This Ethics Code provides a common set of principles and standards upon which psychologists build their professional and scientific work.

This Ethics Code is intended to provide specific standards to cover most situations encountered by psychologists. It has as its goals the welfare and protection of the individuals and groups with whom psychologists work and the education of members, students, and the public regarding ethical standards of the discipline.

The development of a dynamic set of ethical standards for psychologists' work-related conduct requires a personal commitment and lifelong effort to act ethically; to encourage ethical behavior by students, supervisees, employees, and colleagues; and to consult with others concerning ethical problems.

GENERAL PRINCIPLES

This section consists of General Principles. General Principles, as opposed to Ethical Standards, are aspirational in nature. Their intent is to guide and inspire psychologists toward the very highest ethical ideals of the profession. General Principles, in contrast to Ethical Standards, do not represent obligations and should not form the basis for imposing sanctions. Relying upon General Principles for either of these reasons distorts both their meaning and purpose.

Principle A: Beneficence and Nonmaleficence

Psychologists strive to benefit those with whom they work and take care to do no harm. In their professional actions, psychologists seek to safeguard the welfare and rights of those with whom they interact professionally and other affected persons, and the welfare of animal subjects of research. When conflicts occur among psychologists' obligations or concerns, they attempt to resolve these conflicts in a responsible fashion that avoids or minimizes harm. Because psychologists' scientific and professional judgments and actions may affect the lives of others, they are alert to and guard against personal, financial, social, organizational, or political factors that might lead to misuse of their influence. Psychologists strive to be aware of the possible effect of their own physical and mental health on their ability to help those with whom they work.

Principle B: Fidelity and Responsibility

Psychologists establish relationships of trust with those with whom they work. They are aware of their professional and scientific responsibilities to society and to the specific communities in which they work. Psychologists uphold professional standards of conduct, clarify their professional roles and obligations, accept appropriate responsibility for their behavior, and seek to manage conflicts of interest that could lead to exploitation or harm. Psychologists consult with, refer to, or cooperate with other professionals and institutions to the extent needed to serve the best interests of those with whom they work. They are concerned about the ethical compliance of their colleagues' scientific and professional conduct. Psychologists strive to contribute a portion of their professional time for little or no compensation or personal advantage.

Principle C: Integrity

Psychologists seek to promote accuracy, honesty, and truthfulness in the science, teaching, and practice of psychology. In these activities psychologists do not steal, cheat, or engage in fraud, subterfuge, or intentional misrepresentation of fact. Psychologists strive to keep their promises and to avoid unwise or unclear commitments. In situations in which deception may be ethically justifiable to maximize benefits and minimize harm, psychologists have a serious obligation to consider the need for, the possible consequences of, and their responsibility to correct any resulting mistrust or other harmful effects that arise from the use of such techniques.

Principle D: Justice

Psychologists recognize that fairness and justice entitle all persons to access to and benefit from the contributions of psychology and to equal quality in the processes, procedures, and services being conducted by psychologists. Psychologists exercise reasonable judgment and take precautions to ensure that their potential biases, the boundaries of their competence, and the limitations of their expertise do not lead to or condone unjust practices.

Principle E: Respect for People's Rights and Dignity

Psychologists respect the dignity and worth of all people, and the rights of individuals to privacy, confidentiality, and self-determination. Psychologists are aware that special safeguards may be necessary to protect the rights and welfare of persons or communities whose vulnerabilities impair autonomous decision making. Psychologists are aware of and respect cultural, individual, and role differences, including those based on age, gender, gender identity, race, ethnicity, culture, national origin, religion, sexual orientation, disability, language, and socioeconomic status and consider these factors when working with members of such groups. Psychologists try to eliminate the effect on their work of biases based on those factors, and they do not knowingly participate in or condone activities of others based upon such prejudices.

ETHICAL STANDARDS

1. Resolving Ethical Issues

1.01 Misuse of Psychologists' Work
If psychologists learn of misuse or misrepresentation of their work, they take reasonable steps to correct or minimize the misuse or misrepresentation.

1.02 Conflicts Between Ethics and Law, Regulations, or Other Governing Legal Authority
If psychologists' ethical responsibilities conflict with law, regulations, or other governing legal authority, psychologists make known their commitment to the Ethics Code and take steps to resolve the conflict. If the conflict is unresolvable via such means, psychologists may adhere to the requirements of the law, regulations, or other governing legal authority.

1.03 Conflicts Between Ethics and Organizational Demands
If the demands of an organization with which psychologists are affiliated or for whom they are working conflict with this Ethics Code, psychologists clarify the nature of the conflict, make known their commitment to the Ethics Code, and to the extent feasible, resolve the conflict in a way that permits adherence to the Ethics Code.

1.04 Informal Resolution of Ethical Violations
When psychologists believe that there may have been an ethical violation by another psychologist, they attempt to resolve the issue by bringing it to the attention of that individual, if an informal resolution appears appropriate and the intervention does not violate any confidentiality rights that may be involved. (See also Standards 1.02, Conflicts Between Ethics and Law, Regulations, or Other Governing Legal Authority, and 1.03, Conflicts Between Ethics and Organizational Demands.)

1.05 Reporting Ethical Violations
If an apparent ethical violation has substantially harmed or is likely to substantially harm a person or organization and is not appropriate for informal resolution under Standard 1.04, Informal Resolution of Ethical Violations, or is not resolved properly in that fashion, psychologists take further action appropriate to the situation. Such action might include referral to state or national committees on professional ethics, to state licensing boards, or to the appropriate institutional authorities. This standard does not apply when an intervention would violate confidentiality rights or when psychologists have been retained to review the work of another psychologist whose professional conduct is in question. (See also Standard 1.02, Conflicts Between Ethics and Law, Regulations, or Other Governing Legal Authority.)

1.06 Cooperating With Ethics Committees
Psychologists cooperate in ethics investigations, proceedings, and resulting requirements of the APA or any affiliated state psychological association to which they belong. In doing so, they address any confidentiality issues. Failure to cooperate is itself an ethics violation. However, making a request for deferment of adjudication of an ethics complaint pending the outcome of litigation does not alone constitute noncooperation.

1.07 Improper Complaints
Psychologists do not file or encourage the filing of ethics complaints that are made with reckless disregard for or willful ignorance of facts that would disprove the allegation.

1.08 Unfair Discrimination Against Complainants and Respondents
Psychologists do not deny persons employment, advancement, admissions to academic or other programs, tenure, or promotion, based solely upon their having made or their being the subject of an ethics complaint. This does not preclude taking action based upon the outcome of such proceedings or considering other appropriate information.

2. Competence

2.01 Boundaries of Competence
(a) Psychologists provide services, teach, and conduct research with populations and in areas only within the boundaries of their competence, based on their education, training, supervised experience, consultation, study, or professional experience.

(b) Where scientific or professional knowledge in the discipline of psychology establishes that an understanding of factors associated with age, gender, gender identity, race, ethnicity, culture, national origin, religion, sexual orientation, disability, language, or socioeconomic status is essential for effective implementation of their services or research, psychologists have or obtain the training, experience, consultation, or supervision necessary to ensure the competence of their services, or they make appropriate referrals, except as provided in Standard 2.02, Providing Services in Emergencies.

(c) Psychologists planning to provide services, teach, or conduct research involving populations, areas, techniques, or technologies new to them undertake relevant education, training, supervised experience, consultation, or study.

(d) When psychologists are asked to provide services to individuals for whom appropriate mental health services are not available and for which psychologists have not obtained the competence necessary, psychologists with closely related prior training or experience may provide such services in order to ensure that services are not denied if they make a reasonable effort to obtain the competence required by using relevant research, training, consultation, or study.

(e) In those emerging areas in which generally recognized standards for preparatory training do not yet exist, psychologists nevertheless take reasonable steps to ensure the competence of their work and to protect clients/patients, students, supervisees, research participants, organizational clients, and others from harm.

(f) When assuming forensic roles, psychologists are or become reasonably familiar with the judicial or administrative rules governing their roles.

2.02 Providing Services in Emergencies
In emergencies, when psychologists provide services to individuals for whom other mental health services are not available and for which psychologists have not obtained the necessary training, psychologists may provide such services in order to ensure that services are not denied. The services are discontinued as soon as the emergency has ended or appropriate services are available.

2.03 Maintaining Competence
Psychologists undertake ongoing efforts to develop and maintain their competence.

2.04 Bases for Scientific and Professional Judgments
Psychologists' work is based upon established scientific and professional knowledge of the discipline. (See also Standards 2.01e, Boundaries of Competence, and 10.01b, Informed Consent to Therapy.)

2.05 Delegation of Work to Others
Psychologists who delegate work to employees, supervisees, or research or teaching assistants or who use the services of others, such as interpreters, take reasonable steps to (1) avoid delegating such work to persons who have a multiple relationship with those being served that would likely lead to exploitation or loss of objectivity; (2) authorize only those responsibilities that such persons can be expected to perform competently on the basis of their education, training, or experience, either independently or with the level of supervision being provided; and (3) see that such persons perform these services competently. (See also Standards 2.02, Providing Services in Emergencies; 3.05, Multiple Relationships; 4.01, Maintaining Confidentiality; 9.01, Bases for Assessments; 9.02, Use of Assessments; 9.03, Informed Consent in Assessments; and 9.07, Assessment by Unqualified Persons.)

2.06 Personal Problems and Conflicts
(a) Psychologists refrain from initiating an activity when they know or should know that there is a substantial likelihood that their personal problems will prevent them from performing their work-related activities in a competent manner.

(b) When psychologists become aware of personal problems that may interfere with their performing work-related duties adequately, they take appropriate measures, such as obtaining professional consultation or assistance, and determine whether they should limit, suspend, or terminate their work-related duties. (See also Standard 10.10, Terminating Therapy.)

3. Human Relations

3.01 Unfair Discrimination
In their work-related activities, psychologists do not engage in unfair discrimination based on age, gender, gender identity, race, ethnicity, culture, national origin, religion, sexual orientation, disability, socioeconomic status, or any basis proscribed by law.

3.02 Sexual Harassment
Psychologists do not engage in sexual harassment. Sexual harassment is sexual solicitation, physical advances, or verbal or nonverbal conduct that is sexual in nature, that occurs in connection with the psychologist's activities or roles as a psychologist, and that either (1) is unwelcome, is offensive, or creates a hostile workplace or educational environment, and the psychologist knows or is told this or (2) is sufficiently severe or intense to be abusive to a reasonable person in

the context. Sexual harassment can consist of a single intense or severe act or of multiple persistent or pervasive acts. (See also Standard 1.08, Unfair Discrimination Against Complainants and Respondents.)

3.03 Other Harassment
Psychologists do not knowingly engage in behavior that is harassing or demeaning to persons with whom they interact in their work based on factors such as those persons' age, gender, gender identity, race, ethnicity, culture, national origin, religion, sexual orientation, disability, language, or socioeconomic status.

3.04 Avoiding Harm
Psychologists take reasonable steps to avoid harming their clients/patients, students, supervisees, research participants, organizational clients, and others with whom they work, and to minimize harm where it is foreseeable and unavoidable.

3.05 Multiple Relationships
(a) A multiple relationship occurs when a psychologist is in a professional role with a person and (1) at the same time is in another role with the same person, (2) at the same time is in a relationship with a person closely associated with or related to the person with whom the psychologist has the professional relationship, or (3) promises to enter into another relationship in the future with the person or a person closely associated with or related to the person.

A psychologist refrains from entering into a multiple relationship if the multiple relationship could reasonably be expected to impair the psychologist's objectivity, competence, or effectiveness in performing his or her functions as a psychologist, or otherwise risks exploitation or harm to the person with whom the professional relationship exists.

Multiple relationships that would not reasonably be expected to cause impairment or risk exploitation or harm are not unethical.

(b) If a psychologist finds that, due to unforeseen factors, a potentially harmful multiple relationship has arisen, the psychologist takes reasonable steps to resolve it with due regard for the best interests of the affected person and maximal compliance with the Ethics Code.

(c) When psychologists are required by law, institutional policy, or extraordinary circumstances to serve in more than one role in judicial or administrative proceedings, at the outset they clarify role expectations and the extent of confidentiality and thereafter as changes occur. (See also Standards 3.04, Avoiding Harm, and 3.07, Third-Party Requests for Services.)

3.06 Conflict of Interest
Psychologists refrain from taking on a professional role when personal, scientific, professional, legal, financial, or other interests or relationships could reasonably be expected to (1) impair their objectivity, competence, or effectiveness in performing their functions as psychologists or (2) expose the person or organization with whom the professional relationship exists to harm or exploitation.

3.07 Third-Party Requests for Services
When psychologists agree to provide services to a person or entity at the request of a third party, psychologists attempt to clarify at the outset of the service the nature of the relationship with all individuals or organizations involved. This clarification includes the role of the psychologist (e.g., therapist, consultant, diagnostician, or expert witness), an identification of who is the client, the probable uses of the services provided or the information obtained, and the fact that there may be limits to confidentiality. (See also Standards 3.05, Multiple Relationships, and 4.02, Discussing the Limits of Confidentiality.)

3.08 Exploitative Relationships
Psychologists do not exploit persons over whom they have supervisory, evaluative, or other authority such as clients/patients, students, supervisees, research participants, and employees. (See also Standards 3.05, Multiple Relationships; 6.04, Fees and Financial Arrangements; 6.05, Barter With Clients/Patients; 7.07, Sexual Relationships With Students and Supervisees; 10.05, Sexual Intimacies With Current Therapy Clients/Patients; 10.06, Sexual Intimacies With Relatives or Significant Others of Current Therapy Clients/Patients; 10.07, Therapy With Former Sexual Partners; and 10.08, Sexual Intimacies With Former Therapy Clients/Patients.)

3.09 Cooperation With Other Professionals
When indicated and professionally appropriate, psychologists cooperate with other professionals in order to serve their clients/patients effectively and appropriately. (See also Standard 4.05, Disclosures.)

3.10 Informed Consent
(a) When psychologists conduct research or provide assessment, therapy, counseling, or consulting services in person or via electronic transmission or other forms of communication, they obtain the informed consent of the individual or individuals using language that is reasonably understandable to that person or persons except when conducting such activities without consent is mandated by law or governmental regulation or as otherwise provided in this Ethics Code.

(See also Standards 8.02, Informed Consent to Research; 9.03, Informed Consent in Assessments; and 10.01, Informed Consent to Therapy.)

(b) For persons who are legally incapable of giving informed consent, psychologists nevertheless (1) provide an appropriate explanation, (2) seek the individual's assent, (3) consider such persons' preferences and best interests, and (4) obtain appropriate permission from a legally authorized person, if such substitute consent is permitted or required by law. When consent by a legally authorized person is not permitted or required by law, psychologists take reasonable steps to protect the individual's rights and welfare.

(c) When psychological services are court ordered or otherwise mandated, psychologists inform the individual of the nature of the anticipated services, including whether the services are court ordered or mandated and any limits of confidentiality, before proceeding.

(d) Psychologists appropriately document written or oral consent, permission, and assent. (See also Standards 8.02, Informed Consent to Research; 9.03, Informed Consent in Assessments; and 10.01, Informed Consent to Therapy.)

3.11 Psychological Services Delivered To or Through Organizations
(a) Psychologists delivering services to or through organizations provide information beforehand to clients and when appropriate those directly affected by the services about (1) the nature and objectives of the services, (2) the intended recipients, (3) which of the individuals are clients, (4) the relationship the psychologist will have with each person and the organization, (5) the probable uses of services provided and information obtained, (6) who will have access to the information, and (7) limits of confidentiality. As soon as feasible, they provide information about the results and conclusions of such services to appropriate persons.

(b) If psychologists will be precluded by law or by organizational roles from providing such information to particular individuals or groups, they so inform those individuals or groups at the outset of the service.

3.12 Interruption of Psychological Services
Unless otherwise covered by contract, psychologists make reasonable efforts to plan for facilitating services in the event that psychological services are interrupted by factors such as the psychologist's illness, death, unavailability, relocation, or retirement or by the client's/patient's relocation or financial limitations. (See also Standard 6.02c, Maintenance, Dissemination, and Disposal of Confidential Records of Professional and Scientific Work.)

4. Privacy And Confidentiality

4.01 Maintaining Confidentiality
Psychologists have a primary obligation and take reasonable precautions to protect confidential information obtained through or stored in any medium, recognizing that the extent and limits of confidentiality may be regulated by law or established by institutional rules or professional or scientific relationship. (See also Standard 2.05, Delegation of Work to Others.)

4.02 Discussing the Limits of Confidentiality
(a) Psychologists discuss with persons (including, to the extent feasible, persons who are legally incapable of giving informed consent and their legal representatives) and organizations with whom they establish a scientific or professional relationship (1) the relevant limits of confidentiality and (2) the foreseeable uses of the information generated through their psychological activities. (See also Standard 3.10, Informed Consent.)

(b) Unless it is not feasible or is contraindicated, the discussion of confidentiality occurs at the outset of the relationship and thereafter as new circumstances may warrant.

(c) Psychologists who offer services, products, or information via electronic transmission inform clients/patients of the risks to privacy and limits of confidentiality.

4.03 Recording
Before recording the voices or images of individuals to whom they provide services, psychologists obtain permission from all such persons or their legal representatives. (See also Standards 8.03, Informed Consent for Recording Voices and Images in Research; 8.05, Dispensing With Informed Consent for Research; and 8.07, Deception in Research.)

4.04 Minimizing Intrusions on Privacy
(a) Psychologists include in written and oral reports and consultations, only information germane to the purpose for which the communication is made.

(b) Psychologists discuss confidential information obtained in their work only for appropriate scientific or professional purposes and only with persons clearly concerned with such matters.

4.05 Disclosures
(a) Psychologists may disclose confidential information with the appropriate consent of the organizational client, the individual client/patient, or another legally authorized person on behalf of the client/patient unless prohibited by law.

(b) Psychologists disclose confidential information without the consent of the individual only as mandated by law, or where permitted by law for a valid purpose such as to (1) provide needed professional services; (2) obtain appropriate professional consultations; (3) protect the client/patient, psychologist, or others from harm; or (4) obtain payment for services from a client/patient, in which instance disclosure is limited to the minimum that is necessary to achieve the purpose. (See also Standard 6.04e, Fees and Financial Arrangements.)

4.06 Consultations
When consulting with colleagues, (1) psychologists do not disclose confidential information that reasonably could lead to the identification of a client/patient, research participant, or other person or organization with whom they have a confidential relationship unless they have obtained the prior consent of the person or organization or the disclosure cannot be avoided, and (2) they disclose information only to the extent necessary to achieve the purposes of the consultation. (See also Standard 4.01, Maintaining Confidentiality.)

4.07 Use of Confidential Information for Didactic or Other Purposes
Psychologists do not disclose in their writings, lectures, or other public media, confidential, personally identifiable information concerning their clients/patients, students, research participants, organizational clients, or other recipients of their services that they obtained during the course of their work, unless (1) they take reasonable steps to disguise the person or organization, (2) the person or organization has consented in writing, or (3) there is legal authorization for doing so.

5. Advertising and Other Public Statements

5.01 Avoidance of False or Deceptive Statements
(a) Public statements include but are not limited to paid or unpaid advertising, product endorsements, grant applications, licensing applications, other credentialing applications, brochures, printed matter, directory listings, personal resumes or curricula vitae, or comments for use in media such as print or electronic transmission, statements in legal proceedings, lectures and public oral presentations, and published materials. Psychologists do not knowingly make public statements that are false, deceptive, or fraudulent concerning their research, practice, or other work activities or those of persons or organizations with which they are affiliated.

(b) Psychologists do not make false, deceptive, or fraudulent statements concerning (1) their training, experience, or competence; (2) their academic degrees; (3) their credentials; (4) their institutional or association affiliations; (5) their services; (6) the scientific or clinical basis for, or results or degree of success of, their services; (7) their fees; or (8) their publications or research findings.

(c) Psychologists claim degrees as credentials for their health services only if those degrees (1) were earned from a regionally accredited educational institution or (2) were the basis for psychology licensure by the state in which they practice.

5.02 Statements by Others
(a) Psychologists who engage others to create or place public statements that promote their professional practice, products, or activities retain professional responsibility for such statements.

(b) Psychologists do not compensate employees of press, radio, television, or other communication media in return for publicity in a news item. (See also Standard 1.01, Misuse of Psychologists' Work.)

(c) A paid advertisement relating to psychologists' activities must be identified or clearly recognizable as such.

5.03 Descriptions of Workshops and Non-Degree-Granting Educational Programs
To the degree to which they exercise control, psychologists responsible for announcements, catalogs, brochures, or advertisements describing workshops, seminars, or other non-degree-granting educational programs ensure that they accurately describe the audience for which the program is intended, the educational objectives, the presenters, and the fees involved.

5.04 Media Presentations
When psychologists provide public advice or comment via print, internet, or other electronic transmission, they take precautions to ensure that statements (1) are based on their professional knowledge, training, or experience in accord with appropriate psychological literature and practice; (2) are otherwise consistent with this Ethics Code; and (3) do not indicate that a professional relationship has been established with the recipient. (See also Standard 2.04, Bases for Scientific and Professional Judgments.)

5.05 Testimonials

Psychologists do not solicit testimonials from current therapy clients/patients or other persons who because of their particular circumstances are vulnerable to undue influence.

5.06 In-Person Solicitation

Psychologists do not engage, directly or through agents, in uninvited in-person solicitation of business from actual or potential therapy clients/patients or other persons who because of their particular circumstances are vulnerable to undue influence. However, this prohibition does not preclude (1) attempting to implement appropriate collateral contacts for the purpose of benefiting an already engaged therapy client/patient or (2) providing disaster or community outreach services.

6.   Record Keeping and Fees

6.01 Documentation of Professional and Scientific Work and Maintenance of Records

Psychologists create, and to the extent the records are under their control, maintain, disseminate, store, retain, and dispose of records and data relating to their professional and scientific work in order to (1) facilitate provision of services later by them or by other professionals, (2) allow for replication of research design and analyses, (3) meet institutional requirements, (4) ensure accuracy of billing and payments, and (5) ensure compliance with law. (See also Standard 4.01, Maintaining Confidentiality.)

6.02 Maintenance, Dissemination, and Disposal of Confidential Records of Professional and Scientific Work

(a) Psychologists maintain confidentiality in creating, storing, accessing, transferring, and disposing of records under their control, whether these are written, automated, or in any other medium. (See also Standards 4.01, Maintaining Confidentiality, and 6.01, Documentation of Professional and Scientific Work and Maintenance of Records.)

(b) If confidential information concerning recipients of psychological services is entered into databases or systems of records available to persons whose access has not been consented to by the recipient, psychologists use coding or other techniques to avoid the inclusion of personal identifiers.

(c) Psychologists make plans in advance to facilitate the appropriate transfer and to protect the confidentiality of records and data in the event of psychologists' withdrawal from positions or practice. (See also Standards 3.12, Interruption of Psychological Services, and 10.09, Interruption of Therapy.)

6.03 Withholding Records for Nonpayment

Psychologists may not withhold records under their control that are requested and needed for a client's/patient's emergency treatment solely because payment has not been received.

6.04 Fees and Financial Arrangements

(a) As early as is feasible in a professional or scientific relationship, psychologists and recipients of psychological services reach an agreement specifying compensation and billing arrangements.

(b) Psychologists' fee practices are consistent with law.

(c) Psychologists do not misrepresent their fees.

(d) If limitations to services can be anticipated because of limitations in financing, this is discussed with the recipient of services as early as is feasible. (See also Standards 10.09, Interruption of Therapy, and 10.10, Terminating Therapy.)

(e) If the recipient of services does not pay for services as agreed, and if psychologists intend to use collection agencies or legal measures to collect the fees, psychologists first inform the person that such measures will be taken and provide that person an opportunity to make prompt payment. (See also Standards 4.05, Disclosures; 6.03, Withholding Records for Nonpayment; and 10.01, Informed Consent to Therapy.)

6.05 Barter With Clients/Patients

Barter is the acceptance of goods, services, or other nonmonetary remuneration from clients/patients in return for psychological services. Psychologists may barter only if (1) it is not clinically contraindicated, and (2) the resulting arrangement is not exploitative. (See also Standards 3.05, Multiple Relationships, and 6.04, Fees and Financial Arrangements.)

6.06 Accuracy in Reports to Payors and Funding Sources

In their reports to payors for services or sources of research funding, psychologists take reasonable steps to ensure the accurate reporting of the nature of the service provided or research conducted, the fees, charges, or payments, and where applicable, the identity of the provider, the findings, and the diagnosis. (See also Standards 4.01, Maintaining Confidentiality; 4.04, Minimizing Intrusions on Privacy; and 4.05, Disclosures.)

6.07 Referrals and Fees

When psychologists pay, receive payment from, or divide fees with another professional, other than in an employer-employee relationship, the payment to each is based on the services provided (clinical, consultative, administrative, or other) and is not based on the referral itself. (See also Standard 3.09, Cooperation With Other Professionals.)

7. Education and Training

7.01 Design of Education and Training Programs

Psychologists responsible for education and training programs take reasonable steps to ensure that the programs are designed to provide the appropriate knowledge and proper experiences, and to meet the requirements for licensure, certification, or other goals for which claims are made by the program. (See also Standard 5.03, Descriptions of Workshops and Non-Degree-Granting Educational Programs.)

7.02 Descriptions of Education and Training Programs

Psychologists responsible for education and training programs take reasonable steps to ensure that there is a current and accurate description of the program content (including participation in required course- or program-related counseling, psychotherapy, experiential groups, consulting projects, or community service), training goals and objectives, stipends and benefits, and requirements that must be met for satisfactory completion of the program. This information must be made readily available to all interested parties.

7.03 Accuracy in Teaching

(a) Psychologists take reasonable steps to ensure that course syllabi are accurate regarding the subject matter to be covered, bases for evaluating progress, and the nature of course experiences. This standard does not preclude an instructor from modifying course content or requirements when the instructor considers it pedagogically necessary or desirable, so long as students are made aware of these modifications in a manner that enables them to fulfill course requirements. (See also Standard 5.01, Avoidance of False or Deceptive Statements.)

(b) When engaged in teaching or training, psychologists present psychological information accurately. (See also Standard 2.03, Maintaining Competence.)

7.04 Student Disclosure of Personal Information

Psychologists do not require students or supervisees to disclose personal information in course- or program-related activities, either orally or in writing, regarding sexual history, history of abuse and neglect, psychological treatment, and relationships with parents, peers, and spouses or significant others except if (1) the program or training facility has clearly identified this requirement in its admissions and program materials or (2) the information is necessary to evaluate or obtain assistance for students whose personal problems could reasonably be judged to be preventing them from performing their training- or professionally related activities in a competent manner or posing a threat to the students or others.

7.05 Mandatory Individual or Group Therapy

(a) When individual or group therapy is a program or course requirement, psychologists responsible for that program allow students in undergraduate and graduate programs the option of selecting such therapy from practitioners unaffiliated with the program. (See also Standard 7.02, Descriptions of Education and Training Programs.)

(b) Faculty who are or are likely to be responsible for evaluating students' academic performance do not themselves provide that therapy. (See also Standard 3.05, Multiple Relationships.)

7.06 Assessing Student and Supervisee Performance

(a) In academic and supervisory relationships, psychologists establish a timely and specific process for providing feedback to students and supervisees. Information regarding the process is provided to the student at the beginning of supervision.

(b) Psychologists evaluate students and supervisees on the basis of their actual performance on relevant and established program requirements.

7.07 Sexual Relationships With Students and Supervisees

Psychologists do not engage in sexual relationships with students or supervisees who are in their department, agency, or training center or over whom psychologists have or are likely to have evaluative authority. (See also Standard 3.05, Multiple Relationships.)

8.   Research and Publication

8.01 Institutional Approval

When institutional approval is required, psychologists provide accurate information about their research proposals and obtain approval prior to conducting the research. They conduct the research in accordance with the approved research protocol.

8.02 Informed Consent to Research

(a) When obtaining informed consent as required in Standard 3.10, Informed Consent, psychologists inform participants about (1) the purpose of the research, expected duration, and procedures; (2) their right to decline to participate and to withdraw from the research once participation has begun; (3) the foreseeable consequences of declining or withdrawing; (4) reasonably foreseeable factors that may be expected to influence their willingness to participate such as potential risks, discomfort, or adverse effects; (5) any prospective research benefits; (6) limits of confidentiality; (7) incentives for participation; and (8) whom to contact for questions about the research and research participants' rights. They provide opportunity for the prospective participants to ask questions and receive answers. (See also Standards 8.03, Informed Consent for Recording Voices and Images in Research; 8.05, Dispensing With Informed Consent for Research; and 8.07, Deception in Research.)

(b) Psychologists conducting intervention research involving the use of experimental treatments clarify to participants at the outset of the research (1) the experimental nature of the treatment; (2) the services that will or will not be available to the control group(s) if appropriate; (3) the means by which assignment to treatment and control groups will be made; (4) available treatment alternatives if an individual does not wish to participate in the research or wishes to withdraw once a study has begun; and (5) compensation for or monetary costs of participating including, if appropriate, whether reimbursement from the participant or a third-party payor will be sought. (See also Standard 8.02a, Informed Consent to Research.)

8.03 Informed Consent for Recording Voices and Images in Research

Psychologists obtain informed consent from research participants prior to recording their voices or images for data collection unless (1) the research consists solely of naturalistic observations in public places, and it is not anticipated that the recording will be used in a manner that could cause personal identification or harm, or (2) the research design includes deception, and consent for the use of the recording is obtained during debriefing. (See also Standard 8.07, Deception in Research.)

8.04 Client/Patient, Student, and Subordinate Research Participants

(a) When psychologists conduct research with clients/patients, students, or subordinates as participants, psychologists take steps to protect the prospective participants from adverse consequences of declining or withdrawing from participation.

(b) When research participation is a course requirement or an opportunity for extra credit, the prospective participant is given the choice of equitable alternative activities.

8.05 Dispensing With Informed Consent for Research

Psychologists may dispense with informed consent only (1) where research would not reasonably be assumed to create distress or harm and involves (a) the study of normal educational practices, curricula, or classroom management methods conducted in educational settings; (b) only anonymous questionnaires, naturalistic observations, or archival research for which disclosure of responses would not place participants at risk of criminal or civil liability or damage their financial standing, employability, or reputation, and confidentiality is protected; or (c) the study of factors related to job or organization effectiveness conducted in organizational settings for which there is no risk to participants' employability, and confidentiality is protected or (2) where otherwise permitted by law or federal or institutional regulations.

8.06 Offering Inducements for Research Participation

(a) Psychologists make reasonable efforts to avoid offering excessive or inappropriate financial or other inducements for research participation when such inducements are likely to coerce participation.

(b) When offering professional services as an inducement for research participation, psychologists clarify the nature of the services, as well as the risks, obligations, and limitations. (See also Standard 6.05, Barter With Clients/Patients.)

8.07 Deception in Research

(a) Psychologists do not conduct a study involving deception unless they have determined that the use of deceptive techniques is justified by the study's significant prospective scientific, educational, or applied value and that effective nondeceptive alternative procedures are not feasible.

(b) Psychologists do not deceive prospective participants about research that is reasonably expected to cause physical pain or severe emotional distress.

(c) Psychologists explain any deception that is an integral feature of the design and conduct of an experiment to participants as early as is feasible, preferably at the conclusion of their participation, but no later than at the conclusion of the data collection, and permit participants to withdraw their data. (See also Standard 8.08, Debriefing.)

8.08 Debriefing
(a) Psychologists provide a prompt opportunity for participants to obtain appropriate information about the nature, results, and conclusions of the research, and they take reasonable steps to correct any misconceptions that participants may have of which the psychologists are aware.

(b) If scientific or humane values justify delaying or withholding this information, psychologists take reasonable measures to reduce the risk of harm.

(c) When psychologists become aware that research procedures have harmed a participant, they take reasonable steps to minimize the harm.

8.09 Humane Care and Use of Animals in Research
(a) Psychologists acquire, care for, use, and dispose of animals in compliance with current federal, state, and local laws and regulations, and with professional standards.

(b) Psychologists trained in research methods and experienced in the care of laboratory animals supervise all procedures involving animals and are responsible for ensuring appropriate consideration of their comfort, health, and humane treatment.

(c) Psychologists ensure that all individuals under their supervision who are using animals have received instruction in research methods and in the care, maintenance, and handling of the species being used, to the extent appropriate to their role. (See also Standard 2.05, Delegation of Work to Others.)

(d) Psychologists make reasonable efforts to minimize the discomfort, infection, illness, and pain of animal subjects.

(e) Psychologists use a procedure subjecting animals to pain, stress, or privation only when an alternative procedure is unavailable and the goal is justified by its prospective scientific, educational, or applied value.

(f) Psychologists perform surgical procedures under appropriate anesthesia and follow techniques to avoid infection and minimize pain during and after surgery.

(g) When it is appropriate that an animal's life be terminated, psychologists proceed rapidly, with an effort to minimize pain and in accordance with accepted procedures.

8.10 Reporting Research Results
(a) Psychologists do not fabricate data. (See also Standard 5.01a, Avoidance of False or Deceptive Statements.)

(b) If psychologists discover significant errors in their published data, they take reasonable steps to correct such errors in a correction, retraction, erratum, or other appropriate publication means.

8.11 Plagiarism
Psychologists do not present portions of another's work or data as their own, even if the other work or data source is cited occasionally.

8.12 Publication Credit
(a) Psychologists take responsibility and credit, including authorship credit, only for work they have actually performed or to which they have substantially contributed. (See also Standard 8.12b, Publication Credit.)

(b) Principal authorship and other publication credits accurately reflect the relative scientific or professional contributions of the individuals involved, regardless of their relative status. Mere possession of an institutional position, such as department chair, does not justify authorship credit. Minor contributions to the research or to the writing for publications are acknowledged appropriately, such as in footnotes or in an introductory statement.

(c) Except under exceptional circumstances, a student is listed as principal author on any multiple-authored article that is substantially based on the student's doctoral dissertation. Faculty advisors discuss publication credit with students as early as feasible and throughout the research and publication process as appropriate. (See also Standard 8.12b, Publication Credit.)

8.13 Duplicate Publication of Data
Psychologists do not publish, as original data, data that have been previously published. This does not preclude republishing data when they are accompanied by proper acknowledgment.

8.14 Sharing Research Data for Verification
(a) After research results are published, psychologists do not withhold the data on which their conclusions are based from other competent professionals who seek to verify the substantive claims through reanalysis and who intend to use such data only for that purpose, provided that the confidentiality of the participants can be protected and unless legal rights concerning proprietary data preclude their release. This does not preclude psychologists from requiring that such individuals or groups be responsible for costs associated with the provision of such information.

(b) Psychologists who request data from other psychologists to verify the substantive claims through reanalysis may use shared data only for the declared purpose. Requesting psychologists obtain prior written agreement for all other uses of the data.

8.15 Reviewers
Psychologists who review material submitted for presentation, publication, grant, or research proposal review respect the confidentiality of and the proprietary rights in such information of those who submitted it.

9.   Assessment

9.01 Bases for Assessments
(a) Psychologists base the opinions contained in their recommendations, reports, and diagnostic or evaluative statements, including forensic testimony, on information and techniques sufficient to substantiate their findings. (See also Standard 2.04, Bases for Scientific and Professional Judgments.)

(b) Except as noted in 9.01c, psychologists provide opinions of the psychological characteristics of individuals only after they have conducted an examination of the individuals adequate to support their statements or conclusions. When, despite reasonable efforts, such an examination is not practical, psychologists document the efforts they made and the result of those efforts, clarify the probable impact of their limited information on the reliability and validity of their opinions, and appropriately limit the nature and extent of their conclusions or recommendations. (See also Standards 2.01, Boundaries of Competence, and 9.06, Interpreting Assessment Results.)

(c) When psychologists conduct a record review or provide consultation or supervision and an individual examination is not warranted or necessary for the opinion, psychologists explain this and the sources of information on which they based their conclusions and recommendations.

9.02 Use of Assessments
(a) Psychologists administer, adapt, score, interpret, or use assessment techniques, interviews, tests, or instruments in a manner and for purposes that are appropriate in light of the research on or evidence of the usefulness and proper application of the techniques.

(b) Psychologists use assessment instruments whose validity and reliability have been established for use with members of the population tested. When such validity or reliability has not been established, psychologists describe the strengths and limitations of test results and interpretation.

(c) Psychologists use assessment methods that are appropriate to an individual's language preference and competence, unless the use of an alternative language is relevant to the assessment issues.

9.03 Informed Consent in Assessments
(a) Psychologists obtain informed consent for assessments, evaluations, or diagnostic services, as described in Standard 3.10, Informed Consent, except when (1) testing is mandated by law or governmental regulations; (2) informed consent is implied because testing is conducted as a routine educational, institutional, or organizational activity (e.g., when participants voluntarily agree to assessment when applying for a job); or (3) one purpose of the testing is to evaluate decisional capacity. Informed consent includes an explanation of the nature and purpose of the assessment, fees, involvement of third parties, and limits of confidentiality and sufficient opportunity for the client/patient to ask questions and receive answers.

(b) Psychologists inform persons with questionable capacity to consent or for whom testing is mandated by law or governmental regulations about the nature and purpose of the proposed assessment services, using language that is reasonably understandable to the person being assessed.

(c) Psychologists using the services of an interpreter obtain informed consent from the client/patient to use that interpreter, ensure that confidentiality of test results and test security are maintained, and include in their recommendations, reports, and diagnostic or evaluative statements, including forensic testimony, discussion of any limitations on the data obtained. (See also Standards 2.05, Delegation of Work to Others; 4.01, Maintaining Confidentiality; 9.01, Bases for Assessments; 9.06, Interpreting Assessment Results; and 9.07, Assessment by Unqualified Persons.)

9.04 Release of Test Data

(a) The term *test data* refers to raw and scaled scores, client/patient responses to test questions or stimuli, and psychologists' notes and recordings concerning client/patient statements and behavior during an examination. Those portions of test materials that include client/patient responses are included in the definition of *test data*. Pursuant to a client/patient release, psychologists provide test data to the client/patient or other persons identified in the release. Psychologists may refrain from releasing test data to protect a client/patient or others from substantial harm or misuse or misrepresentation of the data or the test, recognizing that in many instances release of confidential information under these circumstances is regulated by law. (See also Standard 9.11, Maintaining Test Security.)

(b) In the absence of a client/patient release, psychologists provide test data only as required by law or court order.

9.05 Test Construction

Psychologists who develop tests and other assessment techniques use appropriate psychometric procedures and current scientific or professional knowledge for test design, standardization, validation, reduction or elimination of bias, and recommendations for use.

9.06 Interpreting Assessment Results

When interpreting assessment results, including automated interpretations, psychologists take into account the purpose of the assessment as well as the various test factors, test-taking abilities, and other characteristics of the person being assessed, such as situational, personal, linguistic, and cultural differences, that might affect psychologists' judgments or reduce the accuracy of their interpretations. They indicate any significant limitations of their interpretations. (See also Standards 2.01b and c, Boundaries of Competence, and 3.01, Unfair Discrimination.)

9.07 Assessment by Unqualified Persons

Psychologists do not promote the use of psychological assessment techniques by unqualified persons, except when such use is conducted for training purposes with appropriate supervision. (See also Standard 2.05, Delegation of Work to Others.)

9.08 Obsolete Tests and Outdated Test Results

(a) Psychologists do not base their assessment or intervention decisions or recommendations on data or test results that are outdated for the current purpose.

(b) Psychologists do not base such decisions or recommendations on tests and measures that are obsolete and not useful for the current purpose.

9.09 Test Scoring and Interpretation Services

(a) Psychologists who offer assessment or scoring services to other professionals accurately describe the purpose, norms, validity, reliability, and applications of the procedures and any special qualifications applicable to their use.

(b) Psychologists select scoring and interpretation services (including automated services) on the basis of evidence of the validity of the program and procedures as well as on other appropriate considerations. (See also Standard 2.01b and c, Boundaries of Competence.)

(c) Psychologists retain responsibility for the appropriate application, interpretation, and use of assessment instruments, whether they score and interpret such tests themselves or use automated or other services.

9.10 Explaining Assessment Results

Regardless of whether the scoring and interpretation are done by psychologists, by employees or assistants, or by automated or other outside services, psychologists take reasonable steps to ensure that explanations of results are given to the individual or designated representative unless the nature of the relationship precludes provision of an explanation of results (such as in some organizational consulting, preemployment or security screenings, and forensic evaluations), and this fact has been clearly explained to the person being assessed in advance.

9.11. Maintaining Test Security

The term *test materials* refers to manuals, instruments, protocols, and test questions or stimuli and does not include *test data* as defined in Standard 9.04, Release of Test Data. Psychologists make reasonable efforts to maintain the integrity and security of test materials and other assessment techniques consistent with law and contractual obligations, and in a manner that permits adherence to this Ethics Code.

10.   Therapy

10.01 Informed Consent to Therapy

(a) When obtaining informed consent to therapy as required in Standard 3.10, Informed Consent, psychologists inform clients/patients as early as is feasible in the therapeutic relationship about the nature and anticipated course of therapy, fees, involvement of third parties, and limits of confidentiality and provide sufficient opportunity for the client/patient to ask questions and receive answers. (See also Standards 4.02, Discussing the Limits of Confidentiality, and 6.04, Fees and Financial Arrangements.)

(b) When obtaining informed consent for treatment for which generally recognized techniques and procedures have not been established, psychologists inform their clients/patients of the developing nature of the treatment, the potential risks involved, alternative treatments that may be available, and the voluntary nature of their participation. (See also Standards 2.01e, Boundaries of Competence, and 3.10, Informed Consent.)

(c) When the therapist is a trainee and the legal responsibility for the treatment provided resides with the supervisor, the client/patient, as part of the informed consent procedure, is informed that the therapist is in training and is being supervised and is given the name of the supervisor.

10.02 Therapy Involving Couples or Families
(a) When psychologists agree to provide services to several persons who have a relationship (such as spouses, significant others, or parents and children), they take reasonable steps to clarify at the outset (1) which of the individuals are clients/patients and (2) the relationship the psychologist will have with each person. This clarification includes the psychologist's role and the probable uses of the services provided or the information obtained. (See also Standard 4.02, Discussing the Limits of Confidentiality.)

(b) If it becomes apparent that psychologists may be called on to perform potentially conflicting roles (such as family therapist and then witness for one party in divorce proceedings), psychologists take reasonable steps to clarify and modify, or withdraw from, roles appropriately. (See also Standard 3.05c, Multiple Relationships.)

10.03 Group Therapy
When psychologists provide services to several persons in a group setting, they describe at the outset the roles and responsibilities of all parties and the limits of confidentiality.

10.04 Providing Therapy to Those Served by Others
In deciding whether to offer or provide services to those already receiving mental health services elsewhere, psychologists carefully consider the treatment issues and the potential client's/patient's welfare. Psychologists discuss these issues with the client/patient or another legally authorized person on behalf of the client/patient in order to minimize the risk of confusion and conflict, consult with the other service providers when appropriate, and proceed with caution and sensitivity to the therapeutic issues.

10.05 Sexual Intimacies With Current Therapy Clients/Patients
Psychologists do not engage in sexual intimacies with current therapy clients/patients.

10.06 Sexual Intimacies With Relatives or Significant Others of Current Therapy Clients/Patients
Psychologists do not engage in sexual intimacies with individuals they know to be close relatives, guardians, or significant others of current clients/patients. Psychologists do not terminate therapy to circumvent this standard.

10.07 Therapy With Former Sexual Partners
Psychologists do not accept as therapy clients/patients persons with whom they have engaged in sexual intimacies.

10.08 Sexual Intimacies With Former Therapy Clients/Patients
(a) Psychologists do not engage in sexual intimacies with former clients/patients for at least two years after cessation or termination of therapy.

(b) Psychologists do not engage in sexual intimacies with former clients/patients even after a two-year interval except in the most unusual circumstances. Psychologists who engage in such activity after the two years following cessation or termination of therapy and of having no sexual contact with the former client/patient bear the burden of demonstrating that there has been no exploitation, in light of all relevant factors, including (1) the amount of time that has passed since therapy terminated; (2) the nature, duration, and intensity of the therapy; (3) the circumstances of termination; (4) the client's/patient's personal history; (5) the client's/patient's current mental status; (6) the likelihood of adverse impact on the client/patient; and (7) any statements or actions made by the therapist during the course of therapy suggesting or inviting the possibility of a posttermination sexual or romantic relationship with the client/patient. (See also Standard 3.05, Multiple Relationships.)

10.09 Interruption of Therapy
When entering into employment or contractual relationships, psychologists make reasonable efforts to provide for orderly and appropriate resolution of responsibility for client/patient care in the event that the employment or contractual relationship ends, with paramount consideration given to the welfare of the client/patient. (See also Standard 3.12, Interruption of Psychological Services.)

10.10 Terminating Therapy

(a) Psychologists terminate therapy when it becomes reasonably clear that the client/patient no longer needs the service, is not likely to benefit, or is being harmed by continued service.

(b) Psychologists may terminate therapy when threatened or otherwise endangered by the client/patient or another person with whom the client/patient has a relationship.

(c) Except where precluded by the actions of clients/patients or third-party payors, prior to termination psychologists provide pretermination counseling and suggest alternative service providers as appropriate.

History and Effective Date Footnote

This version of the APA Ethics Code was adopted by the American Psychological Association's Council of Representatives during its meeting, August 21, 2002, and is effective beginning June 1, 2003. Inquiries concerning the substance or interpretation of the APA Ethics Code should be addressed to the Director, Office of Ethics, American Psychological Association, 750 First Street, NE, Washington, DC 20002-4242. The Ethics Code and information regarding the Code can be found on the APA web site, http://www.apa.org/ethics. The standards in this Ethics Code will be used to adjudicate complaints brought concerning alleged conduct occurring on or after the effective date. Complaints regarding conduct occurring prior to the effective date will be adjudicated on the basis of the version of the Ethics Code that was in effect at the time the conduct occurred.

The APA has previously published its Ethics Code as follows:

American Psychological Association. (1953). Ethical standards of psychologists. Washington, DC: Author.

American Psychological Association. (1959). Ethical standards of psychologists. American Psychologist, 14, 279-282.

American Psychological Association. (1963). Ethical standards of psychologists. American Psychologist, 18, 56-60.

American Psychological Association. (1968). Ethical standards of psychologists. American Psychologist, 23, 357-361.

American Psychological Association. (1977, March). Ethical standards of psychologists. APA Monitor, 22-23.

American Psychological Association. (1979). Ethical standards of psychologists. Washington, DC: Author.

American Psychological Association. (1981). Ethical principles of psychologists. American Psychologist, 36, 633-638.

American Psychological Association. (1990). Ethical principles of psychologists (Amended June 2, 1989). American Psychologist, 45, 390-395.

American Psychological Association. (1992). Ethical principles of psychologists and code of conduct. American Psychologist, 47, 1597-1611.

Request copies of the APA's Ethical Principles of Psychologists and Code of Conduct from the APA Order Department, 750 First Street, NE, Washington, DC 20002-4242, or phone (202) 336-5510.

REFERENCES

Acuff, C., Bennett, B. E., Bricklin, P. M., Canter, M. B., Knapp, S. J., & Moldawsky, S. (1999). Considerations for ethical practice in managed care. *Professional Psychology: Research and Practice, 30,* 563-565.

Adkins, D. C. (1952). Proceedings of the sixteenth annual business meeting of the American Psychological Association, Inc., Washington, DC. *American Psychologist, 7,* 645-670.

American Educational Research Association, American Psychological Association, and National Council on Measurement in Education. (1999). *Standards for educational and psychological testing.* Washington, DC: American Educational Research Association.

American Psychological Association. (1981). Ethical principles of psychologists. *American Psychologist, 36,* 633-638.

American Psychological Association. (1992). Ethical principles of psychologists and code of conduct. *American Psychologist, 47,* 1597-1611.

American Psychological Association. (1993a). Guidelines for providers of psychological services to ethnic, linguistic, and culturally diverse populations. *American Psychologist, 48,* 45-48.

American Psychological Association. (1993b). Record keeping guidelines. *American Psychologist, 48,* 984-986.

American Psychological Association. (1994). Guidelines for child custody evaluations in divorce proceedings. *American Psychologist, 49,* 677-680.

American Psychological Association. (1995). Report of the Ethics Committee, 1994. *American Psychologist, 50,* 706-713.

American Psychological Association. (1996). Report of the Ethics Committee, 1995. *American Psychologist, 51,* 1279-1286.

American Psychological Association. (2001). *Publication manual of the American Psychological Association* (5th ed.). Washington, DC: Author.

American Psychological Association. (2002). Rules and procedures: October 1, 2001 [Ethics Committee Rules and Procedures]. *American Psychologist, 57,* 626-645.

American Psychological Association Committee on Animal Research and Ethics. (1996). *Guidelines for ethical conduct in the care and use of animals* [Brochure]. Retrieved October 2, 2002, from http://www.apa.org/science/anguide.html

American Psychological Association Committee on Professional Standards. (1981). Specialty guidelines for the delivery of services. *American Psychologist, 36*(6), 639-685.

American Psychological Association Practice Directorate and the American Psychological Association Insurance Trust. (2002). *Getting ready for HIPAA: What you need to know now.* Washington, DC: American Psychological Association.

Americans with Disabilities Act of 1990, 42 U.S.C. § 12101 *et seq.*

Anderson, S. K., & Kitchener, K. S. (1996). Nonromantic, nonsexual posttherapy relationships between psychologists and former clients: An exploratory study of critical incidents. *Professional Psychology: Research and Practice, 27,* 59-66.

Appelbaum, P. S., & Rosenbaum, A. (1989). *Tarasoff* and the researcher: Does the duty to protect apply in the research setting? *American Psychologist, 44,* 885-894.

Baier, A. (1985). What do women want in a moral theory? *Nous, 19,* 53-63.

Barnett, J. E., & Hillard, D. (2001). Psychologist distress and impairment: The availability, nature, and use of colleague assistance programs for psychologists. *Professional Psychology: Research and Practice, 32,* 205-210.

Beauchamp, T. L., & Childress, J. F. (2001). *Principles of biomedical ethics* (5th ed.). New York: Oxford University Press.

Beck, A. T., Steer, R. A., & Brown, G. K. (1996). *The Beck Depression Inventory–second edition (BDI-II).* San Antonio, TX: Psychological Corporation.

Bersoff, D. (1994). Explicit ambiguity: The 1992 ethics code as an oxymoron. *Professional Psychology: Research and Practice, 25,* 382-387.

Bersoff, D. N. (1976). Therapists as protectors and policemen: New roles as a result of *Tarasoff? Professional Psychology: Research and Practice, 7,* 267-273.

Bersoff, D. N., & Hofer, P. J. (1991). *Legal issues in computerized psychological testing: The computer and the decision-making process.* Mahwah, NJ: Lawrence Erlbaum.

Bixler, R., & Seeman, J. (1946). Suggestions for a code of ethics for consulting psychologists. *Journal of Abnormal Psychology, 41,* 486-490.

Brabeck, M. (Ed.). (2000). *Practicing feminist ethics in psychology.* Washington, DC: American Psychological Association.

Bronstein, P., & Quina, K. (2003). *Teaching gender and multicultural awareness: Resources for the psychology classroom.* Washington, DC: American Psychological Association.

Brotman, L. E., Liberi, W. P., & Wasylyshyn, K. M. (1998). Executive coaching: The need for standards of competence. *Consulting Psychology Journal: Practice and Research, 50,* 40-46.

Buchanan, T. (2002). Online assessment: Desirable or dangerous? *Professional Psychology: Research and Practice, 33,* 138-154.

Buelow, G. D., & Chafetz, M. D. (1996). Proposed ethical practice guidelines for clinical pharmacopsychology: Sharpening a new focus in psychology. *Professional Psychology: Research and Practice, 27,* 53-58.

Butcher, J. N. (2000). Revising psychological tests: Lessons learned from revisions of the MMPI. *Psychological Assessment, 12,* 263-271.

Butcher, J. N., Dahlstrom, W. G., Graham, J. R., Tellegen, A., & Kaemmer, B. (2002). *Minnesota Multiphasic Personality Inventory (MMPI-2): Manual for administration, scoring, and interpretation* (Rev. ed.). Minneapolis: University of Minnesota Press.

Callahan, D. (1982). Should there be an academic code of ethics? *Journal of Higher Education, 53,* 335-344.

Canter, M. B., Bennett, B. E., Jones, S. E., & Nagy, T. F. (1994). *Ethics for psychologists: A commentary on the APA ethics code.* Washington, DC: American Psychological Association.

Chafetz, M. D., & Buelow, G. D. (1994). A training model for psychologists with prescription privileges: Clinical pharmacopsychologists. *Professional Psychology: Research and Practice, 25,* 149-153.

Chenneville, T. (2000). HIV, confidentiality, and duty to protect: A decision-making model. *Professional Psychology: Research and Practice, 31,* 661-670.

Chernin, J., Holden, J. M., & Chandler, C. (1997). Bias in psychological assessment: Heterosexism. *Measurement and Evaluation in Counseling and Development, 30,* 68-76.

Childs, R. A., & Eyde, L. D. (2002). Assessment training in clinical psychology doctoral programs: What should we teach? *Journal of Personality Assessment, 78,* 130-144.

Combs, D. R., Penn, D. L., & Fenigstein, A. (2002). Ethnic differences in subclinical paranoia: An expansion of norms of the Paranoia Scale. *Cultural Diversity & Ethnic Minority Psychology, 8,* 248-256.

Committee on Ethical Guidelines for Forensic Psychologists. (1991). Specialty guidelines for forensic psychologists. *Law and Human Behavior, 15,* 655-665.

Committee on Legal Issues. (1996). Strategies for private practitioners coping with subpoenas or compelled testimony for client records or test data. *Professional Psychology: Research and Practice, 27,* 245-251.

Council of National Psychological Associations for the Advancement of Ethnic Minority Interests. (2000). *Guidelines for research in ethnic minority communities.* Washington, DC: American Psychological Association.

Daubert v. Merrell Dow Pharmaceuticals, Inc. 509 U.S. 579 (1993).

DeLeon, P. H., Bennett, B. E., & Bricklin, P. M. (1997). Ethics and public policy formulation: A case example related to prescription privileges. *Professional Psychology: Research and Practice, 28,* 518-525.

Department of Health and Human Services. (2001, December). Title 45 Public Welfare, Part 46, *Code of federal regulations, Protection of Human Subjects.* Washington, DC: Government Printing Office.

Department of Health and Human Services. (2003, February 20). Health insurance reform: Security standards; final rule [Rules and Regulations]. *Federal Register, 68*(34), 8333-8381.

Fine, M. A., & Kurdek, L. A. (1993). Reflections on determining authorship credit and authorship order on faculty-student collaborations. *American Psychologist, 48,* 1141-1147.

Fisher, C. B. (1999). Relational ethics and research with vulnerable populations. *Reports on research involving persons with mental disorders that may affect decision-making capacity* (Vol. 2, pp. 29-49). Rockville, MD: National Bioethics Advisory Commission.

Fisher, C. B. (2000). Relational ethics in psychological research: One feminist's journey. In M. Brabeck (Ed.), *Practicing feminist ethics in psychology* (pp. 125-142). Washington, DC: American Psychological Association.

Fisher, C. B. (2002a). A goodness-of-fit ethic of informed consent. *Urban Law Journal, 30,* 159-171.

Fisher, C. B. (2002b). Respecting and protecting mentally impaired persons in medical research. *Ethics & Behavior, 12,* 279-284.

Fisher, C. B. (2003). A goodness-of-fit ethic for informed consent to research involving persons with mental retardation and developmental disabilities. *Mental Retardation and Developmental Disabilities Research Reviews, 9,* 27-31.

Fisher, C. B., & Fyrberg, D. (1994). *College students weigh the costs and benefits of deceptive research.* Presented at the meeting of the American Psychological Association, Washington, DC.

Fisher, C. B., Hatashita-Wong, M., & Isman, L. (1999). Ethical and legal issues. In W. K. Silverman & T. H. Ollendick (Eds.), *Developmental issues in the clinical treatment of children and adolescents* (pp. 470-486). Needham Heights, MA: Allyn and Bacon.

Fisher, C. B., Higgins-D'Alessandro, A., Rau, J. M. B., Kuther, T., & Belanger, S. (1996). Reporting and referring research participants: The view from urban adolescents. *Child Development, 67,* 2086-2099.

Fisher, C. B., Hoagwood, K., Duster, T., Frank, D. A., Grisso, T., Macklin, R., et al. (2002). Research ethics for mental health science involving ethnic minority children and youth. *American Psychologist, 57,* 1024-1040.

Fisher, C. B., Hoagwood, K., & Jensen, P. S. (1996). Casebook on ethical issues in research with children and adolescents with mental disorders. In K. Hoagwood, P.S. Jensen, & C. B. Fisher (Eds.), *Ethical issues in mental health research with children and adolescents* (pp. 135-238). Mahwah, NJ: Lawrence Erlbaum.

Fisher, C. B., Wallace, S. A., & Fenton, R. E. (2000). Discrimination distress during adolescence. *Journal of Youth and Adolescence, 29,* 679-695.

Fisher, C. B., & Younggren, J. (1997). The value and utility of the APA ethics code. *Professional Psychology: Research and Practice, 28*(6), 582-592.

Flanagan, J. C. (1954). The critical incident technique. *Psychological Bulletin, 54,* 327-358.

Fox, R. E., Schwelitz, F. D., & Barclay, A. G. (1992). A proposed curriculum for psychopharmacology for professional psychologists. *Professional Psychology: Research and Practice, 23,* 216-219.

Frankel, M. S. (1996). Developing ethical standards for responsible research: Why? Form? Functions? Process? Outcomes? *Journal of Dental Research, 75,* 832-835.

Friedrich, J., & Douglass, D. (1998). Ethics and persuasive enterprise of teaching psychology. *American Psychologist, 53,* 549-562.

Gilligan, C. (1982). *In a different voice.* Cambridge, MA: Harvard University Press.

Glass, T. A. (1998). Ethical issues in group therapy. In R. M. Anderson, T. L. Needels, & H. V. Hall (Eds.), *Avoiding ethical misconduct in psychology specialty areas* (pp. 95-126). Springfield, IL: Charles C Thomas.

Glosoff, H. L., Herlihy, S. B., Herlihy, B., & Spence, E. B. (1997). Privileged communication in the psychologist-client relationship. *Professional Psychology: Research and Practice, 28,* 573-581.

Graham, T. A. (2001). Teaching child development via the Internet: Opportunities and pitfalls. *Teaching Psychology, 28,* 67-71.

Haas, L. J., & Cummings, N. A. (1991). Managed outpatient mental health plans: Clinical, ethical, and practical guidelines for participation. *Professional Psychology: Research and Practice, 22,* 45-51.

Hadjistavropoulos, T., & Bieling, P. (2001). File review consultation in the adjudication of mental health and chronic pain disability claims. *Consulting Psychology Journal: Practice and Research, 53,* 52-63.

Halpern, S. D., Karlawish, J. H. T., & Berlin, J. A. (2002). The continuing unethical conduct of underpowered clinical trials. *Journal of the American Medical Association, 3,* 358-361.

Hauerwas, S. (1981). *A community of character.* Notre Dame, IN: University of Notre Dame Press.

Hellkamp, D. T., & Lewis, J. E. (1995). The consulting psychologist as an expert witness in sexual harassment and retaliation cases. *Consulting Psychology Journal: Practice and Research, 47,* 150-159.

Hess, A. K. (1998). Accepting forensic case referrals: Ethical and professional considerations. *Professional Psychology: Research and Practice, 29,* 109-114.

Hobbs, N. (1948). The development of a code of ethical standards for psychology. *American Psychologist, 3,* 80-84.

Jeffrey, T. B., Rankin, R. J., & Jeffrey, L. K. (1992). In service of two masters: The ethical-legal dilemma faced by military psychologists. *Professional Psychology: Research and Practice, 23,* 91-95.

Jerome, L. W. (1998). *Seclusion and restraint: Avoiding ethical misconduct in psychology specialty areas.* Springfield, IL: Charles C Thomas.

Johnson, B. W. (1995). Perennial ethical quandaries in military psychology: Toward American Psychological Association-Department of Defense collaboration. *Professional Psychology: Research and Practice, 26,* 281-287.

Jordan, A. E., & Meara, N. M. (1990). Ethics and the professional practice of psychologists: The role of virtues and principles. *Professional Psychology: Research and Practice, 21,* 107-114.

Josephson Institute of Ethics. (1999). *Making ethical decisions.* Marina del Rey, CA: Author.

Kampa-Kokesch, S., & Anderson, M. Z. (2001). Executive coaching: A comprehensive review of the literature. *Consulting Psychology Journal: Practice and Research, 53,* 205-228.

Kant, I. (1959). *Foundations of the metaphysics of morals.* Indianapolis, IN: Bobbs-Merrill. (Original work published 1785)

Keenan, J. (1995). Proposing cardinal virtues. *Theological Studies, 56* D, 709-729.

Kilburg, R. R. (1996). Toward a conceptual understanding and definition of executive coaching. *Consulting Psychology Journal: Practice and Research, 48,* 134-144.

Kitchener, K. S. (1984). Intuition, critical evaluation and ethical principles: The foundation for ethical decisions in counseling psychology. *The Counseling Psychologist, 12*(3), 43-55.

Knapp, S., & VandeCreek, L. (1997). *Jaffee v. Redmond:* The Supreme Court recognizes a psychotherapist-patient privilege in federal courts. *Professional Psychology: Research and Practice, 28,* 567-572.

Knight, G. P., & Hill, N. E. (1998). Measurement equivalence in research involving minority adolescents. In V. C. McLoyd & L. Steinberg (Eds.), *Studying minority adolescents: Conceptual, methodological, and theoretical issues* (pp. 183-211). Mahwah, NJ: Lawrence Erlbaum.

Koocher, G. P., & Keith-Spiegel, P. (1998) *Ethics in psychology: Professional standards and cases* (2nd ed.). New York: Oxford University Press.

Kreck, C. (2000, June 4). "Rebirth" death spurs warning: Abuse charges eyed against therapists using restraints. *Denver Post,* p. A.01.

Krivacska, J. J., & Margolis, H. (1995). The special education consultant in due process hearings: Ethics and expertise. *Consulting Psychology Journal: Practice and Research, 47,* 169-183.

Kumho Tire Co., Ltd. v. Carmichael, 119 S. Ct. 1167 (March 23, 1999).

Lakin, M. (1994). Morality in group and family therapies: Multiperson therapies and the 1992 ethics code. *Professional Psychology: Research and Practice, 25,* 344-348.

Lamb, D. H., & Catanzaro, S. J. (1998). Sexual and nonsexual boundary violations involving psychologists, clients, supervisees, and students: Implications for professional practice. *Professional Psychology: Research and Practice, 29,* 498-503.

Lang, S. (1993). Questions of scientific responsibility: The Baltimore case. *Ethics & Behavior, 3,* 3-72.

Leigh, I. W., Corbett, C. A., Gutman, V., & Morere, D. A. (1996). Providing psychological services to deaf individuals: A response to new perceptions of diversity. *Professional Psychology: Research and Practice, 27,* 364-371.

Liss, M. (1994). State and federal laws governing reporting for researchers. *Ethics & Behavior, 4,* 133-146.

MacIntyre, A. (1984). *After virtue* (2nd ed.). Notre Dame, IN: University of Notre Dame Press.

MacIntyre, A. (1989). *Whose justice? Which rationality?* Notre Dame, IN: University of Notre Dame Press.

Maheu, M. M. (2001). *Exposing the risk, yet moving forward: A behavioral e-health model.* Retrieved October 21, 2002, from http://www.ascusc.org/jcmc/

Margolin, G. (1982). Ethical and legal considerations in marital and family therapy. *American Psychologist, 37,* 788-801.

May, W. F. (1984). The virtues in a professional setting. *Soundings, 67,* 245-266.

Mill, J. S. (1957). *Utilitarianism.* New York: Bobbs-Merrill. (Original work published 1861)

Needleman, H. M. (1993). Reply to Ernhart, Scarr, and Geneson. *Ethics & Behavior, 3,* 95-101.

Newman, J. L., Gray, E. A., & Fuqua, D. R. (1996) Beyond ethical decision making. *Consulting Psychology Journal: Practice and Research, 48*(4), 230-236.

Nickelson, D. W. (1998). Telehealth and the evolving health care system: Strategic opportunities for professional psychology. *Professional Psychology: Research and Practice, 29,* 527-535.

O'Connor, M. F. (2001). On the etiology and effective management of professional distress and impairment among psychologists. *Professional Psychology: Research and Practice, 32,* 345-350.

Office for Protection From Research Risks, Department of Health and Human Services, National Institutes of Health. (1993). *Protecting human research subjects: Institutional review board guidebook.* Washington, DC: Government Printing Office.

Orme, D. R., & Doerman, A. L. (2001). Ethical dilemmas in the U.S. Air Force clinical psychologists: A survey. *Professional Psychology: Research and Practice, 32,* 305-311.

Patterson, D. R., & Hanson, S. L. (1995). Joint Division 22 and ACRM guidelines for postdoctoral training in rehabilitation psychology. *Rehabilitation Psychology, 40,* 299-310.

Pearlman, L. A., & Saakvitne, K. W. (1995). Treating therapists with vicarious traumatization and secondary traumatic stress disorders. In C. R. Figley (Ed.), *Compassion fatigue: Coping with secondary traumatic stress disorder in those who treat the traumatized* (pp. 150-177). Philadelphia: Brunner/Mazel.

Perrin, G. I., & Sales, B. D. (1994). Forensic standards in the American Psychological Association's new ethics code. *Professional Psychology: Research and Practice, 25,* 376-381.

Ponterotto, J. G., Casas, J. M., Suzuki, L. A., & Alexander, C. M. (2001). *Handbook of multicultural counseling* (2nd ed.). Thousand Oaks, CA: Sage.

Rabasca, L. (1999). Help for coping with stresses of today's practice. *Monitor, 30,* 3. Retrieved from http://www.apa.org/monitor/mar99/coping.html

Ramsey, P. (2002). *The patient as person: Explorations in medical ethics* (2nd ed.). New Haven, CT: Yale University Press.

Randsdell, S. (2002). Teaching psychology as a laboratory science in the age of the Internet. *Behavior Research Methods, Instruments & Computers, 34,* 145-150.

Rehabilitation Act of 1973, Pub. L. No. 93-112, 29 U.S.C.A. § 794, regulations implementing Section 504 appearing at 34 CFR Part 105 (1993).

Rest, J. R. (1983). Morality. In P. H. Mussen (Series Ed.) and J. Flavell & E. Markham (Vol. Eds.), *Handbook of child psychology: Vol. 4. Cognitive development* (pp. 520-629). New York: John Wiley.

Savin-Williams, R. C., & Diamond, L. M. (1999). Sexual orientation. In W. K. Silverman & T. H. Ollendick (Eds.), *Developmental issues in the clinical treatment of children and adolescents* (pp. 241-258). Boston: Allyn and Bacon.

Schur, G. M. (1982). Toward a code of ethics for academics. *Journal of Higher Education, 53,* 319-334.

Sechrest, L., & Coan, J. A. (2002). Preparing psychologists to prescribe. *Journal of Clinical Psychology, 58,* 649-658.

Seitz, J., & O'Neill, P. (1996) Ethical decision-making and the code of ethics of the Canadian Psychological Association. *Canadian Psychology, 37,* 23-30.

Shapiro, D. E., & Schulman, C. E. (1996). Ethical and legal issues in e-mail therapy. *Ethics & Behavior, 6,* 107-124.

Sherman, M. D., & Thelen, M. H. (1998). Distress and professional impairment among psychologists in clinical practice. *Professional Psychology: Research and Practice, 29,* 79-85.

Sieber, J. E. (1982). Kinds of deception and the wrongs they may involve. *IRB: A Review of Human Subjects Research, 4,* 1-5.

Sinclair, C., Poizner, S., Gilmour-Barrett, K., & Randall, D. (1987). The development of a code of ethics for Canadian psychologists. *Canadian Psychology, 28,* 1-8.

Skorupa, J., & Agresiti, A. A. (1993). Ethical beliefs about burnout and continued professional practice. *Professional Psychology: Research and Practice, 24,* 281-285.

Soisson, E. L., VandeCreek, L., & Knapp, S. (1987). Thorough record keeping: A good defense in a litigious era. *Professional Psychology: Research and Practice, 18,* 498-502.

Sonne, J. L., & Pope, K. S. (1991). Treating victims of therapist-patient sexual involvement. *Psychotherapy, 28,* 174-187.

Sprague, R. L. (1993). Whistleblowing: A very unpleasant avocation. *Ethics & Behavior, 3,* 103-134.

Staal, M. A., & King, R. E. (2000). Managing a multiple relationship environment: The ethics of military psychology. *Professional Psychology: Research and Practice, 31,* 698-705.

Stefan, S. (2000). *Unequal rights: Discrimination against people with mental disabilities and the Americans with Disabilities Act.* Washington, DC: American Psychological Association.

Tarasoff v. Regents of the University of California (Tarasoff II), 551 P.2d 334 (Cal. 1976).

Taylor, R. E., & Gazda, G. M. (1991). Concurrent individual and group therapy: The ethical issues. *Journal of Group Psychotherapy, Psychodrama, & Sociometry, 44,* 51-59.

U.S. Department of Defense. (1997a). *Mental health evaluations of members of the Armed Forces* (DoD Directive 6490.1). Washington, DC: Government Printing Office.

U.S. Department of Defense. (1997b). *Requirements for mental health evaluations of members of the Armed Forces* (DoD Instruction 6490.4). Washington, DC: Government Printing Office.

VandeCreek, L., & Knapp, S. (1993). Tarasoff *and beyond: Legal and clinical considerations in the treatment of life-endangering patients* (Rev. ed.). Sarasota, FL: Professional Resource Press.

Walzer, M. (1983). *Spheres of justice: A defense of pluralism and equality.* New York: Basic Books.

Webber, D. W. (1999). *AIDS and the law: 1999 cumulative supplement* (3rd ed.). New York: Panel.

Wechsler, D. (1991). Wechsler Intelligence Scale for Children, third edition (WISC-III). San Antonio, TX: Psychological Corporation.

William Daubert, et ux. etc. et al. Petitioners v. Merrell Dow Pharmaceutical Inc. Supreme Court of the United States, No. 92-102, decided on June 28, 1993.

Workforce Investment Act of 1988, 29 U.S.C. 2938.

Index

ABOUT THE AUTHOR

Celia B. Fisher, Ph.D., Director of the Fordham University Center for Ethics Education and the Marie Doty University Chair in Psychology, served as Chair of the American Psychological Association's (APA) Ethics Code Task Force responsible for the 2002 revision of the APA Ethical Principles of Psychologists and Code of Conduct. She also has served as Chair of the New York State Board for Licensure in Psychology, the National Task Force on Applied Developmental Science, and the Society for Research in Child Development Committee for Ethical Conduct in Child Development Research, and as a member of the APA Ethics Committee. Dr. Fisher is a member of the Department of Health and Human Services Secretary's Advisory Committee on Human Research Protections, the National Institute of Mental Health (NIMH) Data Safety and Monitoring Board, and the Institute of Medicine Committee on Clinical Research Involving Children and has served on numerous federal grant review committees. Dr. Fisher has written commissioned papers on research ethics with mentally impaired and vulnerable populations for the President's National Bioethics Advisory Commission and for NIMH on points for consideration in the ethical conduct of suicide research and research involving children and adolescents. She has coedited five books and authored more than 100 scholarly chapters and empirical articles on cognitive and social development across the lifespan and on research and professional ethics with special emphasis on informed consent procedures and confidentiality and disclosure policies. With support from the National Institute for Child Health and Human Development (NICHD), she is studying how to assess and enhance the abilities of adults with developmental disabilities to consent to research. With funding from the National Science Foundation (NSF) and the National Institutes of Health (NIH), she has developed research ethics instructional materials for undergraduates, graduate students, senior scientists, and institutional review boards. In July 2001, she cochaired the APA, NIMH, Fordham University national conference Research Ethics for Mental Health Science Involving Ethnic Minority Children and Youth (*American Psychologist*, December 2002). She has developed assessment instruments to evaluate how teenagers and parents from different racial/ethnic backgrounds prepare for and react to racial discrimination, examined the validity of child abuse assessment techniques in institutional and forensic settings, and with support from the NSF has partnered with culturally diverse community members to understand their perspectives on the ethics of adolescent risk research.